TRAINER'S

COMPLETE GUIDE TO

MANAGEMENT

AND

SUPERVISORY DEVELOPMENT

CAROLYN NILSON

TRAINER'S COMPLETE GUIDE TO MANAGEMENT AND SUPERVISORY DEVELOPMENT

PRENTICE HALL
Englewood Cliffs, New Jersey 07632

Prentice-Hall International (UK) Limited, *London*
Prentice-Hall of Australia Pty. Limited, *Sydney*
Prentice-Hall Canada, Inc., *Toronto*
Prentice-Hall Hispanoamericana, S.A., *Mexico*
Prentice-Hall of India Private Limited, *New Delhi*
Prentice-Hall of Japan, Inc., *Tokyo*
Simon & Schuster Asia Pte. Ltd., *Singapore*
Editora Prentice-Hall do Brasil, Ltda., *Rio de Janeiro*

10 9 8 7 6 5 4 3 2 1

Library of Congress Cataloging-in-Publication Data

Nilson, Carolyn D.
Trainer's complete guide to management and supervisory development /
Carolyn Nilson.
p. cm.
Includes bibliographical references and index.
ISBN 0-13-410663-6
1. Executives—Training of. 2. Supervisors—Training of. I. Title.
HD38.2.N536 1992 92-15854
658.4'07124—dc20 CIP

ISBN 0-13-410663-6

PRENTICE HALL
Professional Publishing
Englewood Cliffs, NJ 07632
Simon & Schuster, A Paramount Communications Company

Printed in the United States of America

DEDICATION

This book is dedicated to my husband, Noel,
born to manage—by nature a facilitator,
always a curious and often a reluctant student—
with thanks for the special way in which he cares.

About the Author

Carol Nilson, Ed.D. is a veteran trainer with a wide experience base in traditional and state-of-the-art training assignments. Among the corporations and agencies she has served as consultant are: American Management Association, The ARINC Companies, Chemical Bank, Chevron, Dun & Bradstreet, Nabisco, National Institute of Education, National Westminster Bank, New Jersey Bell, New Jersey State Department of Education, U.S. Department of Education, and the World Bank.

Dr. Nilson was Director of Training for a systems consulting firm with a broad-based Fortune 500 clientele in the New York metropolitan area. In this position she supervised a staff of training consultants and was responsible for management, design, and delivery of training services to managers and supervisors throughout the region.

She also held the position of Manager of Simulation (CBT) Training at Combustion Engineering, where she managed the training operation and created high-level computer-based training for an international base of managers and supervisors in the chemical process industry. At CE, she was a key member of the corporate Artificial Intelligence team with specific responsibilities for design of an expert system in learning and trainee evaluation.

Dr. Nilson was also a Member of Technical Staff at AT&T Bell Laboratories where she was part of the Standards, Audits, and Inspections Group of the Systems Training Center. In this capacity, she developed, implemented, and promoted quality standards in course design and delivery throughout AT&T through internal consulting work with managers and supervisors, through presenting courses and seminars, by organizing conferences, and through creating a variety of print and electronic communication efforts. At Bell Labs she taught the course, Techniques of Instruction. Throughout her career, she received commendations for her work with professional staff and managers for whom English was a second language.

Carolyn Nilson is the author of four other books on training: *Training Program Workbook and Kit,* Prentice Hall, 1989; *Training for Non-Trainers,* 1990, *How To Manage Training,* 1991, *How To Start a Training Program In Your Growing Business,* 1992, and of numerous papers, articles, and reports on education and training. She received her doctorate from Rutgers University with a specialty in measurement and evaluation.

What This Guide Will Do For You

In the search for effective supervisors and managers, an often overlooked key is the management trainer and the quality of management training itself. This book provides rich and varied tools to enable this critical resource—the management trainer—to design and deliver high-quality, cost-effective management and supervisory training. Good trainers are major contributors to outstanding return on investment in your management and supervisory training. Good training will speed the development of the increasingly complex resource of human capital in an increasingly diverse workplace. The *Trainer's Complete Guide to Management and Supervisory Development* will show you, the corporate trainer, the most appropriate techniques for designing and delivering superior training for the leaders in American business today.

This guide is based on the premise that busy managers require training that enables them to deal confidently with change, with technology, and with the people issues that confront them. Busy managers and supervisors need training that goes to the heart of these matters, doesn't waste time, and provides them with opportunities to practice new skills.

Techniques in this guide are presented as complete, practical instructional ideas. Each chapter includes training plans to make the job of training easier and the results of training more valid.

The training methods described here address the most pressing issues of management toward the year 2000—critical, current issues of human resources practice and productivity that well-trained managers and supervisors can influence. Management training techniques presented here focus on the most practical and most relevant business skills and people skills, emphasizing the payoff of good training in the real world of fast-changing organization structures, global competition, electronic working environments, and the changing complexion of the workforce.

The purpose of this guide is to provide clarity and structure for the proven methods of teaching and learning that lie behind today's practices of successful supervisors and managers. It blends theory and application. It recognizes the challenge faced by corporate human resources practitioners to provide excellent training to business leaders whose time for study and reflection is severely limited by competitive and operational demands in today's fast-moving business environment. Its format invites immediate use. *It is a self-help guide for management trainers.* It can make your job of training design, delivery, and administration the effective partner in business growth that it should be.

DESIGNED FOR IMMEDIATE USE

The *Trainer's Complete Guide to Management and Supervisory Development* will shape management and supervisory training for you. A wealth of well thought-out training plans, trainer's worksheets, and trainee handouts are ready for you to put into immediate use. The guide is a made-to-order reference to classroom techniques, CBT and video techniques, one-on-one training, independent study, off-site training, training evaluation methods, and a host of other methods for effective instruction. This is a tool for forging new management skills for the managers and supervisors entrusted to your corporate training programs, and for enabling you to do your job better as a management trainer.

The *Trainer's Complete Guide to Management and Supervisory Development* will help you as an instructor to empower your managers and supervisors through good training—training that is targeted to today's demands, training that is anchored in the best of proven techniques of instruction, and training that can be designed and delivered with cost constraints in mind.

Above all, the guide is practical. By using it, you will become a better facilitator, presenter, designer, evaluator, and more effective as an instructional leader. This guide will help you to become more visible and valued as a bottom-line developer of a critical business resource—the potential of your company's managers and supervisors.

FOR SEASONED MANAGEMENT TRAINERS AS WELL AS TRAINING NEWCOMERS

The *Trainer's Complete Guide to Management and Supervisory Development* is aimed at all trainers with responsibility or interest in strategic and effective supervisory and management training. Experienced trainers will find this guide an interesting stimulus to their creativity, and an update to training issues emerging from global competitive challenges, new workplace demographics, and the broadening electronic base of business resulting from the proliferation of information technologies. Newcomers will find it an invaluable source of shortcuts to good training design and delivery, and a convenient "on-the-job training" document. It will help all trainers learn to model the kinds of successful behaviors that effective managers and supervisors need to demonstrate.

This guide is also a useful tool for training managers and human resources managers as you deal with the major issues facing training organizations today—increasing productivity of your training staff, decreasing throughput time from development to finished course, and improving quality of instruction and instructional products. It leads you into designing a strong and viable future for the training organization through delivery of highly effective management and supervisory training. It's a "how to" working document you will not want to be without!

HOW THIS GUIDE IS ORGANIZED

Eight Chapters Related to Managers' Responsibility Areas

The guide is organized into eight chapters following the major areas of responsibility for supervisors and managers. Since this is a training guide (and not a "how to be a better manager" book), the essence of each chapter is the management training techniques in each of these responsibility areas that work best with managers and supervisors. The focus of training methods is varied. The guide describes, explains, shows examples, and provides practical guidelines for techniques to be used in generic as well as highly specialized situations, in one-on-one training, in small groups, in large classrooms, with printed material, with video-based, computer-based, or other electronic delivery systems. The guide provides information on brokered training, on using consultants, and on personalizing packaged training products purchased from vendors. The special needs and constraints of management and supervisory training is, of course, the focus as various delivery techniques are presented. Relationships are drawn throughout the text between the various responsibilities of the manager's job and the training techniques that will best help teach him or her to do that job.

Overview

Each chapter begins with an overview of the responsibility area, highlighting current trends, legislation, and challenges facing the manager or supervisor.

Key Training Issues for This Responsibility Area

Tied to this and following the overview is an expansion of key training issues resulting from the trends, legislation, and challenges. New and nontraditional methods are described in relationship to tried-and-true management training methods that have been successful in the recent past. Case examples from corporate training practices are used for illustration. Throughout, the text emphasizes problem identification and problem solving, effective use of evaluation, dynamics of collaboration, and how to transfer the essence of training to today's workplace.

Training Plans

Each chapter includes training plan ideas presented as bulleted lists, checklists, guidelines, or procedural steps that will enable the trainer to quickly turn the training technique into an instructor's guide or course outline. How to tailor training to the various levels and styles of adult learners and how to conduct appropriate evaluations are included with each Training Plan.

The Training Plan is a synthesis of a particular managerial responsibility area, providing a content framework and a succinct presentation of training techniques relevant to that area. Each training plan includes many proven instructional techniques, which are highlighted in italics; if you want additional information on a particular technique, simply turn to the Index of Training Techniques at the back of the book, which will refer you to sections of the book where that technique is described in detail.

Following is the structure of the information provided in each Training Plan:

- Overview of training methodology
- Time required to deliver this training
- Level of trainee
- Training objectives
- Learning objectives for the trainee
- Methods to evaluate the trainee's progress
- Training tips and exercises

Trainer's Worksheets and Trainee Handouts

Included with each Training Plan are trainer's worksheets (charts, forms, procedures, guidelines) and trainee handouts to elaborate and illustrate the text where appropriate.

List of Training Techniques

The following training techniques and related concepts are included in the *Trainer's Complete Guide to Management and Supervisory Development*. What makes this guide unique is that these techniques are presented **in the context of management and supervisory issues and challenges,** thus providing the management trainer with the most direct and effective link between the manager's job *today* and the design and delivery of management training.

CBT	quality improvement	simulation
modeling	learning readiness	apprenticing
role play	mentoring	language study
coaching	peer training	questionnaires
interviews	mastery lists	documentation
skill checklists	training software	giving feedback
getting feedback	policies	planning
making decisions	problem solving	IVD
managing change	seminars	television
quality teams	learning centers	orientation
managing projects	facilitating	lecturing
demonstrating	motivating adults	tutoring
hands-on training	cognitive objectives	writing
brainstorming	stimulus/response	job aids
workshops	difficult groups	rating scales
conferences	learning styles	presentations
case study	criterion-reference	exercises
psychomotor objectives	norm-reference	tests
sports psychology	conference	goals
independent study	institute	field trip
print materials	thinking skills	followup
learning to learn	overheads	slides
co-instructing	affective objectives	video

An alphabetic **Index of Training Techniques** beginning on page 279, precedes the Guide's general index to help you find a specific technique you might be looking for.

Contents

Expanded Contents

List of Trainer's Worksheets and Trainee Handouts

Author's Preface

The art of training people at work is changing as the workplace and as work itself are changing in today's people-intensive, data-based, customer-sensitive businesses. It's no longer enough to know how to stand up in front of a group and deliver a course, do an effective presentation with attractive slides, or make the decision to hire a vendor with the least impact on your bottom line. There's a great deal more, in terms of the art—or the big picture of training today—and in terms of the craft of instruction—or the techniques of training, that is required to meet the highest level training needs of the human resource leaders of the 1990s.

This is a techniques book for the corporate trainer whose job is to train the company's managers and supervisors. It is different from other techniques books because it zeros in on how to use a specific training technique as it applies to the areas of contemporary management that demand the attention of today's business leaders. Complete training plans marry the technique itself to the management issue. The corporate trainer will be able to focus on a particular area of his or her company's management responsibility and quickly have a training plan of attack to help the manager or supervisor know and do what needs to be done.

In a sense, this is a "how to... how to..." book—how to train managers how to manage. It is a training technique book that makes the leap to application in the most demanding areas of management and supervisory behavior today. This book brings the art and craft of teaching directly to the context of the 1990s most pressing human resources challenges.

In this book I have shunned the temptation to write a discourse on the nature of American productivity, the effects of our computer revolution on how managers manage and how people learn, the striking changes in the profile of the workforce, the unprecedented opportunities in the global marketplace, and the human resources challenges spinning off the quality initiatives around the country. However, all of these shapers of the corporate trainer's leadership role are in the book, but in a transparent way that allows you to see through them to the essence of how to do the training of the people who must meet the company's special business challenges.

The book is loaded with all sorts of techniques that recognize technology's influence, a diverse workforce, faster production and processing, faster turnaround, interval reduction, fewer layers from the top to the bottom line, vertical groupings of task-oriented employees, teams, and interorganizational relationships that require flexibility to manage. Within each section of the book you'll find many different teaching techniques to help you deal with helping your managers and supervisors stay current and competent.

The book is designed to be immediately useful to the trainer. It will tell you why this particular technique is valuable for learning the particular content to which it is matched, why the training department will benefit from doing it this way, and why a manager or supervisor cares about learning this particular thing. This book will simply let you do your job better.

Chapter 1

Training Managers and Supervisors to Manage Quality

Largely due to the outstanding job of publicity by the U.S. Department of Commerce's Malcolm Baldrige Quality Award organizers, large corporations, small companies, and service businesses nationwide are on the quality bandwagon. Fuelled by the latest revelation of dirty tricks by foreign competitors and the American consumer's appetite for products that look good and work well, companies throughout the country are reorganizing and retraining themselves to pay more attention to their customers. There is a great proliferation of courses, programs, and "thrusts" throughout corporate America in the name of quality.

Managers are squarely in the middle between the old profit and productivity goals and the new quality standards—between the old ways of monitoring and measuring and the deep-down gut feeling that business should change. Many managers have responded to the quality clarion call by sending themselves or their employees off to quality seminars and by hiring consultants and vendors to give them advice and on-site training in quality. Many managers have shown by their actions that they believe the quality movement is a good thing.

How can managers get beyond the basics of quality, and more important, how can we teach managers to do what they need to do in order to do it right the first time for their own organizations? As trainers, we need to distinguish between types of quality training such as quality awareness training, quality leadership training, quality management training, how to use quality tools, and training for quality improvement. In our approach to management training, we must develop the same keen sense of problem identification and organizational analysis that we expect our managers to develop as they manage quality initiatives. We, too, need the long-term strategic approach to training managers to implement quality, as they need the long view to make organizational changes that foster quality achievements. Like them, we must guard against embracing the latest bag of tricks purported to contain all the wisdom of "doing quality" in a three-day seminar.

With our managers, we need to review the definitions of quality, be able to articulate the various values of quality, choose and apply appropriate measures, to ask the right questions, and to analyze and restructure organizations so that quality happens. We need to prevent quality from being the latest toolkit, slogan, or program. Quality training that fails is training that is unconnected, disjointed, unplanned, whiz-bang, and reactionary. The rest of this section describes the quality context in today's business environment and illuminates the challenges for management trainers.

A BRIEF HISTORY OF QUALITY TRAINING

Quality has been around for a long time. Anyone who's worked in a factory or on a government contract is probably more than a little familiar with quality control and the counting, measuring, and statistical interpretations generally applied to manufactured products. SQC, or statistical quality control, is the grandfather field of most of today's broader views of quality. SQC is the concept against which newer approaches to quality measurement and design are compared.

Quality and Statistical Process Control

To understand what's new in approaches to quality is to understand the nature of the changes in the American workplace. In recent years, the fundamental change in the nature of American work has been the change to a service economy and away from a manufacturing one. SQC has evolved into SPC, statistical *process* control, taking the idea of quality control (of product) into the realm of quality control of process. The product versus process distinction is a fundamental concept in your ability to move management training and the management of quality beyond the basics.

In the grand scheme of things, SQC and SPC are generally placed today within the continuum of quality training in the "tools" curriculum because of their historical reliance on the application of statistics to analyze and describe, particularly to analyze and describe production and the processes such as design and engineering that had a direct impact on products. In past years, these approaches might have been the only approaches to quality in a company.

Today, however, many factories have become assembly or warehousing operations, not manufacturing operations, and processes have become at least as important as products. Managers who are looking out for process quality have had to adapt the former product quality approaches to their new challenges in process operations. The statistical base of product quality control has moved on into process quality control. However, the narrowness of the control of completed product approach of SQC has remained with the evolved SPC, relegating SPC to the quality tools training agenda. It is important for management trainers to understand the conceptual and historical base of quality in the American workplace before designing training for quality.

Of course, the clarification of what was meant by process quality brought with it a systems view of "process" and a systems convention of seeing work as an end-to-end endeavor, not simply a culminating piece of goods. As people thought about process, the system model of inputs, throughputs, outputs, and feedback within a dynamic environment seemed appropriate. Inputs and outputs could be isolated for descriptive purposes, customers and suppliers could be factored into the process quality loop, and seeing a process in its component parts held out the possibility of finding and fixing the problems with parts before those parts interacted. Training for this kind of quality means more than learning how to use statistical tools at the point of production. Feedback means more than reporting quantity of defective product.

In addition, process quality carries with it a need for management of more than raw materials, machinery, plant, and equipment. Process quality management involves paying attention to communication, information access and dissemination, cooperation and collaboration, setting priorities, using time, brokering knowledge, planning, and a host of other fluid business activities that are grounded in the human resources of a company, not in its capital resources. Service is different from product, but we can use what we've learned about product quality in our quest for process quality. Quality management and quality leadership are terms that managers need to come to grips with and that management trainers need to understand.

Total Quality Management

Other characteristics of the American manager in the 1990s suggest the need for an expanded managerial role when it comes to quality. The organization men of the 1950s are nearly all retired—the earlier management profile of planning, controlling, coordinating, and organizing has given way to a managerial profile characterized by flexibility, variety, interruptions, discontinuity, and quick study. Today fewer managers handle a greater range of work, and information has exploded to such a degree that most managers trying to avoid overload rely on informal and oral media to stay informed. Employees have gotten the message that they themselves can have a say in the way they do their jobs, and they believe in empowerment. Managers have their old names, but not their old games. Managers seem to be running faster just to stay in place.

The total quality management (TQM) concept is the response to this new management profile. TQM easily becomes the watchword in a company in which a quality program audit turns up such things as

- no uniform quality improvement process
- lack of a cohesive corporate quality structure
- no support structures dedicated to quality
- redundant development especially in human resources functions such as training
- incomplete training curricula in quality as well as in other process areas
- extensive and expensive use of outside consultants

Quality improvement takes its place as a critical quality function, requiring its own kind of training. TQM becomes an umbrella for end-to-end company-wide quality efforts, clearly bringing the narrow focus of SQC that served an earlier day so well into a floodlight of involvement with today's organization in its entirety. Quality is no longer the job of the R&D folks or the engineers; it is everybody's job, part of everybody's job description. As Ford says, "Quality Is Job One."

VARIOUS APPROACHES TO QUALITY: DEMING, JURAN, CROSBY

Quality's popular gurus of the 1990s, Crosby and Juran, and their predecessor statistician Deming, all seem to agree that a company must focus on improving processes and that this must be done continuously throughout a company. The Baldrige Quality Award categories, too, suggest this "organization development" approach. Baldrige's seven categories are:

1. leadership
2. information and analysis
3. strategic quality planning
4. human resource utilization
5. quality of products and services
6. quality of results
7. customer satisfaction

Companies competing for the Baldrige must show success in each of these categories. The scoring of applications is weighted in favor of customer satisfaction (300 points), quality results (180 points), and human resource utilization (150 points). Quality results, for example, includes such items as "product and service quality results"; "business processes, operational, and support service quality results"; and "supplier quality results."[1] The Baldrige clearly supports the systems view of quality and values the people interfaces and processes that make quality happen.

Within this popular view of the definition of quality, some technical definitions make more sense. All definitions of quality begin with the customer and include a reference to the customer's requirements translated into some kind of standards or specifications for product or service. All definitions of quality contain the concept of prevention of errors. All definitions include frequent measurements. Here are some of the subtleties. Quality is:

- Conformance to requirements, not goodness (Crosby, Winter Park, FL)
- Zero defects, not acceptable levels of quality (Crosby, Winter Park, FL)[2]
- A planned pattern of action to ensure confidence that the product conforms to technical requirements (IEEE, NY)[3]
- Minimizing losses incurred by the customer due to deviation of the product performance from its target (Taguchi, Japanese father of Robust Design)
- Systematic quality planning, quality control, and quality improvement (J.M. Juran, Wilton, CT)
- Fitness for use (J.M. Juran, Wilton, CT)

Translated into product and process characteristics that workers can do something about, these definitions suggest dimensions such as features, serviceability, durability, reliability, conformance, aesthetics, timeliness, availability. Managers must find ways to turn quality slogans such as "walk the talk," "the customer is always right," and "do it right the first time" into real ways to improve quality in the company's output—its products and services, and all of the processes that make this output happen.

A good place to start is to focus on the internal links in chains of production or service. For example, the accounting department needs accurate and timely timesheets from employees in order to do its work. That supply link has to work well, according to quality standards governing accuracy and scheduling, in order for the producer (payroll specialists) to prepare its product for the next link in the chain, management personnel who certify the payroll for processing. Those management personnel are customers of the accounting department, and they expect to receive data in a form that is correct (zero defects), easy to analyze (fitness for use), and according to all established procedures for efficiency. Each operation of business has internal "suppliers" and "customers."

Most operations have products, targets, or outcomes. All business processes can be broken down into smaller units that emphasize quality standards regarding inputs and outputs. When managers are given the challenge to implement a Total Quality Management approach, this is where they generally have to begin. And by the accumulated wisdom of numerous quality improvement attempts over the years, we know that finding and correcting errors early and preventing them in the first place cost far less than dealing with internal and external failures downstream at product or service acceptance time.

A MANAGER'S GENERAL APPROACH TO MANAGING FOR QUALITY

Thus, the challenge becomes how to restructure the organization so that those inputs and outputs of individual processes within the total company can be analyzed, monitored, and measured according to standards of quality. Managers must focus on improving quality by:

- creating structure and strategy to guide the improvement efforts
- critically analyzing many small operations that feed into larger ones
- finding and removing obstacles to progress
- providing targeted, sequential, and comprehensive training to all employees
- trusting employees to exhibit high levels of ability in their jobs
- recognizing and supporting those who take personal and organizational risks in the advancement of quality
- forcefully and visibly demonstrating their own leadership commitment to making lasting improvements

In practice, this means that managers have to sit down and set goals for quality based on customer—internal or external—requirements. This is a totally different approach, a paradigm shift for most companies, from the approach based on "how much output our current headcount can produce," or "three months from now our department quota is $750,000 in sales." Managers then must break down the broad goals into specific goals—for departments, work groups, product lines, geographic regions, components of products, suppliers, and so on.

Practically speaking, what managers do once they've gotten the specific goals well defined, is to develop a set of questions the answers to which prove that the specific goal has been reached. During this process of tying questions and answers to goals, a manager will identify resources that he or she needs to reach each goal, and will begin to plan for acquiring and maximizing these resources. The cost of quality becomes a strategic factor in quality improvement.

The next most obvious thing that a manager does is to identify, assemble, and prioritize all of the metrics that must be used to answer questions related to goals, and to specify a detailed plan of data collection that feeds into these metrics. Some very wise person once said that "what gets measured gets done."

And finally, managers must design reports that make use of the various measurements that have linked the goals, the resources expended, and the metrics employed. Only after the strategy of managing for quality has been defined can the hard work of communication, training, and recognition begin. Lofty-sounding slogans about quality never substitute for a goal-centered, metrics-dependent quality strategy. Quality leadership is hard work.

MAKING SENSE OF QUALITY PROBLEMS

Managers who ask many questions generally get a lot of answers. The trick for managers is to know the different categories of answers that they're looking for, and to focus their questions so that their respondents do in fact provide them with information that they can use. When they finally do get some answers, they'll begin to paint "big pictures" involving problems surrounding major themes, such as:

- culture
- teamwork
- leadership
- organizational structure

- measurement
- skills
- reward systems
- resources
- technology
- communication

Here are some typical findings when managers go searching for quality problems:

- there's no obvious crisis
- upper management isn't pushing it
- profits and quotas are stronger immediate driving forces
- corporate mind-set is top-down authority
- teamwork takes too much time
- people around here are good "fire fighters" but are lousy planners
- this company prospered on hard technical values, not on soft market values
- quality is the job of the quality assurance department, not my job
- we don't have time or resources to inspect during production; end-of-process control statistics have always worked for us
- problems are considered enemies, not friends

The wise manager will focus on defects during questioning about both products and processes. These are some questions that might be useful:

- what are the most frequent defects?
- what are the apparent causes of the defects?
- who, including me, is responsible for the cause of the defect?
- how much will it cost to fix the defect?
- how do I know that a defect exists?
- do others agree with my analysis?
- have I sought other informed opinions about this specific defect?
- who can best correct this defect?

Quality improvement means that action plans are in order to make continuous corrections. It means that managers must "put their money where their mouth is" regarding quality—that they cannot delegate away the tough analysis, planning, and allocation tasks of molding resources and people in more effective ways to achieve quality. Juran, for example, suggests that these essential tasks should not be delegated (from *Juran on Quality Leadership®: How to go from here to there* videotape, The Juran Institute, Inc., Wilton, CT, 1987):

- serve on the quality council
- approve the strategic quality goals
- allocate resources
- review progress
- give recognition
- serve on project teams
- revise the merit rating system
- bring quality goals into the strategic business plan

SECRETS OF CREATING QUALITY LEADERS

It should be clear that teaching managers and supervisors to manage quality is not going to be accomplished in a short seminar either on site or at a "quality college." Management trainers have a formidable task ahead when it comes to training your company's leaders to transform the company into doers of as well as believers in quality.

The most sensible approach to this kind of training is the curriculum approach, recognizing that many kinds of training experiences must be offered at varying levels of sophistication to match the varying levels of understanding and experience with quality that your managers represent. Quality training cannot be a one-shot deal.

A useful differentiation of types of quality training might be:

- quality awareness training
- quality planning techniques
- how to use quality tools (statistics, process metrics, various analytical charts and graphs, quality software, and so on)
- training to create quality improvement structures

Whatever curriculum scheme you choose, be sure to begin by co-opting your company executives to commit themselves to promoting and participating in your training efforts. It should be clear to them and to your training staff that organizational and personal growth are at stake here, and that both of these changes require considerable time to accomplish. Quality training is not something that can be quickly bought.

Why Quality Training Should Take Time

Teaching managers to manage quality—or quality training—is a complex training task with challenges that are common to several other areas of organizational life. These are the areas of:

- *change theory,* including how to be an effective change agent or interventionist;
- *psychological growth,* including how to progress from insecurity to being able to make personal contributions, integrating the old with the new;
- *behavior change,* including the development of skills and attitudes that lead from new knowledge to new ways of doing things;
- *organization development,* including arranging the systems, resources, processes, and products of an organization to support quality initiatives.

Each of these areas has a host of behavioral science research behind it, with all of the theories, hypotheses, models, reports, and results that such study suggests. It is not the purpose of this chapter to review these fields of endeavor; this overview is presented here simply to suggest to the reader that teaching managers to manage quality requires a breadth of perspective into many areas of human growth within organizational life, and that the teaching task itself must be sufficiently complex that it accommodates the differentiation suggested by the four areas listed above.

Managers need time to assimilate both the personal changes and the organizational rearrangements that managing quality generally demands. Teaching managers how to be change agents is no small job, nor is it one that can be done in a single session. Giving managers the new skills they need in order to be able to change themselves, to behave in ways that are different from their current and past ways of acting, requires supportive and facilitative training that extends for as long as the support and facilitation are needed. This kind of training surely cannot be done quickly. And training that enables managers to analyze organizations, envision new structures and procedures, energize new relationships, and implement new organizational systems needs the benefit of trial and feedback in a learning context. Learning new measurement tools takes practice and time.

So, the challenge facing the management trainer in quality training is that the nature of the learning itself is complex and best dealt with over a period of time, and the topics that managers need to know are best dealt with as a variety of courses within a curriculum and spread out over time so that time becomes a factor in the success of the training.

A Model for Learning

Educational researchers David Krathwohl, Benjamin Bloom, and Bertram Masia in the 1960s did major work in what they called "the affective domain," or the kind of learning involving the areas of interest, beliefs, attitudes, and values. This "domain" was contrasted to the motor skills development area (psychomotor domain) and to the cognitive, or intellectual, skills development area of learning. The "affective" areas were also typically seen by Americans as private matters, and not in the province of either public education or the business world.[4]

Businesses, especially, were thought not to be in the business of caring about one's beliefs, and if a prospective employee didn't exhibit the proper attitudes and values during the job interview, he or she simply wasn't hired. Businesses were not in business to reform people. In the days when there were plenty of people to fill plenty of jobs, corporate managers could pick and choose from an employee pool with existing intellectual abilities, current skills, and a good match when it came to values.

There were exceptions, of course. IBM, in fact, in the 1950s and 1960s, was well known as one of the few companies that had a well-developed training program to turn employees' thinking around once they got on board. IBM essentially had an "affective domain" training program for all employees to turn them into IBMers. Other companies both envied them and hated them, and their employees learned company songs, dress codes, and began to conduct themselves consistently over time according to a well-structured and well-taught code of business values, IBM-style.

The researchers put it this way: mastering affective objectives means that a person "does do" things in a certain way, not that he or she "can do" them. Training people so that they can do things is considered cognitive or psychomotor training, but training people so that over time they are motivated by beliefs so that they *do* it is affective training.

There is a parallel in marketing theory, where the goal is to take a person from an understanding of certain intellectual aspects of a new product through the adoption of certain consumer behavior—not only a "can do" mentality, but also a "does do" mentality. Marketers pay a lot of attention to the transition the consumer makes between legitimizing or mentally accepting the new product and perhaps trying it out and the adopting behavior that will ultimately cause that buyer to repeatedly use the product. Massive doses of print advertising, psychological buy-in campaigns, and testimonials from other satisfied users are aimed at the new consumer to encourage "adoption" behavior. Like a program to teach managers and supervisors to become quality managers, the campaign to convince a consumer to use a new product depends on a carefully planned affective education process over time.

Training to influence affective behavior begins with making the trainee aware of the need for change, of sparking the trainee's interest in the topic. Translated into quality training, this means courses or programs in "quality awareness." From awareness, the affective continuum progresses through willingness to respond, to satisfaction in response, and on to accepting and even preferring the new value. These learning steps

—willingness, satisfaction, acceptance, and preference—cannot happen quickly or without some trial of new behavior and affirmation from one's peers and superiors that the new behavior is good. It is these mid-stages of affective learning, or the responding and valuing stages, where the tough stuff of training must occur. Quality training programs that fail to make a difference often fail to pay enough attention to these stages in the design and implementation of training.

Krathwohl's model, in brief, includes these stages of learning:

1. **receiving**, including awareness, willingness to receive, and controlled or selected attention,
2. **responding,** including acquiescence in responding, willingness to respond, and satisfaction in response,
3. **valuing**, including acceptance of a value, preference for a value, and commitment,
4. **organization,** including conceptualization of a value, and organization of a value system, and
5. **characterization by a value complex,** including generalized set and characterization whereby an individual integrates, consistently uses, and is known by the new values in all aspects of his or her behavior.

Training managers and supervisors to manage quality involves planned, sequential courses in all five stages of "affective" learning. This kind of training requires differentiation of content and variety in instructional processes, and it must occur over time. It cannot happen in a two-day seminar, a week, a month, or sometimes even a year. Trainers who are committed to training managers and supervisors to manage quality must be ready to expend considerable resources of time and energy over an extended period of time—18 months to three years is not uncommon—in order to adequately train your management staff to behave differently regarding quality.

A BROAD QUALITY CURRICULUM AS A FOUNDATION FOR CHANGE

Simply stated, a curriculum is a plan for learning. In the quality context, the curriculum for managers and supervisors to learn quality in its broadest sense must be a set of learning experiences that teach them about quality as well as enable them to become quality practitioners. Along the way, they also will need to be teachers of quality information and practice to those who report to them. Management trainers must be both subject matter experts in all of the subjects of quality and process facilitators as managers and supervisors assume the practical roles associated with quality leadership. Your curriculum will need to reflect these two aspects of training.

Comments in the popular business press by Baldrige Quality Award winners generally contain references to the power of training, and particularly to extended training. For example, in the April 1991 issue of *Training and Development Journal,* p.12, 1990 winners are quoted:

> **Wallace Company**: "Wallace has invested more than $700,000 and 19,000 hours of training and education in our associates."
>
> **Cadillac Motor Car**: "We made a cultural change, . . . increasing employee involvement 600 percent. We gave our people the system, knowledge, and empowerment to make things happen. . . . Only by continuing to learn can America continue to lead."

And President George Bush commented on other Baldrige winners: "IBM is competitive because of quality coupled with education and training . . . ; and Federal Express's secret is its training. . . . These companies prove that America has a new style of working and thinking. . . . Companies are only as strong as the intelligence, judgment, and character of their employees."

The number of applicant companies going after the Baldrige stands at around 200,000 in 1991. Clearly, American companies are getting the message that comprehensive change, of the kind the Baldrige Award puts forth, is something worth working for.[5]

It should be obvious that the management trainer in developing a quality training program functions in many roles—coordinator, researcher, marketer, evaluator, producer of materials, program designer, course writer, instructor, change agent—to name some of the most common. When it comes to curriculum design, all of these roles will be affected; each will come into play in various ways during implementation of the quality curriculum. Because of these differing roles, curriculum design is approached in a systematic fashion to ensure adequate attention to the complexities of the task of teaching managers to manage quality.

EIGHT STEPS TO DESIGNING QUALITY CURRICULUM

The basic system of instructional system design (ISD) is applied here to the task of curriculum design, with the added dimension of specifying the scope and sequence of the specific quality courses. Steps in curriculum design for a quality training program might look like this:

1. Analyze the needs of the entire management force, including their needs as trainers in quality for those who report to them,
2. State the objectives of the quality training program in terms of cultural or systemic change and personal change,
3. Choose the content to be covered; specify its scope, and arrange the topics in sequence,
4. Determine what kinds of learning you want to happen, and arrange these into low-level skills, mid-level skills, and high-level skills,
5. Merge the topics and the kinds of learning into courses and groups of courses,
6. Organize the courses into logical and hierarchical groups, specifying any that require prerequisites,
7. Choose which instructional delivery methods might be used to teach each course, and
8. Specify evaluation criteria and methods connected with the objectives of each separate course or training experience.

Of course, as you design a curriculum, keep in mind the nature of your target audience, the manager or supervisor. Remember the various typical roles of a manager—the information disseminator role, the interpersonal relator role, and the decision maker role—and the true nature of most managerial work—that is, the need to accomplish within short attention spans; a preference for face-to-face, not written, information; and a reticence to demonstrate changed behavior without the boss's approval. Obviously, corporate cultures and social value systems vary, and it behooves the wise corporate trainer to get as accurate and corroborated a reading as possible describing the organization as a whole, and just what it is that managers and supervisors must deal with as they create the change that managing quality brings.

One way to approach the quality management curriculum design task is to represent the company as a cube of building blocks, with height, width, and depth dimensions. Along the height dimension, assign one cell to the business function for which a specific manager is responsible, for example, customer service, manufacturing, sales, human resources, finance. Look at your company's organization chart for the function titles that apply to you. Along the width dimension, specify the breakdown of the quality training itself, for example, quality awareness, quality planning techniques, quality tools, and quality improvement processes. Along the depth dimension, suggest the groupings in your target audience, for example, senior executives, managers, and supervisors. Other dimensions can be added as needed for curriculum planning.

A simplified version of the Quality Training Cube might look like this:

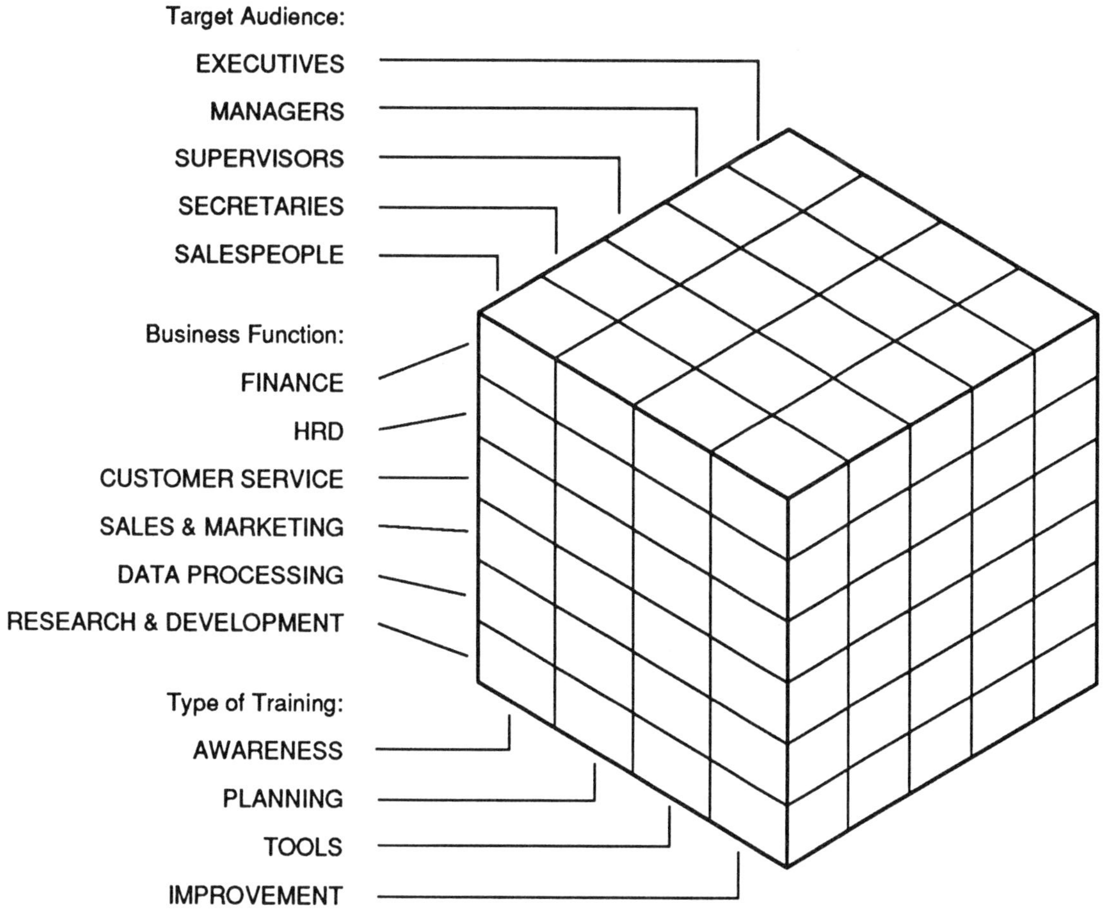

This kind of representation will enable you to see at a gross level where your curriculum will be applied, and will give you a general guide for establishing both a calendar for training implementation and a curriculum chart of courses for each department. From a chart like this you should be able to see what kinds of numbers of trainees you'll be preparing for, and whether or not those numbers might suggest classroom training or a more individualized approach to courses. This kind of cubical representation is based on the work of J.P. Guilford, namely his "Structure of Intellect" theory.[6]

Following is a list of some typical quality courses found scattered within a quality curriculum:

- Creating a Quality Environment
- Quality Assurance
- Quality Audit
- Quality Control
- Quality Leadership
- Quality Measurement
- Quality Motivation and Recognition
- Quality Orientation
- Quality Policy
- Quality Principles
- Quality Planning
- Quality Processes
- Quality Teams
- Quality in Theory and Practice
- Statistical Process Control (SPC)
- Statistical Quality Control (SQC)

Look in any corporate management development curriculum or in the numerous brochures from consulting services and training vendors and you'll see a host of variations on these themes.

As you develop each course, list the five or six major things you want trainees to be able to do at the conclusion of the course, and specify the criterion against which each of these major learning tasks will be measured. List the skills that each of the tasks demands, and code the skills as low-, mid-, or high-level skills. Make yourself a curriculum planning chart with columns "Learning task," "Measurement criterion," and "Skills." Use a new chart for each course. In brief, the curriculum planning chart might look like this:

Course title ________________________________

Learning task	*Measurement criterion*	*Skills / code l m h*
1.	1. o	1. o
		o
	o	o
	o	
2.	2. o	2. o
		o
	o	o
		o
	o	o
	o	o
3.	3. o	3. o
	o	

You will find that within each course, there are some low-level skills, mid-level skills, and high-level skills. Be sure to structure the content so that low-level skills are taught first, even in a course that seems like a "high-level" course. Remember, it's the progression of skills that must be learned that determines the kinds of instruction, not the high-sounding title of the course or the salary level of the trainee. Many quality courses for senior executives are in fact low-level courses from an instructional design perspective.

The point is that when you devise a new curriculum such as a quality curriculum, you'll need to develop some design formats and design document standards in order to adequately handle the curriculum scope and sequence issues surrounding the range of quality courses from awareness to adoption behaviors. Your end product, the quality curriculum, will probably be presented as a flowchart-type chart of interrelated boxes, one for senior executives, one for managers, and one for supervisors. Each course should have the number of days training is expected to take, and each curriculum should estimate how many days the typical trainee will be in training. In addition, you should note which of the courses are required and which are elective and which courses are prerequisite to other courses.

ESTABLISHING ORGANIZATIONAL SUPPORT FOR THE QUALITY PROGRAM

A carefully ordered quality curriculum is only the first step in teaching managers and supervisors to manage quality. Equally important as the curriculum itself are the organizational support functions that are often performed by corporate trainers. One way to think about the deployment of quality training is to think of it as a "rollout" of learning experiences lasting over five years. A three- to five-year period should be enough time for those all-important adoption behaviors to take hold—the willingness to respond and to take pleasure in new response, the preference for choosing new values, and the ability to consistently act in a new way. These kinds of behaviors need more than the leadership of instructors and good instructional design; they also require facilitators of learning who operate within organizations to support change. Beyond the courses in quality principles, quality planning techniques, and SQC tools, there must be a quality improvement program that infiltrates the entire organized worklife of a company. There is a role for management trainers to facilitate this process by management of communication, follow-up, and feedback during the trial phase of doing things differently in the name of quality.

The Philip Crosby Associates in Winter Park, Florida have a useful structure through which to see the trainer's role as facilitative change agent, not just course instructor. Crosby suggests "Fourteen Steps" to quality improvement that managers must follow in order to change the workforce. Most of these steps do not require training in the traditional classroom sense, but rather are efforts to lead people into the adoption of changed attitudes and behaviors about quality. If training goes on during these quality improvement efforts, it most probably follows the model for education in the affective domain presented earlier in the chapter. Crosby's fourteen steps:[7]

Step 1: **Management Commitment.** Get management commitment by carefully communicating the need for defect prevention, resulting in visible, sustained personal participation in the company's broad quality improvement efforts.

Step 2: **Quality Improvement Team.** Form an action-oriented quality improvement team made up of department heads whose purpose is to cause the necessary actions for change to take place.

Step 3: **Quality Measurement.** Establish quality measurements for each area of activity; take measurements periodically, record results, make corrective actions, and document improvements in a highly visible way.

Step 4: **Cost of Quality Evaluation.** Work with the company controller to establish what constitutes the cost of quality.

Step 5: Quality Awareness. Communicate through all sorts of internal media (videotape, posters, reports, flyers) with employees about the costs of nonquality, creating an understanding of the basis for error.

Step 6: Corrective Action. Encourage and empower employees through an open reporting process to bring any problem to the surface in order to solve it. Remove obstacles and disincentives to suggesting corrective actions.

Step 7: Establish an Ad Hoc Committee for the Zero Defects Program. Select three or four members from the quality improvement team to plan and execute a communication campaign to show employees why doing it right the first time is the only way to go. Give this committee the responsibility to study the wide implications of zero defects, and to plan and implement ZD day.

Step 8: Supervisor Training. Train all levels of supervisors and managers to be able to explain each of the fourteen steps in quality improvement.

Step 9: Zero Defects (ZD) Day. Establish a highly visible day of commitment in which everyone in the company shows by their actions that they are committed to the new standard of performance, zero defects. Make it a "new attitude" day.

Step 10: Goal Setting. Have supervisors meet with their people to establish realistic, measureable goals. Suggest 30-, 60-, and 90-day goals.

Step 11: Error Cause Removal. All employees are given a simple one-page form on which to describe any problem that keeps them from performing error-free work. Any problem written down is acknowledged within 24 hours and a solution to it is handled by any appropriate person in the company. This process is continuous.

Step 12: Recognition. Recognize with nonfinancial awards any persons who meet their goals or perform outstanding acts.

Step 13: Quality Councils. Bring the quality professionals and team chairpersons together on a regular basis to communicate with each other and to determine ways to improve the total quality program.

Step 14: Do It Over Again. Repeat the steps about every 18 months to account for organization changes and turnover. Repetition makes the quality program perpetual and helps ingrain it into the organization.

Endnotes

[1]U.S. Department of Commerce, National Institute of Standards and Technology, The Malcolm Baldrige National Quality Award, *1991 Application Guidelines*, p. 5.

[2]Philip B. Crosby, *Quality Is Free*. New York: Mentor, 1979. Reproduced with permission, McGraw-Hall, Inc.

[3]Reprinted with permission, IEEE, from *IEEE Standard for Quality Assurance Plans.*

[4]Krathwohl, D., B. Bloom, and B. Masia, *Taxonomy of Educational Objectives: Handbook II: Affective Domain,* Copyright © 1964 by Longman Publishing Group. Reprinted with permission.

[5]Reprinted from *The Training and Development Journal,* Copyright April 1991, the American Society for Training and Development. Reprinted with permission. All rights reserved.

[6]J.P. Guilford, *Intelligence, Creativity and Their Educational Implications.* Edits Publishers, 1968. Adapted with permission.

[7]Philip B. Crosby, *Quality Is Free,* New York: Mentor, 1979, p. 112-19. Reproduced with permission, McGraw-Hill, Inc.

TRAINING PLANS

Four training plans sample the lessons that could be developed in the four basic areas of any quality curriculum: quality awareness, quality planning, quality tools, and quality improvement. Each uses a different training technique to deliver its instructional message. Worksheets are appended as appropriate.

Training Plans for Chapter 1 include:

management issues	*training techniques*
1.1 Quality awareness	External seminar
1.2 Quality planning	PC-based quality software
1.3 Quality tools	Corporate learning center
1.4 Quality improvement	Using a consultant

TRAINING PLAN 1.1

Sending Managers and Supervisors to an External Seminar on Quality Awareness

This training plan is an outline of the key considerations, procedures, and responsibilities of the training department when you choose to send your managers and supervisors to an *external seminar.*

A training plan begins with objectives for training itself as well as objectives for the learner, and with evaluation methods tied to the learning objectives. Teaching points related to the content of a manager's or supervisor's area of responsibility provide the foundation for topics covered during training. Sample exercises suggest ways to deliver this kind of instruction. In this training plan, a sample seminar agenda is substituted for teaching points and exercises to show the reader the value of the complete training plan.

OVERVIEW OF TRAINING METHODOLOGY

Management trainers generally have the option of developing and delivering training in-house or of sending trainees off premises to an external seminar developed and delivered by a vendor of training programs. There are some reasons why one choice or the other should be made. In a quality curriculum, it often makes sense to use external seminars as a delivery methodology for part of the training.

In this example, a one-day external seminar called "Principles of Quality" was chosen for these reasons:

- Our own development staff was limited and would have had to do more research before they could write such a seminar.
- The topic is one in which being current is important, and we feel comfortable going with a vendor who is at the forefront of the quality movement.
- Our options among vendors are many; the field is competitive right now and we have many choices.
- We like the idea of going to a seminar with managers and supervisors from other companies. In this quality awareness stage of learning, we believe that we can learn from other companies. That's a bonus of training!
- We know some other companies that have used this vendor for the same seminar. The vendor's reputation is solid.
- The one-day format in a hotel near the company means that we don't have to pay travel and living accommodations, so that price is affordable.
- In awareness training, we believe that having an outsider deliver the quality message will carry more weight than if one of our own executives or management trainers did it.

TIME REQUIRED TO DELIVER THIS TRAINING

One day
Seven hours of instruction are planned, plus a one-hour lunch, in a hotel conference center.

TRAINEE LEVEL

Since this is an open seminar, widely advertised to many companies, it is difficult to control the trainee level. You can therefore expect to find managers and supervisors of all sorts here. Because it is a basic-level seminar, that is, a seminar in the basic principles of quality management, you can assume that most people in the audience will know very little about quality management. One of the benefits of this kind of training is the cross-communication of ideas and experiences that trainees from various companies share with each other during training. Thirty to fifty trainees are expected. Encourage your managers and supervisors to go and learn everything they can from the instructor and everyone else.

TRAINING OBJECTIVES

- To introduce trainees to the ideas of Crosby, Deming, and Juran, the three recognized quality gurus of the 1980s and 1990s, and to the Baldrige Quality Award criteria.
- To present the concept of the cost of quality, focusing especially on the cost of prevention.
- To present the concept of process quality, contrasted with product quality, and to develop standards of measurement for various kinds of processes familiar to the trainee audience.
- To describe various inspection processes and documentation forms.
- To discuss various quality policies and the reasons for writing such a policy.
- To discuss the role of recognition and reward in managing quality.

LEARNING OBJECTIVES FOR THE TRAINEE

Note: Learning objectives for the trainee are generally stated on the brochure, either in a list or in the text describing the seminar. For this kind of management training seminar, you should be sure that the focus is on what management *can do,* that is, tied to the descriptions of quality principles should be a challenge that your managers can rise to as they begin to take action back home.

The learning objectives in the brochure should probably look something like this:

- To examine the ideas of today's quality gurus, Crosby, Deming, and Juran, and the Baldrige Quality Award criteria with the aim of selecting relevant concepts to apply in the manager's own situation.
- To apply the concept of the cost of quality by analyzing several examples from Baldrige Award winners with the aim of identifying the major sources of preventable errors.
- To describe common standards of product and process quality, contrasting one with the other.
- To identify at least two processes in the manager's area of responsibility that could have quality standards set for them.
- To establish process quality standards in one of these areas.
- To examine various in-process inspection processes and documentation forms from other companies, noting pros and cons of each with the aim of possibly adapting some in the manager's own area of responsibility.

- To examine and discuss various quality policies with the aim of developing one's own personal guidelines for policy creation.
- To discuss the role of recognition and reward in managing quality.

METHODS TO EVALUATE THE TRAINEE'S PROGRESS

The best chance you have of evaluating your trainees' progress at an external seminar that is out of your control is to follow up that seminar with training of your own or with a developmental assignment back in your own company that requires the attendees at that seminar to use what they learned there in your own company's affairs.

In Krathwohl's affective taxonomy (discussed earlier in this chapter), you need to move your trainees from "receiving" and "responding" to the "valuing" stage of learning, and as they demonstrate their ability to value the quality concepts they've learned, they'll need plenty of recognition and support for their efforts. The wise management trainer will be there at the crucial point of their trying out their new learning. Remember, you're trying to change behavior here on your premises, so you cannot just send your managers and supervisors off to an external seminar and expect someone else to facilitate that behavior change. In marketing theory, there's a principle that says that dissonance is greatest right after joining, meaning that at the point a consumer tries out the new product he or she needs the most reassurance that they made the right decision to purchase it. Trying out newly learned behavior is the same situation—that valuing and commitment stage of learning requires support and reassurance in order for it to stick.

It's also a good idea to ask the vendor for a copy of your trainees' seminar evaluation forms so that you can spot any potential areas of misunderstanding or incomplete information to clarify later.

TRAINING TIPS

This plan suggests the daily agenda for this vendor-developed seminar. Training tips and exercises are purposely omitted from this training plan for the purposes of contrast between a course developed in-house and one such as this, purchased from a vendor. *Trainer's Worksheet 1.1* provides a sample agenda.

Trainer's Worksheet 1.1

SEMINAR AGENDA, PRINCIPLES OF QUALITY

8:30–9:30	Overview of Crosby, Deming, Juran and the Baldrige Quality Award
9:30–10:30	The Cost of Quality: Theory and Practice
10:30–10:45	*Break*
10:45–noon	Setting Standards and Measures for Process Quality
noon–1:00	**Lunch**
1:00–2:30	Monitoring, Inspection, and Documentation
2:30–2:45	*Break*
2:45–3:30	Creating a Quality Policy
3:30–4:15	Recognition and Reward
4:15–4:30	Seminar Evaluation

Note: The sample agenda shows about as much as you can expect from a seminar brochure. That is, a good brochure will list or spell out in text the objectives for the learner, and will give you some idea of how much time will be spent on the various topics of the seminar. If you expect the seminar to be very interactive, perhaps making use of small group work during the lessons on setting standards and measures for process quality or on creating a quality policy, you will never know from the information above. You'll need the training plan of the seminar in order for you to see how the instructor will go about presenting the topics listed in the agenda.

Many a seminar that seemed to be interactive and learner-focused from the topics listed in the brochure turned out to be a lecture and very much instructor-focused. Your best hedge against disappointment is to carefully investigate your vendors before hiring them. Sometimes all you have to do is ask the vendor about the training techniques used in this particular seminar.

Talking with a vendor's other customers is also a good idea before you sign up your managers. Remember, a lecture is the easiest form of instruction to deliver and also the most cost-effective from the vendor's point of view, but it is probably the least effective way for anyone to learn anything, and it is especially inappropriate as a delivery method for instruction that is meant to eventually result in behavior change.

TRAINING PLAN 1.2

Using PC-Based Quality Software to Help Managers Plan for Quality Program Implementation

This training plan is an outline of the key elements, methods, and procedures involved in training managers and supervisors to plan for quality program implementation by using their own individual *personal computer quality software.* The outline is structured to enable the trainer to create lesson plans, an instructor guide, or course outline from it.

While the software is designed for the manager to use himself or herself, it is not enough to simply hand it to the manager and expect that manager to be able to use it, no matter how user-friendly the software design is. This training plan, therefore, outlines the approach to teaching a manager or supervisor how to use PC-based software.

OVERVIEW OF TRAINING METHODOLOGY

One of the biggest problems managers face as they embark on planning a comprehensive quality program throughout their departments or company is the problem of choosing the right things to measure. Nearly every business activity has something measurable about it, and if you think hard enough, you'll be able to quantify most anything. The trick in quality planning is to identify measures for things that make a significant difference in reaching quality goals set by the people at work.

If you do not have realistic quality goals, and not just profit goals (profit should be the result, not the goal), you can very easily end up choosing the wrong things to set standards for and to measure. The power of the personal computer in accessing information, matching, extrapolating, and revising is a natural ally to the manager who is trying to decide what's important to meeting new goals.

The training operation itself is a good example of the knotty decisions facing a manager who would be a quality planner. There are many familiar things to count; for example:

- numbers of trainees in class per year
- numbers of class hours, numbers of days per week in operation
- frequency of trainee choice for each course in the schedule
- numbers of poor evaluations
- numbers of rave reviews per instructor
- numbers of complaints about the food or the facilities

One could argue that perhaps none of the above-mentioned quantifications really matter when it comes to the quality of training and if trainees have learned anything. Yet, we could do all sorts of analyses on these numbers, do regression lines, and plot one measure against another on tidy graphs. If we do not have the ability to look at our selection of what to measure against our quality goals, we can easily spin our wheels measuring and analyzing data that tells us nothing about our quality progress.

If we look again at the training department operations, we can also see that processes such as creating a course or registering a trainee have measureable elements, and that these processes might be more relevant to making satisfied customers and be more likely to be tied to quality goals. If you engage in formative evaluation during the design of a course, you can find many things to measure, such as:

- numbers of development hours expended
- numbers of design errors in the topic outline
- numbers of times the course objectives had to be rewritten
- numbers of typos during production

If doing it right the first time is your goal, then you'll want to choose some of these development elements to measure. That's a very different kind of measure than the yearly average number of trainees per instructor—a number frequently publicized in training department annual reports. Doing it right the first time has very little to do with headcounts.

The point is to choose the right things to measure. The PC-based quality planning software approach is one that might work for you. Teaching managers and supervisors to use such software is best done in a group where trainees have their own PC and the software already loaded. A group computer training room of 8-12 stations is advisable if you have only one instructor. More stations and trainees can be accommodated if there are training aides available.

TIME REQUIRED

Six hours of hands-on classroom training, one trainee per computer; in addition, learning time on the job is also required as managers begin to use the software. In this, each manager will vary in the time required, depending on his or her general computer literacy and on the quality of his or her data.

TRAINEE LEVEL

This kind of teaching is done simultaneously in two areas: the content and processes of quality planning, and the content and procedures of the software. Trainees will be at different mastery levels in each of these areas; for example, a manager who is not computer literate and cannot type might be a genius at planning.

There are two steps you can take to make your job easier:

1. Choose a software package that quickly and actively engages the user by presenting the user with important and interesting challenges in the first screens. (The March issue of *Quality Progress* magazine of the American Society for Quality Control annually features a current list of quality software.)
2. Require that trainees bring with them a current set of data from their own departments that they can practice on in class. Specify this carefully ahead of time so that trainees come with customized data.

Your goal should be to get trainees' hands on the computers within the first half hour of class and let the clarity and enticement of the software take over; varying trainee levels will not be a problem if each trainee can quickly make something happen on the PC. And those trainees who are way above the others in computer literacy will be able to enjoy using the software creatively and in many different ways on their own data. It's a fact of life that you will have to deal with different trainee levels in this kind of training, but by using high quality materials, you should be able to manage the level situation with minimal instructional difficulty.

TRAINING OBJECTIVES

- To teach trainees to use quality planning software
- To enable each trainee to get around within the software
- To facilitate the trainee's correct use of documentation and reference manuals associated with the software
- To guide trainees in use of their own data with this software in order to see the possibilities for quality planning that the software provides (if trainees need help in choosing data, *Trainee Handout 1.2* provides suggestions)

LEARNING OBJECTIVES FOR THE TRAINEE

- To use quality planning software with my own data
- To access all screens and work my way around all commands, functions, and menus in the software
- To manage the system—get in, get out, review, branch, skip ahead, enter data, and generate output
- To use appropriate user documentation and manuals for help and for guidance
- To produce useful reports by asking the right questions

METHODS TO EVALUATE THE TRAINEE'S PROGRESS

Evaluating trainees' progress is best done at many times during the delivery of training, and in a friendly and somewhat informal way. This is called *formative evaluation* because it is evaluation that helps to form or shape instruction. Formative evaluation is developed in relationship to a specific learning objective, thus contributing to the effective accumulation of understanding and skill during a lesson.

In this kind of instruction, you will find yourself giving feedback and reassurance to trainees every few minutes, because there are so many different levels of competence represented by them and because you are dealing with two kinds of content, the computer content and the quality planning content. You will also find yourself being very active physically, as trainees need your watchful eye on their fingers and computer screens as they try out new commands and responses to system prompts. It's important to their progress that you do a lot of looking over shoulders, moving rapidly around the room, instructing as you go, and letting your evaluation of their actions propel you into the next training point. In this kind of training, end-of-process evaluation is almost useless, because it's the accumulation of small successes that will build trainees' confidence to go forward.

Keep your training plan very simple so that you can remember it on the move, or write down the major topics on a flipchart that you can see all the time. Remember that in the computer training, you are dealing with some psychomotor skills (eye-hand coordination, finger dexterity) as well as cognitive skills in the planning content area. Managers who do not use computers regularly will probably need a lot of practice time, need to develop some self-confidence, and need you to be patient with their psychomotor skills infancy. Good evaluation plays a major role in helping such trainees gain self confidence. Be sure that you're there when they need you. Help them to correct mistakes early and set them on a corrective path right away.

More Training Tips That Will Help You and Your Trainees

- Provide a comprehensive and graphically pleasing job aid (brochure, tent card, chart) listing how to perform the most common functions, so that when a trainee has succeeded in one operation, he or she can refer to the job aid and easily go on to the next operation without necessarily involving you in the training loop.
- Get trainees used to checking themselves by using a job aid, either for procedures, definitions, or formulas.
- Use these training crutches to facilitate formative evaluation and self-evaluation.
- Hook up a projection screen to your own computer so that you can demonstrate procedures and results to the entire group of trainees at once.
- Set up the training situation so that you are on the move most of the day, getting around to all trainees many times.

You'll know that trainees have learned when they begin using their own data for studies of their own choosing as they move through the software.

TRAINING TIPS	*EXERCISES*
1. Describe the three major tools of this training: the PC and its software, the documentation and job aid, and their own data.	1. Be sure that trainees have all documents readily at hand, system documentation, the job aid, and their own data. Wait until each person has gotten the briefcase opened and closed again and is comfortably set up with all materials at hand. Readiness is an important part of psychomotor training.
2. Within the first half hour of class, after introductions and housekeeping tasks, get the trainees' hands on the computer.	2. Give them a goal, for example, to go to one screen beyond the menu screen by choosing the second menu option, labelled "organizational overview." Refer trainees to a specific page in the documentation (user guide) that tells them how to get to the menu screen. Let them experiment on their own. Tell them that you'll be getting around the room to help, and that trainees who get there first should feel free to offer help to slower ones. Get to this point yourself on the projection screen, so that trainees know what the screen looks like—they'll evaluate their own progress.

3. When everyone is at the "organizational overview" description, step out of the computer training mode and into the quality planning content mode of instruction. You'll find yourself doing this many times during this training. Be aware of when you do this, so that you can begin the cognitive instruction at the appropriate level—comprehension before making judgments, description before explanation, and so on.	3. Talk about what this software can do, point out—perhaps on the projection screen or in the documentation manuals—how the system defines inputs, key activities, and outputs. Try to get trainees to envision some of their own data categorized as inputs, activities, or outputs. Get trainees to begin to match up their experience base with the described elements of the software.
4. Ask trainees to go back to the main menu and access a different screen, the "Customer Profile" screen.	4. Explain any keystroke shortcuts now, and be sure that the slower trainees know how the arrow keys, tab, backspace, and enter keys work in facilitating easy access throughout the system. More facile trainees will already be moving ahead, trying out some questions and answers on the next screen. Bring the entire class to the same point before you begin the cognitive instruction again.
5. Show trainees how to enter customer data as it is called for as you step through the "Customer Profile" section. Ask trainees to enter some of their own data, and to create several graphs as the system prompts. Then play "what if" with some of their data, changing it slightly to illustrate how the software instantly adjusts to show you a new option.	5. Use your PC and the projection screen to display your inputs and the system results as you talk your way through the procedures, step by step. Go slowly, make it seem easy and logical, and let trainees do it on their PCs also if they choose. The point of this exercise is to show the power of the software at data manipulation, so don't worry if all trainees don't try to do it themselves—this is essentially a cognitive exercise, not a psychomotor one. You're after comprehension here, not eye-hand coordination.
6. Continue on for the rest of the day in this fashion, moving between one kind of instruction and the other, drawing trainees ever more deeply into using their own data in response to system cues and questions.	6. At some point during instruction, show-trainees how to access and use libraries glossaries, tutorials, and help screens. Be sure that especially the novice computer user knows where to find information about the system in the documentation and on the job aid. Build the capability for self-study among all trainees.

Trainee Handout 1.2

MANAGER'S PROCESS MEASUREMENT CHECKLIST

Quality planning begins with your customer: first, your external customer who buys your product or service, and second, your internal customer—those departments and persons who receive the output of your work in common pursuit of that end product or service which gets sold. On the input side of the quality system, external suppliers provide materials and internal departments and persons provide their part of the company's product or service for you to work on. Customers and suppliers often hold the key to what to measure.

Look in every organization of the company for processes that can be measured on such dimensions as:

____ accuracy
____ completeness
____ timeliness
____ accessibility
____ clarity
____ ease of use
____ customer's judgment regarding fitness for use
____ supplier's record of providing exactly what you want
____ schedules
____ documentation
____ goals
____ procedures
____ meetings
____ inventories
____ praise, commendation
____ training
____ sufficiency (lack of redundancy)
____ consistency
____ reliability
____ reasonableness
____ necessity
____ efficiency

TRAINING PLAN 1.3

Setting Up a Corporate Learning Center for Quality Tools

This training plan is an outline of the key elements, methods, and procedures involved in *maintaining a corporate learning center* specifically to house quality tools that managers need to plan for and implement quality improvements. The learning center is designed to be a place for self-study with minimal training assistance.

One specific quality tool, the Pareto Diagram, from among the list of standard tools, is used as an example throughout this training plan. A glossary of common tools is provided in *Trainee Handout 1.3* at the end of this training plan.

OVERVIEW OF TRAINING METHODOLOGY

The corporate learning center is one environment in which self-study, or independent study, is encouraged. In order for this to be truly an effective learning time, management trainers should pay careful attention to learning objectives and training supports for the kinds of learning they expect to happen there, as they do in the many varieties of instructor-led training.

There are certain characteristics of adult learners that suggest that independent study could be the methodology of choice. These are that:

- Adults like to be in charge of their own learning
- Adults want workplace learning to be directly related to their jobs
- Adults would rather be at their work stations than in a workplace classroom
- Adults hate to risk looking foolish in front of their peers

Independent study in a well-maintained learning center addresses each of these characteristics. Individual carrels with breathing room, that is, not strung out in egg-crate fashion, provide independence for the learner and encourage a feeling that "I'm in charge here." Workers can come to the learning center when they need to learn a new skill or for information at the moment their jobs require it. An accessible learning center makes it seem like a worker is not wasting time by sitting in class. And finally, individuals can brush up on a rusty skill or learn a new one in the privacy of self-study, without having to be embarrassed by admitting a lack of skill in a group setting for training.

Learning the tools of quality management is one good application for the learning center. Many managers will believe that they are already "doing quality," when, in fact, they have forgotten how to use certain tools or have just plain ignored certain measures or procedures. The quality area is one in which a manager likes to be in control and does not like to admit to sins of omission. Both the nature of the learner and the nature of the quality content lend themselves to success with a learning center.

These are some general guidelines for operating an effective corporate learning center:

1. Involve the target trainees (managers and supervisors) in selecting the learning materials to include in the center.
2. Choose a variety of equipment, but beware of "bells and whistles." Be sure that equipment is easy to operate, sturdy, and comes with a maintenance contract.

Choose the kinds of equipment that most trainees will be familiar with using. Choose equipment designed to be used for the purpose of self-study; don't try to economize by getting equipment that is good for auditorium use and large groups.

3. Preview all films, slides, videotapes, audiotapes, and videodiscs to be sure styles of dress, business behavior, and content are current and nondiscriminatory. Don't believe the salesperson; see and hear for yourself before you buy it.
4. Develop your own trainee instruction card for each item of media or software. Make this a recognizable hallmark of your learning center, so that trainees look for it each time they use the center. On this card tell how to operate the equipment and summarize the key points of content of the material. List several learning objectives for the trainee on this card. Place this card in the same obvious spot in each learning station and hand it out with each piece of media or software.
5. Assign a clerk the job of keeping the learning center organized and functioning smoothly. This could be a part-time job for someone, or part of someone's job. This person would function as a media librarian and equipment maintenance and repair coordinator. It would be this person's responsibility to see that films and tapes were rewound after trainee use, that media were all filed correctly, and that maintenance records were properly kept. This person could also maintain the usage log for the center, and be the contact person when a trainee wanted to come and use it. Maintenance of a learning center catalog could also be part of this person's job.
6. Assign the job of hot-line counselor to someone in the training department. Liberally post the person's name and phone number throughout the learning center, and include it by all telephones in the center. Encourage trainees to call the hot-line counselor at any time during training when they have a procedural or content problem. Allow this person enough flexibility to do what needs to be done to support the learner (sit beside him or her, set up a meeting, talk him or her through the problem/solution). Be sure that the counselor's office is close to the learning center.

TIME REQUIRED

Any amount of time; generally two hours at one sitting is maximum for independent study. Short, focused learning sessions seem to be more productive for most people.

TRAINEE LEVEL

Trainees who come to a learning center to learn quality tools will be at a basic-skill level regarding the specific tool they're investigating, but at all levels of understanding and skill regarding the range of tools you have in your learning center.

TRAINING OBJECTIVES

- To maintain a corporate learning center for independent study of quality tools
- To equip the center with current hardware, software, media, and print materials appropriate for independent study
- To provide coordination and counseling support on call at all times for users of the center

- To promote on a regular basis through print and electronic notices the use of the learning center

LEARNING OBJECTIVES FOR THE TRAINEE

- To comprehend the features and characteristics of any specific quality tool required for the job
- To experiment with the quality tool in an independent study mode
- To apply the tool to job-related data during independent study
- To learn at the time learning is required

Note: The rest of this training plan focuses on one specific quality tool, the Pareto Diagram.

The Pareto Diagram is a vertical bar graph based on the principle that 80 percent of quality failures or errors are based on 20 percent of the problems. That is, the Pareto principle separates the vital few from the trivial many. The graphic representation of this principle helps you focus on that vital 20 percent in order to direct attention to the most important problem areas in which you are likely to find the most sources of error. In quality management and in life, we tend to get bogged down with the trivial many, finding it hard to assign weight to problems, and end up spending too much time and energy enmeshed with trivia. The Pareto Diagram helps direct your attention to the vital few.

In form, it is a bar graph characterized by the arrangement of data in columns in descending rank order, that is, the tallest column is the most important. In addition, a line plot drawn from left to right from the tallest bar indicates the cumulative frequency of errors across all bars.

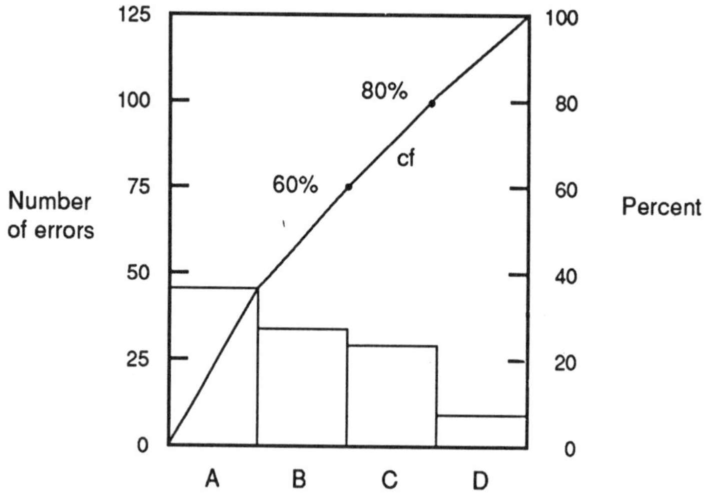

Simplified Pareto Diagram

In a self-study environment, the trainee can expect to find videotapes, interactive videodiscs, and computer software (CBT) that would be helpful in learning quality tools. Any self-study package should have the following characteristics:

TRAINING TIPS	*EXERCISES*
1. Overall purpose	1. See examples of the 80/20 principle.
2. Descriptive features	2. Point out the labels for each axis, show the bars indicating relative importance, and show the line plot indicating cumulative frequency.
3. Data required	3. Describe and explain why certain kinds of data are required to construct and interpret the Pareto Diagram.
4. Examples	4. Show examples of Pareto Diagrams made from sample sets of data. Be sure that trainees have clear instructions for branching, skipping over sections, and reviewing material as they use any interactive medium.
5. Practice	5. Lead the trainee through practice lessons, providing feedback either electronically or through an accompanying answer sheet.
6. Challenge to use one's own data	6. Provide a summary sheet or a procedures page so that the trainee can use the tool easily with his or her own data. Be sure that the hot-line counselor's number is available.
7. Record of use	7. Request the trainee to sign in and sign out, indicating the tool used and the business problem which precipitated the visit to the learning center.

Trainee Handout 1.3

GLOSSARY OF QUALITY TOOLS

These are the basic quality tools that any program of independent study should contain. These tools could be made available in a learning center or could be purchased in quantity and distributed to each manager for use at any time.

1. **Cause and Effect Diagram** (Fishbone Diagram)

   The cause and effect (fishbone) diagram helps you to identify the probable causes of a problem. Graphically it resembles a fish skeleton, with the quality problem (the effect) represented by the spine and the various causes of the problem represented by the ribs or bones on either side of the spine. To identify causes, work either from a frequency checksheet or a brainstorming group. Show relationships within major causes, resulting in a dispersion type fishbone diagram.

2. **Control Chart**

   The control chart shows departures from a standard in the continuing performance of a process. Its most common form is the X-bar and R chart which monitors the mean value and the range between minimum and maximum values. The control chart is based on the idea that fixable problems can be identified because they will cross the upper or lower control limits established for a process when that process becomes unstable.

3. **Flowchart**

   A flowchart is a representation of all of the steps in a process. Two flowcharts, an ideal process and an actual process, can be effectively contrasted to analyze the source of a problem. Obviously, an expert in dealing with the process in question must design the control charts for comparison. The flowchart uses simple symbols to represent actions: ovals start and stop actions; boxes are steps in the process; diamonds are decisions; and arrows are the direction of the action. All feedback loops must have an escape, and the entire chart must be connected.

4. **Histogram**

   A histogram is a bar graph of measurements. Typically, the measurements or categories of measurements are across the horizontal axis and the frequency of occurrence is on the vertical axis. A histogram is usually constructed from a frequency table of occurrences within the boundaries of categories. From a histogram, you can see a quick overview of variation in your data, as normal processes can be expected to produce a histogram resembling the shape of the normal curve.

5. **Pareto Diagram**

   The Pareto Diagram is a vertical bar graph and line plot indicating the cumulative incidence of error found in various parts of processes. It is based on the principle that it is better to concentrate corrective action on

Trainee Handout 1.3 (continued)

the vital few 20 percent of problem areas which generate 80 percent of the problems, than on the trivial many where numerous errors, but unimportant ones, are present. It is generally derived from a frequency of error checksheet of data collected over time.

6. **Scatter Diagram**

   A scatter diagram is a plot of points representing the relationships between variables. Scatter diagrams are derived from data collected in pairs that are suspected of having a relationship to each other. One variable is represented by the horizontal axis and the other variable is represented by the vertical axis. A point is placed on the graph for each item in the sample, indicating the measure of both variables. If the picture of all the points resembles a straight line, diagonally from lower left to upper right, the relationship between the variables is assumed to be strong, that is, as the variable on one axis changes, the variable on the other axis changes also.

7. **Other basic analysis tools**

   A well-equipped learning center for quality tools should probably also provide the basic statistical analysis tools:

   - measures of central tendency and dispersion (mean, median, mode, range and standard deviation)
   - the normal curve
   - percents and percentiles
   - reliability
   - regression lines

   Even well-seasoned managers and supervisors might have gotten out of the habit of measurement and analysis, so stay one jump ahead of them by providing good self-study packages in these measurement basics. You might want to also purchase some videotapes on the use of quality circles, quality councils, and quality improvement teams. Be sure the hot-line counselor is available for these too.

TRAINING PLAN 1.4

Using a Consultant During Implementation of Your Quality Improvement Program

This training plan is an outline of the key considerations involved in *hiring a consultant* to work with your managers and supervisors during implementation of your quality improvement program. Because this is the area of quality endeavor in which you expect managerial behavior to change and that changed behavior to be repeated over time, you are indeed engaged in a training program—an organizational learning program. As a corporate trainer, you should be instrumental in choosing the consultant and in planning the consultant's work.

All of the quality gurus and the Baldrige folks are clear about building into their systems for quality improvement the ongoing individual and group efforts that promote and facilitate long-term change. Time and new organizational structures such as quality councils and quality teams are required for defining problems, finding and correcting errors, developing and testing theories, establishing measures and controls, training, communicating, and empowering employees. It is the kind of situation in which a consultant can be used successfully.

A review of the seven Baldrige Award categories of a quality management system is instructive: leadership, information and analysis, strategic quality planning, human resources utilization, quality assurance of products and services, quality results, and customer satisfaction (U.S. Department of Commerce, National Institute of Standards and Technology, *1991 Application Guidelines*). When quality improvement is discussed, it is always in the context of a "system," seen as a complex web of interacting forces, activities, and people. The concept of quality improvement involves the concept of "over time."

Often in an undertaking of such magnitude, a consultant's position outside of the organization works in your favor. To be sure, the consultant you choose must know your company well and be acceptable to a broad range of employees, not just executives and managers. He or she must be a roll-up-the-sleeves, slosh-around-in-the-mud sort of person who can hassle through a statistical puzzle as well as give corrective feedback to your top executives. The right kind of objective but hands-on consultant can be charged with seeing the whole picture of organizational change potential, something your own staff cannot do because of their visceral and emotional attachment to their work. The right kind of consultant can intervene at the right times and back off at the right times, giving the visibility and the responsibility for change to employees themselves.

A good consultant can help you re-orient your total organization so that employees at all levels are structured for quality improvement; can help you define specific quality improvement projects; set up and monitor project teams; and mobilize the resources —including training and recognition processes—to engage in all of the analysis activities and corrective functions that quality improvement demands. And best of all, a good consultant will know when to leave your company and turn over a rejuvenated and redirected organization to your own managers.

OVERVIEW OF TRAINING METHODOLOGY

When you view the challenge of quality improvement as an instructional challenge, you can subject the chosen methodology to the rigors of a training plan. The taxonomy of educational objectives in the affective domain, developed by Krathwohl and colleagues and discussed earlier in this chapter, is the learning model upon which quality improvement can be superimposed. Each of the five successive stages in this model contains more learning, so that by the end of the fifth stage, the individual learner is able to integrate and consistently use the new values in his or her behavior. And this is what you want to happen during a quality improvement program too.

These are some of the services a consultant could provide on your quality improvement assignment:

- Leadership guidance one-on-one with your executives
- Seminars and workshops for small and large groups
- Analysis meetings with your customers and suppliers
- Planning
- Program audit
- Policy evaluation
- Training individuals in use of quality tools
- Feedback and follow-up to reinforce new behavior
- Statistical analysis
- Facilitation for quality councils, teams, circles, brainstorming meetings
- Promotion and public relations
- Internal communication
- Contacts for benchmarking visits
- Providing videos, books, software, and other vendor products in quality improvement
- Documentation and reports for executives, board members, stockholders

Trainee Handout 1.4-A is a checklist of items to consider when issuing a contract to a consultant.

TIME REQUIRED

At least six months, and probably closer to two years.

TRAINEE LEVEL

Quality improvement obviously must involve every employee at every level in the company. However, the primary audience for this consultant's work is the manager or supervisor, that is, one who has the job responsibility for producing product or service results. This trainee audience will be at varying levels of understanding regarding quality improvement goals, concepts, and tools.

TRAINING OBJECTIVES

- To provide consultant services over a two-year period for a company-wide quality improvement program, with special focus on managers and supervisors
- To be involved initially and throughout the consultant's tenure in organizational

analysis, monitoring and evaluation of results, and design and development of training courses and activities to implement the quality improvement program

- To promote and facilitate the quality improvement program through the affective domain learning model from awareness to adoption of new values (see *Trainee Handout 1.4-B*)

LEARNING OBJECTIVES FOR THE TRAINEE

- To improve the company through a comprehensive quality improvement program extending over a two-year period of time
- To work with the consultant and all company personnel, particularly providing guidance for those who report to me
- To participate fully in all analysis and evaluation tasks to determine causes of quality problems
- To implement and test solutions to quality problems
- To learn and apply new tools and procedures for quality improvement
- To establish and implement new systems and procedures for monitoring and sustaining quality improvements, including new reward and recognition systems

METHODS TO EVALUATE THE TRAINEE'S PROGRESS

As with other more conventional and more compressed training programs, an organizational learning program such as this quality improvement effort depends upon formative evaluation to move its instructional component forward. Formative evaluation of learning objectives such as these listed above still relates to each specific objective, even though the objectives are nearly all high-level ones requiring the trainee to master some more basic objectives first.

A review of the Krathwohl model (*Trainee Handout 1.4-B*) illustrates this. For example, the third learner objective, "to participate fully in all analysis and evaluation tasks to determine causes of quality problems," can be measured in terms of how fully the learner participated and whether or not he or she did or could participate in all analysis and evaluation tasks. The raw number and the identification of which tasks tell only part of the story.

According to the model, your objective for the learner is at the highest level (5.2) of affective learning, "characterization," whereby the learner does use a newly-learned value set. If that learner cannot do this, you'll want to find out why, and provide additional training to make up for the deficit in that trainee's learning. For example, consider the following reasons why the learner did not use the new value set:

- Perhaps the learner did not yet fully accept the reasons for his or her own full participation in all analysis and evaluation tasks. Look at level 3.1 in the model, "acceptance of a value."
- Perhaps there was a misunderstanding at some cognitive level; perhaps the trainee still believed that the old organizational lines of responsibility were in effect and that the quality assurance department really had responsibility for quality problem analysis.
- Perhaps you, the trainer, neglected to spend enough time simply describing the new organizational structure.

- Perhaps the trainee was out sick the day of the vice-president's vertical conference at which all of this and the cutover dates were explained.
- Perhaps this particular trainee was still at level 1.1, "awareness" or lacked the feedback regarding his or her own response (level 2.3) that might have enabled that learner to adopt the behavior change sooner.
- Perhaps this trainee didn't know how to use several key analysis tools and was reluctant to admit this lack of ability, so refrained from full participation.

Your ability as an evaluator of individual behavioral objectives, a formative evaluator, is critical in this kind of organizational learning program because that kind of periodic look at learning results will help to keep the entire learning program on track with corrective and supplemental training all along the way.

TRAINING TIPS

Training tips and exercises in this case will take the form of the consultant's plan of action for the two-year period. As the contractor, you might want to have detailed plans and timelines for each three-month period. One such plan might look like this:

Months 1, 2, 3 : Choosing three quality improvement areas

Key activities (Training tips)	***Techniques (Exercises)***
• All managers list possible problem areas	• Hold brainstorming sessions with managers across the company; mix operational areas
• Collect data	• Conduct interviews; send questionnaires; study files
• Report and interpret data	• Hold training sessions to learn interpretation tools, i.e., Pare to Diagram, review basic statistical measures of central tendency and dispersion
• Convene the Quality Improvement Council	• Promote the quality improvement program throughout the company; get visible involvement from executives in all promotion activities and commitment to serve on the Council
• Choose the three areas for concentration of quality improvement efforts	• Let Council decide this based on reports, and have them set the time line for the total program

The succeeding phases of the Quality Improvement Program would be developed in similar fashion, with your translation of the consultant's plans into training development methodology that you can monitor and evaluate, and to which training can make a considerable contribution.

Trainee Handout 1.4-A

CHECKLIST FOR CONSULTANT CONTRACT

____ 1. Brief (1-2 sentences) description of the project.

____ 2. Description of the consultant's role (e.g., provide technical writing support to three course developers; test the system).

____ 3. Specific time requirements that consultant is expected to work (e.g., part-time three mornings per week, 8 a.m. to noon, for six weeks).

____ 4. Estimated rates per hour, per day, and total (e.g., at $50 per hour, $400 per day, or 40 days at $16,000 total).

____ 5. Overtime restrictions and rates.

____ 6. Travel expense agreement. Rates, contact person, conditions of travel.

____ 7. Expectations regarding office space, and secretarial and word processing support.

____ 8. A staff contact/internal project manager.

____ 9. Project start date and end date.

____10. Contract extension conditions.

____11. Billing procedures and formats.

____12. Protection of intellectual property, or nondisclosure statement (i.e., consultant guarantees he or she will not disclose any of your company's proprietary information to any other person or corporation).

____13. Contract acceptance signatures and dates—yours and the consultant's.

Carolyn Nilson, *Training Program Workbook & Kit*, Englewood Cliffs, NJ: Prentice Hall, a Division of Simon & Schuster, 1989, p. 403.

Trainee Handout 1.4-B

KRATHWOHL's, et al. MODEL OF THE TAXONOMY OF EDUCATIONAL OBJECTIVES IN THE AFFECTIVE DOMAIN

1.0 Receiving	1.1	Awareness	
	1.2	Willingness to receive	
	1.3	Controlled or selected attention	
2.0 Responding	2.1	Acquiescence in responding	APPRECIATION, INTEREST
	2.2	Willingness to respond	
	2.3	Satisfaction in response	
3.0 Valuing	3.1	Acceptance of a value	ADJUSTMENT, VALUE, ATTITUDES
	3.2	Preference for a value	
	3.3	Commitment	
4.0 Organization	4.1	Conceptualization of a value	
	4.2	Organization of a value system	
5.0 Character-ization by a value complex	5.1	Generalized set	
	5.2	Characterization	

Chapter 2

Training Managers and Supervisors to Manage Diversity

America has always had a genius for making opportunity available to those who seek it, in our public life and in the great economic and educational institutions of our society. In fact, we guarantee equal opportunity through legislative and judicial processes that govern all Americans no matter where they live or work. Dealing with diversity is something Americans believe in, and something which we generally do rather well.

Our problems in managing work and diverse workers is not so much a difficulty with diversity as it is a human aversion to dealing with change. In the case of equity-based diversity-induced change, we have a deeper problem in figuring out what to do and how to do it in order to further the great human dignity and individual worth principles that have traditionally guided our enterprise.

To be sure, the human resources profile of the American workforce has changed in the last decade and will continue to change as we approach the year 2000. Many respected sources have given us statistics and interpretive information around them—the Bureau of Labor Statistics, the Census Bureau, the Hudson Institute (*Workforce 2000*), the National Center on Education and the Economy, Congress's Office of Technology Assessment, and the College Board, to cite only a few. All agree that the composition of the workforce will be less white male, more female, older, poorer, and less educated than in the recent past. All agree that diversity brings with it acute needs for basic skills in English language writing, reasoning, and expression, and with other basic skills such as basic mathematics and problem solving. All reports indicate that numbers of Asians, African-Americans, and Hispanics in the workforce will increase at higher rates than numbers of whites, and, in fact, real numbers of whites in the workforce will decrease because of low birth rates of white babies during the 1960s and 1970s. Work itself is changing, with a higher percentage of jobs requiring no more than a high school education, but with a small percentage of jobs at the high professional and technical end of the scale requiring advanced thinking skills and graduate degrees. We seem to be losing the great middle.

The nature of the changing workplace can seem overwhelming. At the same time that work is changing, the people who do it are changing too, but probably not in parallel. The dichotomies are hard to understand—consider the following examples:

- we send work "off shore" because we can get high productivity and high quality workers, yet Asians and Hispanics are flocking especially to our border and coastal states in large numbers for better work opportunities

- entry-level jobs in fast food chains, retail stores, and factories go begging, yet numbers of homeless working-age men and women swell to as many as 10,000 per night in New York City shelters[1]
- our appetite is ravenous for Japanese cars, cameras, and VCRs, but our computer software labs are still the best in the world
- women are working in huge numbers in a broad range of jobs, but few are present as CEOs and board chairpersons
- we impose import tariffs to protect our component manufacture, such as laptop computer screens, yet many of our major hardware manufacturers can make more profit by "outsourcing" entire projects—getting around the tariff issue and keeping quality up—but resulting in a net loss of work for American workers
- we encourage foreign companies to build their products, for example, cars, in factories on U.S. soil, but complain when their products satisfy American consumers better than competitive American products do

These seemingly opposite pulls are typical of the upheaval in the human resources foundation of the American workplace and they present managers and supervisors with human resources management challenges unlike any that the current crop of business leaders has seen before. It is difficult to separate one's emotional, psychological, and sociological responses from one's business decision making. Diversity in the workplace is greater than it has ever been before, and it demands better management.

HOW TO MEET THE CHALLENGES OF THE CHANGING WORKFORCE

This chapter focuses on managing the workforce—the diverse kinds of people who make up the human resources base of American business. Management trainers have an unusual opportunity to help mold the workforce into a high-quality, productive, and effective business asset that appreciates in value over time. Managers and supervisors are clearly looking for and are in need of help, and trainers generally have the skills to do the helping. What's often lacking on the parts of both the managers and supervisors and the trainers is a clear vision and definition of what the diversity is really all about—and the variety and depth of how much really has to be done. This chapter offers some definitions and some guidance.

Valuing Differences Among Workers

Valuing differences is generally thought of as awareness and accepting obvious differences among people. It is generally focused at the individual, personal level, as contrasted with the group or organizational level.

Training in valuing differences often includes the following approaches:

- role playing involving adopting another's point of view
- creating multi-ethnic task forces to work out a specific problem
- holding panel discussions on common topics by persons who obviously represent differing constituencies
- using videotapes showing how different employees would solve the same business problem according to their own cultural biases
- providing behavioral checklists and language immersion courses to managers who travel to other countries for business prior to their departure

- conducting training-related sensitizing events, such as ethnic foods luncheons or workshops in dealing with deaf or blind employees

Training for valuing differences has a personal consciousness-raising feel to it.

Affirmative Action

Affirmative action has been the chief anti-discrimination strategy of corporate America for several decades, spurred on by the U.S. government. The assumptions upon which it was built focused on the redress of apparent employment inequities based on sexual and racial prejudice against women and minorities by the mainstream white male business power structure.

Affirmative action strategies carried with them hiring and promotion quotas and a host of exclusionary development programs designed to right past wrongs regarding the target groups. In spite of real gains by women and minorities because of affirmative action, it currently has a rather negative press and has become stereotyped, even by many of its beneficiaries, as an unfortunate exercise in imposing the stigma of differential treatment within the quota concept and in pushing unqualified people into positions of certain failure. Affirmative action carried with it the unfortunate consequence of "reverse discrimination" litigation and other forms of backlash in numerous companies. Many businesses today are choosing not to use the term "Affirmative Action" any more.

Managing Diversity

Managing diversity, first and foremost, is a concept that begins with the word managing. It is seen as a total approach to making things happen in organizational life, and it carries with it all of the current employee empowerment and facilitative management philosophies. Managing diversity is concerned with planning, allocating resources, designing work, providing leadership, monitoring, evaluating, creating and promoting policy, setting standards, establishing priorities, and a host of other standard management tasks that are needed for organizations to function well.

Managing diversity implies a comprehensive approach to making the workplace a setting in which all kinds of workers can achieve the best they are able to achieve according to their abilities and aspirations in pursuit of common corporate goals. It has an organizational thrust, rather than a personal one. Managing diversity encompasses more than race and gender—it reflects the new diversity of the American workplace and includes diversity of age, lifestyle, ethnicity, educational background, learning style, language, religion, handicapping condition—and race and gender. Issues of inclusion versus exclusion, access versus lack of access for all kinds of employees are the issues in managing diversity. The melting pot of assimilation is challenged by the salad bowl of distinguishing differences.

ORGANIZING A TRAINING CONFERENCE TO CREATE A CLIMATE FOR MANAGING DIVERSITY

The training methodology chosen to address the challenge of teaching managers and supervisors to manage diversity is a training conference. Trainers should think of a conference as an instructional methodology, not simply a means of disseminating information of corporate public relations. And when you do this, you will approach conference planning with all of the care and systematic decision making as you would approach building an instructional plan for classroom training.

Conferences teach people many things: new skills, new understandings, new attitudes, new modes of interaction, new ways of communicating and cooperating. Learning at a conference includes task learning as well as process learning, intentional instruction and learning because of one's own ability to reach out or to synthesize information presented in "messy" form. Conferences are ideal media through which group instruction can be presented.

The built-in bonus of the conference format is that, given a little direction and focus, individual attendees ("trainees") can learn a great deal from the conference because they themselves are choosing to participate in only the workshops, lectures, and events of priority interest to them. As adult learners, conference-goers have a wonderful opportunity to exhibit one of the basic principles of adult learning, and that is, that adults like to be in charge of their own learning.

Conferences have the potential, as no other methods of training have, of enabling trainees to take the first steps towards changing their behavior because of what they learned. In the conference format for instruction, trainees have a rich opportunity to network with others who are interested in the same things, and who often represent a critical implementation factor that would be hard to find through normal day-to-day workplace interactions. Conferences can be efficient vehicles for establishing a climate for understanding and action.

Four Reasons Why the Conference Format Works

The conference format addresses some of the other key characteristics of adult learners in ways that make it comfortable for trainees to learn. These characteristics are:

1. Adults want training that's directly related to the work that they do. At a conference, they can choose to attend only the most relevant parts of the program.
2. An adult learner has a preferred style of learning. At a conference, trainees self-select into learning situations where they believe they can succeed.
3. Adult learners at work need to be valued as workers and contributors to the common good, in spite of what they don't know and within the context of continuing education. At a conference, co-workers have a chance to talk about and get feedback about their successes and challenges and to share in the camaraderie of pursuing new skills and knowledge together.
4. Adult learners want reminders of learning, so that they can have an easier chance of integrating what's new into their old ways of doing things. At a conference, trainees usually have many opportunities to gather up reports, handouts, mementos, business cards, books, and other memory-joggers which are useful at a later time as they attempt to adopt new behaviors learned at the conference.

Making the Conference Format Serve Your Objectives for Learning

As you decide how to teach your managers and supervisors how to manage diversity, you'll be faced with determining the business reasons driving the desire for training and you will have to figure out what realistic, doable learning goals will be. Neither of these tasks is easy, and it is difficult to keep emotions and biases out of your deliberations. When you determine what exactly the business drivers are, list them. Expect items such as:

- "to give recruiters a competitive edge by sending the signal that this company values and has opportunity for all persons"
- "to minimize employee turnover, especially in technical ranks"
- "to improve personal productivity"

Then, establish objectives for the kinds of learning you want to happen, and go about designing conference experiences to accomplish your learning objectives.

Realize that in a conference all trainees will not take advantage of everything you have designed for them. The benefit of a conference is that the learning is flexible, that trainees take what they want or need from a conference. Often you have no way of predicting what experiences will attract which employees; often the dynamics of the conference itself affect who goes where when the conference is up and running.

Planning the Conference

Trainer's Worksheet 2.0 will help you with the initial stages of conference planning. Keep in mind that effective conferences are minutely planned, to the last detail. Even in a short one- or two-day conference, it's a good idea to have one chairperson who deals with overall management tasks and two different assistant chairpersons, one for program content and one for facilities/food. Early in your thinking about a conference, be sure to get agreement from your own management about the title and objectives of the conference, and write them down. Then later when decisions have to be made about whether or not to include a certain vendor or speaker, you'll have a firm purpose in mind for the conference and all further planning will be that much easier. Don't neglect the critical deliberations about objectives early in your planning; and plan early to assign responsibility for the myriad elements within each major category of conference planning.

Ensuring Diversity in the Conference Itself

When you begin interacting with various other managers and with your conference committee, you will uncover your own biases and stereotyped behaviors, and those of your colleagues. Be ready for this, because it sometimes catches you by surprise. If you are in a company that has been dominated by a white male power structure, try to enlist the help of some nonwhite males in your earliest planning stages so that you have a better chance of checking your perceptions, your terminology, and your expectations, and of filtering out at least some of the problems so that you don't inadvertently design bias into the conference.

Here are some general management guidelines that can be useful during planning:

- Think in terms of individuals speaking only for themselves, that is, a person of "difference" is never representative of an entire group, race, gender, or category of worker. Remind yourself constantly that diversity is about the beauty of differences, not the convenience of sameness.
- Always try to expand and broaden your definitions. The aim is to include but not to assimilate.
- Look at each operational system in your company for potential sources of lack of diversity. Focus on such things as marketing, public information, internal communication, sales, accounting, promotion, termination, turnover, recruitment, performance appraisal, training, mentoring, company-related social events. By looking at each system separately, you'll find problems that can be addressed.
- Go beyond the mindset and past practices of preferential treatment of one group or another. If your proposed speaker, vendor, or small group session deals with special considerations, quotas, or other preferred status, you're on the wrong track. Managing diversity is about motivation to excel, not to conform; about equal opportunity to build a future, not about redress of past grievances.

Endnote

[1]Thomas Morgan, "Fear and Dependency Jostle in Shelters," *The New York Times*, November 4, 1991, p. B2.

Trainer's Worksheet 2.0

CONFERENCE PLANNING WORKSHEET

Title: ______________________________

Objective(s): ______________________________

____

Audience: ______________________________

____

Date: ______________________________

Location: ______________________________

____

Planning Element	Person Responsible	Start Date	End Date	Comment

Management: ______________________

- Budget, Finances ______________________________
- Mailing List ______________________________
- Registration ______________________________
- Evaluation ______________________________
- Public Relations ______________________________
- Message Center ______________________________
- Mementos ______________________________

Program: ______________________

- Schedule ______________________________
- Content/Topics ______________________________
- Speakers ______________________________
- Audio/Visual Media ______________________________
- Exhibits ______________________________
- Handouts ______________________________

Facilities/Food: ______________________

- Meeting Rooms ______________________________
- Meals, Coffee Breaks ______________________________
- Accommodations ______________________________
- Parking ______________________________
- Reception, Hospitality ______________________________
- Transportation ______________________________

adapted from Carolyn Nilson, *Training Program Workbook and Kit*, Englewood Cliffs, NJ: Prentice-Hall, a division of Simon & Schuster, 1989, p. 245.

TRAINING PLANS

During your content planning, consider all of the options open to you regarding delivery format, and design tasks and processes that are appropriate for the varying subjects of your particular conference. The rest of this chapter includes sample training plans for typical conference sessions and events in the area of managing diversity. As you decide upon the topics to include in your conference, expand certain topics according to your business "drivers" for the conference and the priority of your conference objectives. Consider covering some topics in luncheon addresses or keynote speeches. Consider running a video festival around one or two topics, consider poster sessions, wine and cheese round tables, a training games room, a managing diversity bookshop, an ethnic foods smorgasbord. Don't get stuck in the lecture format for group sessions: think of all conference events and activities as group training challenges, and make the most of your opportunity to choose creative options for instructional techniques.

In the following topics, the standard training plan format has been altered slightly to accommodate the special characteristics of the conference. General worksheets follow all of the training plans.

These are some possible topics to include in a conference on managing diversity:

	management issues	*training techniques*
2.1	What You Need to Know About the Law, e.g., Civil Rights Act of 1991	Action-based overheads and effective use of handouts
2.2	Supervisors on the Hot Seat: Realities of Day-to-Day Diversity Management	Role play using "blind" identities; Using videos to increase awareness
2.3	How to Assess an Organization's "Managing Diversity" Needs	Workshop in organization analysis
2.4	How to Write a "Managing Diversity" Policy	Panel discussion and workshop in writing policy
2.5	How to Prepare a Manager's "Personal Action Plan"	Workshop in creating a Personal Action Plan

TRAINING PLAN 2.1

What You Need to Know About the Law, e.g., The Civil Rights Law of 1991

This training plan is an outline of the key elements, methods, and procedures required to train managers and supervisors, in a conference setting, to address the issue of civil rights legislation through a small or large group session using *action-based overhead transparencies and handouts.*

At any conference on managing diversity, current legislation—state and federal—should be examined carefully. The recently passed federal Civil Rights Act of 1991 is chosen here as an example.

OVERVIEW OF TRAINING METHODOLOGY

Because of the perceived importance of the topic, you can expect a small group session on it to attract a large crowd, and, in fact, you might want to turn this topic into one that the entire conference audience attends. The trick with such a topic is to make it more than simply an information dump. This is where establishing learning objectives for the topic will pay off. This training plan shows you how to use overheads and handouts as more than information.

TIME REQUIRED TO DELIVER THIS TRAINING

30 - 40 minutes
This training can be delivered through a small group session or as an entire-conference large group session.

TRAINEE LEVEL

The audience for this session is anyone who attends this conference. The potential trainee level, therefore, is as broad as the conference mailing list and as imbalanced as the biases and experiences of those on it. When planning a conference, one of your first considerations is what mailing list you will use—exactly for whom will you design this conference.

The assumption here is that the audience will be managers and supervisors, but in a profound human dignity context such as managing diversity, you will probably find that your trainee learning threshold or "learning readiness" level will vary greatly within what on the surface might seem to be a rather homogeneous audience. In such a conference, you will run up against "learning curve" problems in which an individual's biases, fears, or insecurities will prevent effective learning, flattening the learning curve.

TRAINING OBJECTIVES

- To present an overview of the Civil Rights Act of 1991 using action-based overhead transparencies and handouts
- To engage all trainees in analysis of the new legislation

LEARNING OBJECTIVES FOR THE TRAINEE

- To read highlights of the Civil Rights Act of 1991
- To identify new provisions of the law, contrasting them with current civil rights legislation
- To analyze the new legislation, determining areas of one's own responsibilities which these new features will affect

METHODS TO EVALUATE THE TRAINEE'S PROGRESS

In keeping with the formative evaluation thrust of good instruction, you'll want to give trainees—even in a large group of 100 or more people—some indication that they are meeting the objectives for learning. You'll be able to see trainees engage in marking up the handouts, leafing through pages, reading, making margin notes, and so on—you'll be able to hear the activity associated with learning.

When you are fairly well assured that trainees are learning in the way you expected them to, give the group some feedback—"Yes, that's right," "No, on the second page," "Look's like you have it there," and so on. When a speaker functions as an instructor, and not simply a dispenser of information, that speaker interacts with the audience in an evaluative fashion in order to encourage more and better movement towards more and better learning.

TRAINING TIPS	*EXERCISES*
1. Ask trainees to get the copy of the Civil Rights Act of 1991 out of their conference folders to follow along with you.	1. Before the conference, be sure that folders include a copy of the legislation for everyone. At the start of your presentation have several assistants move forward in the aisles with visible extra copies of the legislation. The first step is being sure that every trainee recognizes the legislation.
2. Introduce the legislation by walking forward toward the trainees, holding a copy in your hand. Suggest to them that your focus during the next half hour will be on what's different about this legislation from current law.	2. Leaf through the law itself, pausing at key provisions which you intend to cover in a few minutes. Suggest that trainees leaf through their copies with you. Say the section number and title of major topics. In this way, you have just described your content outline in a concrete way, helping the learner to see the priority of provisions.

3. Begin your overhead presentation by showing a short list (four or five items only) of terms that form the key issues in the debate over civil rights, 1990s-style. Some of these could be:

   - disparate impact
   - burden of proof
   - business necessity
   - job-related
   - compensatory damages

   Read the list to them slowly and deliberately.

3. Give your trainees the chance to see the terms written out, singled out and emphasized (after having heard them said by you, and perhaps after having seen the terms in the context of the law itself). Suggest that they might want to use a highlighter pen to point out these terms as you go over them in the law.

   The idea here with all of the "stage business" is to draw trainees into an active involvement mode so that, hopefully, they will want to continue acting on behalf of civil rights. It would have been much easier to simply mail a copy of the new legislation to each manager and supervisor, with instructions to begin doing business according to it. That's an information dump, not training.

4. Show about 10 overheads made from the law, with key sections, e.g., "disparate impact," greatly enlarged.

4. Go slowly as you introduce each major issue, use a non-permanent colored pen to underline or highlight key phrases or ideas. Give trainees your interpretation of how that issue or idea will impact your business in the immediate term and long term.

5. Contrast the new provisions with current law, briefly, pointing up only the issues of contention.

5. The reason for doing this is to help trainees cement in their minds what is new. In learning conceptual information, it often helps to see what a thing is not, as well as what it is.

   Talk trainees through the differences, or use contrasting copies of the current legislation (use different color acetates, stick-on highlighter acetate patches, or different color marking pens).

6. Conclude the session by showing overheads of interpretations of the new law. Use newspaper articles, magazine articles, publications from your senator's office, or words from your corporate attorney. Be sure that references are clearly visible in case anyone wants to read the documents you've cited.

   Give trainees several names of persons in the company whom they can call for more information with the new legislation.

6. Steer your comments around to what needs to be done around this company in order to comply with the nuances of the new law. End by commenting on the big picture in the 1990s world of civil rights in the workplace.

TRAINING PLAN 2.2

Supervisors on the Hot Seat: Realities of Day-to-Day Diversity Management

This training plan is an outline of the key elements, methods, and procedures required to train managers and supervisors, in a conference setting, to come to grips with the day-to-day realities of managing diversity. It is a plan for instruction that will be especially useful to supervisors or to managers who must get involved in the daily direction and facilitation of the work of others. The instructional techniques presented here feature *observation of videotapes of individuals at work and role plays* during the group session.

A conference on managing diversity should have many practical small group sessions in which trainees can test their assumptions, practice new attitudes and behaviors, and begin to see how they themselves can make changes in the way they do business in order to achieve a workplace where all employees can succeed. This training plan is for such a session. In past times, it might have been called "sensitivity" training, or "awareness" training.

As you plan this kind of session, keep your conference objectives in mind and choose topics that obviously fit. Keep the focus on the supervisor's interaction with those reporting to him or her; get down to the nitty-gritty of interpersonal, one-on-one relationships. Dispense with the grand principles and legal terminology. What you're after in this session is instruction in how to act on a day-to-day basis in order to manage diversity well.

Some topics you might consider are these:

- Should we have a "mommy track"?
- Can we afford not to offer child care?
- How do I come across to handicapped workers?
- How long can I retain workers with AIDS?
- Why don't Hispanic workers work here?
- What can we do about our practice of unequal perqs?
- Do we know how to recruit older workers?
- Why do only males show up for technical training?

OVERVIEW OF TRAINING METHODOLOGY

For this small group session, focus on as many topics as you have time for; for example, make this a two-hour session and deal with about four topics. If this looks like it will be a popular session, run it twice during the conference, perhaps once in a morning time slot and once in an afternoon time slot.

The main thrust of this kind of session is self-awareness regarding one's contributions to problems with managing diversity, and personal identification and involvement with some kind of solution. Keep the group rather small, perhaps a maximum of 20 people. Don't deny that you have problems; the clue is to identify the problems correctly so that you can begin to solve them.

This training plan suggests two of many ways to increase a person's self awareness about human relations issues. One approach is role playing, using "blind" role assignments; another approach is guided viewing of videotapes created for this purpose (available from numerous sources).

In role playing, the instructor hands out roles to trainees so that they can't see who they are supposed to be (baseball caps with the role written on the front, or stickers for trainees' foreheads). The idea in this kind of role play is for the role "player" to experience what it feels like to be perceived as different—everyone else in the room can see the player's identity. Role players together focus on solving a typical work problem, such as:

- Teaching a new hire how to use the word processing system
- Sharing your office mate's telephone answering machine and documentation books
- Arranging a car pool and using it
- Reaching consensus on what to include in a departmental needs analysis regarding child care
- Agreeing on a format for a report on what the major human resources challenges are for the next six months and on the priority listing of the challenges

The task is to go about solving the group's problem, but reacting to the "blind role" in a stereotyped, even if subtle, way—probably similar to the current way of reacting to that particular role. Be sure to de-brief after the role play exercise.

In guided videotape viewing, the instructor generally works from a handbook or video guide furnished with the tape. In such a tape, you'll probably be looking for evidence of the personal and business benefits of diversity, strategies for recognizing and valuing individual strengths, and models of effective communication within a diverse workforce. Look for videotapes and guidebooks that are as broad or as narrow as your objectives, and lead your trainees according to the suggestions for discussion in the guidebook. There are many good tapes on the market, so be choosy. Using the tapes and discussion guide is a good way to start this particular small group session.

TIME REQUIRED TO DELIVER THIS TRAINING

Probably two hours, but could be extended to three hours.

TRAINEE LEVEL

The audience for this small group session is any manager or supervisor who has self-selected into the group, plus walk-ins who show up the day of the conference without having previously registered. You can expect supervisors to outnumber managers because of their immediate interest in dealing directly with significant numbers of persons reporting to them on a day-to-day basis. The trainee audience will exhibit varying levels of sensitivity and ability to manage diversity. Their titles and job functions may be the same, but their bias levels and attitudes will show a wide range.

TRAINING OBJECTIVES

- To show a videotape or tapes on managing a diverse workplace and guide trainees in a discussion according to the guide book that comes with the video. (20-30 minutes of tape)
- To lead trainees in a problem-solving role play, using "blind" role assignments.

(Divide a group of 20 into 3 work groups, each of which works on a different problem.)

- To debrief all trainees after the role play, with the goal of facilitating self-awareness of one's biases and obstacles to effective management of diversity.
- To lead trainees into the initial stages of planning for follow-up action that's achievable.

LEARNING OBJECTIVES FOR THE TRAINEE

- To identify one's own biases and personal obstacles to effectively managing diversity.
- To view the videotape objectively and analytically.
- To engage in blind role play in order to experience the effect of bias in a typical workplace problem-solving situation.

METHODS TO EVALUATE THE TRAINEE'S PROGRESS

In this kind of personal revelation training, it is difficult to tell how much people are learning during the exercises. Often, gregarious and extroverted personalities are quick to enter into the training experiences and it appears as though they are learning a great deal, while some other more quiet types of trainees say very little and seem reluctant to participate. The quantity of participation doesn't always indicate the quality of participation, so you have to be aware of both kinds of responses to exercises such as "sensitizing" or "awareness" exercises—sometimes the quiet participant will in fact learn faster and ultimately achieve more than the noisy one.

Your task as instructor is to encourage both kinds of trainees—and all those in between the extremes. One reason to keep class size small is so that you can give feedback to individuals as they work their way through new ways of thinking and communicating. This is especially helpful in the three small role play groups. (If you have more than three small groups, enlist the help of another trainer/facilitator to work with you. One person can handle only about three groups.) During this time, spend a few minutes with each small group, supporting the new insights of each person. Throughout the session, look for clues that individuals are achieving a better understanding of themselves. Bias, unfortunately, is a fact of life. Do not criticize inappropriate responses; rather, focus on those moments when individuals seem to be awakening to new possibilities.

TRAINING TIPS	*EXERCISES*
1. Review the learning objectives so that trainees know that this session is not simply the dissemination of information.	1. Since this is a small group, use a flipchart which can be brought up closer to the audience than a screen. Save the overhead or slide presentation for larger groups. Write the objectives on the chart as you say them. Ask trainees if they have other personal objectives. Add them to the flipchart.

2. Show the videotape on managing a diverse workforce.

2. Use handout materials and instructor guide furnished with the videotape. If there are no guides, create a simple list of questions raised by the video and hand these out to trainees to review as they watch the tape.

3. Lead trainees in a brief discussion of the tape, focusing on taped individuals' behaviors, biases, and points of view.

   Your aim in this part of the session is to get trainees thinking about that one-on-one interaction—which the role play coming next will approach from a more direct "sensitivity" angle.

3. Use your own list of reference questions or study guides furnished by the video producer.

   Keep in mind that a videotape is a good introductory stimulus, and that your goal in interacting with trainees at this early part of the small group session is to be sure that they didn't miss any key concept. Videos are good at showing and telling, that is, at defining and explaining, but often in a compressed fashion. Viewers can easily get distracted from the main messages by the enticement of the medium—the glamour and the action. You also have to be careful that you don't dampen the spirits and enthusiasm of trainees by over-analysis of the messages. Be sure to leave this part of the training on a high note of interest and motivation. Videos are usually very good at inspiring and raising the sights of viewers.

4. Divide the group into three small groups for role play. Give each trainee a baseball cap with a role written on it. Choose any that are important to your company, such as:
   - age 59
   - Black male
   - Chinese Ph.D.
   - company president
   - new hire
   - in a wheelchair
   - blind
   - single mother, 4 kids
   - job-sharer
   - poor reader
   - Spanish-speaking
   - HIV-positive
   - ex-convict

4. Tell the groups that they will be given a typical workplace problem to solve during the next 15 minutes, and that they are each to function as a problem-solving team. Ask each group to choose a leader. They are to initiate action as they normally would, but be very aware of the constraints that their team members' roles impose on them.

   The task goal is to come to some agreement on a problem solution. The process goal is to feel the effect of prejudice.

5. At the end of the role play, call trainees back into the larger group and lead them in a general discussion of their feelings about the effect of bias on their ability to deal with the task at hand.	5. During the role play, trainees will experience the discomfort of being excluded, ignored, or perhaps listened to in a stereotypical way that has nothing to do with ability. Instruct trainees to be ready for these feelings and to try to remember the context in which they occurred. Tell trainees to identify their roles at the end of the exercise.
6. Conclude the discussion with a call to action in their own ways of interacting and for the good of their organizations.	6. Don't make the action part too structured. Go for a general commitment to change based on an individual's new sensitivity to the detrimental effects of bias in the workplace.

TRAINING PLAN 2.3

How to Assess an Organization's "Managing Diversity" Needs

This training plan is an outline of the key elements, methods, and procedures required to train managers and supervisors, in a conference setting, to assess their own organization's needs regarding managing diversity. This particular training plan is for a *workshop that uses actual data from individuals' own departments* to frame the problems and solutions to various diversity management challenges. It is cast as either a small group session, that is, a workshop session, during the conference, or as a pre-conference workshop.

This kind of working session requires participants to have done some preparation work before coming to training. This is sometimes difficult for people to do, so this particular training methodology requires some up-front work on the part of conference planners. It is often a good idea to select the people whom you want to attend this session, get agreement from their supervisors to attend the "reporting out" part of the session too, and communicate briefly with each potential attendee at least one week in advance of the conference regarding the materials he or she will bring to the workshop. This kind of working session is enhanced by the tangible support of the trainees' management and by their presence at part of the workshop. This kind of training is especially important if your conference objectives include items such as "to organize for action" or "to create plans for implementation of new practices." In classic training theory, "transfer" is speeded from training encounter to job by the visible support of management.

In a workshop of this kind, trainees are encouraged to identify the errors they've made in the past; to recognize incongruities in their behaviors, styles, and attitudes; and to look equally to long-term solutions as well as short-term fixes. In addition, trainees are asked to commit to the following:

- replacing prediction and control with flexibility and facilitation
- supporting change and risk
- removing barriers to contribution
- rewarding persistence
- working to create new norms and values
- ousting current gatekeepers
- redefining jobs

Current management assumptions and systems are under intense scrutiny in such a workshop.

In such a workshop, it becomes painfully clear that traditional assumptions about success at work are not necessarily shared by a diverse workforce. For example, doing better is a good thing—a solid American value—is not necessarily valued the same way by persons who believe in the greater good of stability and a sense of style, both of which require a more static set of processes than the continuous and unsettling striving for success that "doing better" suggests. Or, the great egalitarian American principle of freedom with responsibility in terms of making a difference in public life and at work is often at odds with many persons in a diverse workforce whose cultural heritage stresses the legitimacy and right of hierarchical authority and the surety and efficiency of class-based society. In workshops of this sort, you can expect trainees to wrestle with significant change in workplace culture, especially as they attempt to deal not with managing for assimilation, but with managing diversity.

OVERVIEW OF TRAINING METHODOLOGY

The workshop using actual data is chosen as a training methodology for the subject of managing diversity for several reasons:

- the subject of *managing* diversity is one that can benefit from suggestions of fellow managers in the workshop; that is, in this kind of subject, two heads are often better than one in problem solving, and the whole turns out to be greater than the sum of its parts in terms of effect on the company
- the structure of a workshop—with its examination of models, causes and effects, and systematic analysis of data—can often help people who tend to get emotionally involved in the surrounding issues to see more clearly what needs to be done
- the feeling of "we're in this together" that comes from shared focus by a variety of individuals gives support to other trainees in the group
- the scheduled invited presence of upper management motivates trainees to work efficiently towards proposed solutions during the workshop so that they all have something of importance to say during that "reporting out" section of the workshop

The other important ingredient of the structure of this workshop is its use of a *model* for organizational needs analysis. One such model is that developed by R. Roosevelt Thomas, Jr., President of The American Institute for Managing Diversity at Morehouse College in Atlanta. Part of the training methodology of the workshop is use of a model through which to organize one's data and focus one's thoughts. Early in the workshop, the model will have to be described and explained to trainees. Thomas's model, of organizational culture as tree roots (*Trainee Handout 2.3-A*), lends itself nicely to a colored slide or a large poster as a visual aid to instruction.

When you teach students about a model, think of the instruction as divided into two parts, the *conceptual* model itself, and the *skills* involved in how to use the model. Conceptual, or knowledge-based learning is taught differently from the way skills are taught. Good training methodology consciously separates the two parts of this instruction when the objectives for learning include understanding of the model as well as its use. Because this particular training is delivered as a workshop (and not simply a lecture), and trainees are expected to apply the model, not just know what it looks like, both kinds of instruction are required.

Here are some guidelines.

When teaching concepts, follow these steps:

1. Name the model. Use visual aids.
2. Tell its preferred application and the "big picture" of why it can be helpful.
3. Describe the critical properties of the model (for example, roots, trunk and branches, environment).
   —define or explain any unfamiliar terms (for example, assumptions)
   —elaborate on each property so that trainees can see the whole and the interrelationships among the parts
4. Give an example(s) of the model as it applies to a current business situation with which students are familiar.
5. Contrast the model with something that it is not (for example, a flowchart).
6. Synthesize information from steps 1 - 5 to verify the concept.

Stated in outline form, the essentials of concepts are:

1. name
2. big picture application
3. critical properties and their interrelationships
4. positive example
5. negative example
6. synthesis

Skills, on the other hand, are taught differently. When teaching skills, follow these steps:

1. Check students on their knowledge of the concept (review, ask questions, point out key ideas, check definitions).
2. State the aim of learning the skill; specify the intended outcome (for example, to produce an organizational needs assessment report).
3. Tell students what procedures they'll have to use.
4. Show examples of completed work.
5. Teach procedures, step by step.
6. Guide students in practice
   —give frequent feedback to each student
   —get students to correct mistakes right after they've happened
   —strive for 100 percent mastery of procedures
7. See that students can perform the skill.

Stated in outline form, the essentials of skills are:

1. conceptual understanding
2. aim/outcome
3. definition of procedures
4. completed example
5. learning the procedures step by step
6. practice
7. demonstrated mastery

TIME REQUIRED TO DELIVER THIS TRAINING

Four hours, including one hour of "reporting out" to higher management; probably 9 A.M. to noon with the reporting out session over lunch, noon to 1 P.M.

TRAINEE LEVEL

Try to get commitment from pairs of attendees, the supervisor/manager and his or her manager (top management for the one-hour reporting out session at the end of the workshop). Make it clear in preconference publicity that this session is designed as a practical, hands-on working session whose benefits will be felt sooner if top management participates during the final hour. Encourage your target audience to get their management's commitment to attend; however, open the session to any supervisor or manager who can benefit from learning and applying the model and who will do the required workshop preparation. Restrict the workshop to peers and their managers because of the potentially sensitive nature of the file data to be used in the workshop. It works best with 8 - 12 trainees, plus their managers at lunch.

TRAINING OBJECTIVES

- To present a model for organizational needs assessment that is appropriate to use in analyzing managing diversity needs within a manager's/supervisor's organization.
- To lead trainees through applying the model to one small needs analysis task using data from their own organizations which they have brought with them to the workshop.
- To facilitate a "reporting out" luncheon session to which trainees have invited their management, the goal of which is for trainees to show their managers how their organizations can change in order to maximize the benefits of a diverse workforce.

LEARNING OBJECTIVES FOR THE TRAINEE

- To apply a model for organizational needs assessment to one's own communication process, using actual organizational data
- To identify one or more cultural roots of one's own organization as they apply to the communication process
- To describe the organizational analysis process and the results to upper management at a "reporting out" luncheon meeting
- To articulate a vision for managing the communication process within a diverse workforce, from the point of view of one's own organization

METHODS TO EVALUATE THE TRAINEE'S PROGRESS

The ultimate evaluation for this learning is whether or not the trainee participates in the reporting out session and in what depth of understanding. Some reports will be shallower than others; some will be broader and more inclusive because input data was organized better or because some trainees work faster than others. This is a session that lends itself well to a summative evaluation approach in addition to the formative evaluation feedback and encouragement during the needs assessment process.

When presenting the model—identifying its parts, defining terms, and showing examples—the best way to find out if trainees understand is to simply ask them. At several points during your presentation, just look at someone and ask, "Is this clear?" Or ask a trainee to give you an example of rites, traditions, an organization system, or strategy. If trainees can elaborate on a definition by giving an example, chances are that learning has occurred. Don't wait until you've finished presenting the whole model—evaluation at that point won't help drive instruction. Remember, in formative evaluation, you depend on the in-process evaluation during the give and take of instruction to "inform" your approach for the remainder of the lesson.

It is a good idea to have a handout of the model, completely labelled, for each trainee. There's no point in asking trainees to memorize the model; simply give it to them as a reference document and encourage them to use it.

As trainees are working in pairs or triads to apply the model to their own situations, walk around the room to be sure all trainees are engaged in the task. Listen for a quiet hum of discussion. If a trainee triad is unusually quiet, it probably means that the data is not in a good form for easy use or that group members are starting at too high a level, that is, they are attempting to articulate a vision before they've gotten to the root assumptions. If this happens, help trainees get back on track by telling them to think small at first. Extract small similarities out of the data, rearrange it so that smaller categories are defined, organize it differently. Focus on only the most obvious assumption. Remind all trainees that determining one clear assumption during this exercise is all that's required. More assumptions are better, but the model will have been learned at a basic level as soon as one assumption has been defined. At the skill level of actually using the model, practice can be expected to yield better learning; therefore, encourage trainees to identify more than one assumption.

TRAINING TIPS	***EXERCISES***
1. Present the model, "Organizational Culture as Tree Roots" (*Trainee Handout 2.3-A*) or any other model of your choice that can lead to needs assessment of an organization, one function or key process at a time.	1. Make this into a slide, transparency, or large wall chart. Systematically define the terms.
2. Suggest that the key organizational process of communication is one to which this model can be effectively applied in order to get at the assumptions that feed the communication process within the organization.	2. Ask trainees to get out the data from their own organizations. (Two weeks before the conference, ask trainees to bring with them some file data which they will analyze during the workshop with other managers.) Suggest that data analysis is only a first step in doing any needs assessment, and that these kinds of data might be appropriate to bring to the workshop: • performance review narrative comments from all employees in the organization • memos and letters • time sheets • complaints • promotional pieces (newsletters, articles, videos) generated by the organization Circulate this list to trainees prior to their coming to the workshop as a suggestion of the kinds of information to bring with them.

3. Present the challenge to trainees of analyzing the communication system in one's own organization to find the cultural roots of the real way communication happens in the organization. (Use data from your own organization to prepare the example to use in the workshop.)

3. Give the example of using back issues of the newsletter to identify the types of heroes or heroines implicit in the choices for articles. Make a list of the types and do a frequency count in order to see priority. Identify one apparent assumption indicated by this data. Use the model as an organizational analysis tool, reviewing how you used the parts of the model. Challenge trainees to use the model in a similar way.

   Expect assumptions such as
   —bosses are always the heroes
   —heroes outnumber heroines three to one
   —heroes usually come from high-tech operations

4. Pair off trainees so that discussion is detailed and based on actual data. Expect some trainees to be unprepared; assign a third person (unprepared) observer to each pair in order to give all trainees experience in at least the decision-making about the data.

4. Give them at least two hours to work on their data, systematically using the model with first, the topic of communication, then another key process such as marketing, employee development, or production control. (Be happy if they can just get through one key process, but be sure to suggest other processes that need to be analyzed.)

5. Guide trainees in documenting the way in which they went about this task, with the aim of being able to give a short presentation of their results, that is, the identification of assumptions, to management after lunch. Keep the entire luncheon presentation to about 45 minutes; encourage trainee reporters to be succinct.

5. Make available to trainees flipcharts, transparencies, and so on, for them to use in the "reporting out" to management. Give them a time limit, for example, 5 minutes. Use a standard documentation form, shown in *Trainer's Worksheet 2.3-B* and *Trainee Handout 2.3-C*.

6. After lunch has been served but while people are eating, begin the reporting out session. (Seat upper management in a V-shaped table so that they are all facing the podium. Seat trainees with their backs to the podium since they will be getting up and down during reporting out.) Show them the model. Then turn over the session to trainees.	6. Introduce the reporting out session by thanking upper management for their presence and support for managing diversity. Suggest that what they are about to see is the phenomenon of the whole is greater than the sum of its parts—that together, by critical analysis of many parts, organizations of this company can begin to move towards an effectively managed diverse workforce.
7. Conclude the session by challenging trainees and upper management alike to continue the dialogue about diversity, the good and bad assumptions upon which our management is built, and to devise plans to change the constraining assumptions and to expand upon the good ones.	7. Offer yourself as a recorder (on flipchart) to begin the list of planning priorities as they are mentioned during trainees' short presentations. Several days after the conference, make copies and send them to all persons at the luncheon session.

Trainee Handout 2.3-A

ORGANIZATIONAL CULTURE AS TREE ROOTS

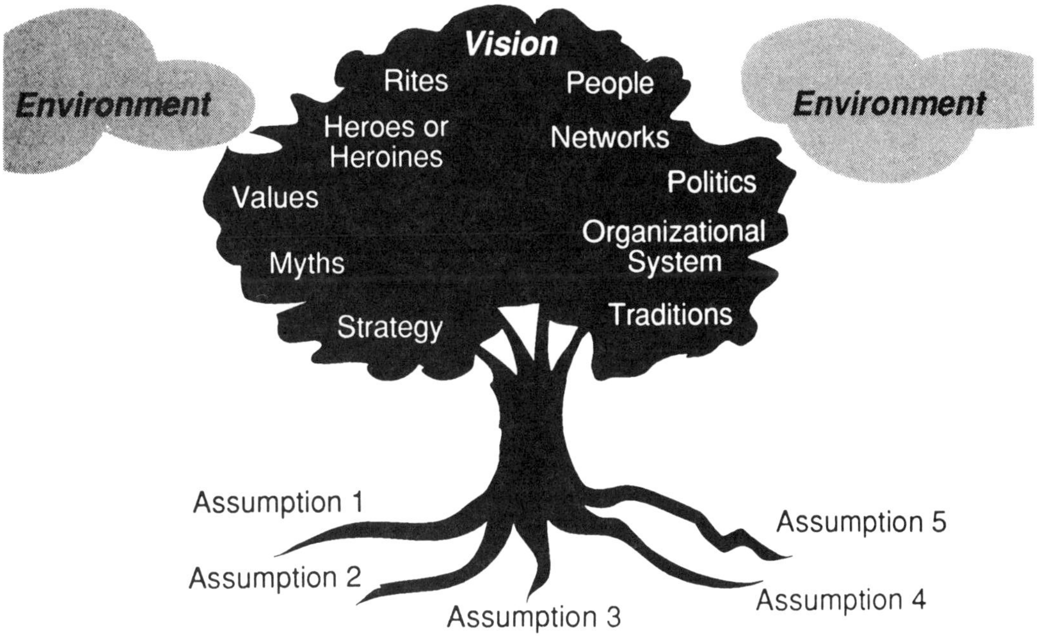

Excerpted, by permission of the publisher, from *Beyond Race and Gender,*

Trainer's Worksheet 2.3-B

"REPORTING OUT" DOCUMENTATION FORM

Trainees working under a time constraint towards doing a presentation to their managers will probably be helped by a form or forms on which to record notes and key words to guide their thinking as they develop a presentation. In this case, do what you can to keep their presentations focused on the assumptions underlying communication in their organizations. It will be tempting to digress into other areas, but you'll want to guide trainees into dealing with one area at a time, and delving into it according to the "branches" or "canopy" part of the tree.

The accompanying *Trainee Handout 2.3-C* shows some of the areas where documentation might be helpful. Expand each of the four documentation areas as needed. Encourage note-taking by trainees in order to stay focused.

Trainee Handout 2.3-C

DOCUMENTATION FORM FOR PRESENTATION TO MANAGEMENT

SOURCES OF DATA FOR THIS STUDY

1.

2.

3.

4.

FINDINGS (RELATIONSHIPS)

1.

2.

3.

4.

APPARENT ASSUMPTIONS

1.

2.

3.

4.

TARGETS FOR CHANGE

1.

2.

3.

4.

TRAINING PLAN 2.4

How to Write a Managing Diversity Policy

This training plan is an outline of the key elements, methods, and procedures required to train managers and supervisors, in a conference setting, to create a managing diversity policy. The task of writing policy is set within a small group session of one hour that includes a *panel discussion followed by a group-focused, instructor-led writing exercise.*

This is a very structured session with a high degree of instructor leadership and a low degree of trainee interaction. The session, however, is designed to involve all trainees in writing policy, even though instruction is one-way, that is, from instructor to group with very little lateral interaction, trainee to trainee. The topic of writing policy lends itself very well to one-way instruction because the end product is somewhat standardized, it is procedural, and the trainee audience can be thought of as homogeneous (same level) when it comes to writing policy. (Those who select themselves into this session are all probably managers who don't yet have a managing diversity policy; in spite of different departments and perhaps different salary levels within the company, they are alike when it comes to needing to know how to write policy.)

The session also includes a panel discussion. The reason this is included is for interest and expansion of thinking prior to the lecture-type presentation and narrow focus of writing the policy statement. Lectures alone are generally very dull; managers and supervisors especially seem to want action in their training.

OVERVIEW OF TRAINING METHODOLOGY

The training methodology for this session is discussed here in two parts, the methodology for a panel discussion, and the methodology for a lecture-type instructional session in writing policy.

This kind of panel discussion is chosen for several reasons:

- It adds interest to an otherwise dull presentation format
- It fosters examination of ideas and various points of view
- It adds a reality dimension to a somewhat intellectual exercise (i.e., policy deliberations) as panelists share experiences
- It gives trainees an opportunity to identify experts or contact people who can be helpful to them as they try to develop policies similar to those of the panelists

As management trainer, you are the one who coordinates the preparation work of the panel. To make the most out of your panel, follow these guidelines:

1. Decide what you want the focus of the panel discussion to be before you make the first contact with any potential panelist. In this case, your purpose might be "to discuss how to get started in writing a managing diversity policy" including
    - who are the key players
    - how do you tap into the real business objectives of the company
    - what are the good words that absolutely must be included
    - what are the disaster zones and obstacles

2. Give each panelist a list of these objectives well in advance of the session so that their preparation can be guided by your objectives.
3. If you intend to open the floor to questions from your trainees to the panel, have at least two questions prepared in advance in case no one from your trainee audience can think of any to ask. Ask these yourself to get things rolling—and if things don't get rolling after your two questions, stop the panel part of the session and go on to the policy-writing part.
4. Function as panel leader and moderator. Keep all panelists on an equal basis, so that no one monopolizes the discussion and that no one point of view dominates the discussion. Maintain leadership and control of the panel.
5. Establish time limits for each presentation and stick to them. Use a bell or electronic timer.
6. Be prepared to make concluding remarks and to summarize everyone's comments. Make this short and use it as a transition to the policy-writing lesson that comes next.
7. Prepare an accurate introduction of each panelist.
8. Thank each panelist individually at the end of the discussion and question-and-answer period.

The balance of this small group session is a lesson in writing policy. Divide the training time roughly in half: half for the panel and half for the writing exercise. As panelists disperse, make some obvious physical move such as bringing a flipchart directly center front in the room or turning out lights and projecting an overhead transparency of a policy format such as *Trainee Handout 2.4.* At half-time, help the trainees to shift mental gears into the next learning situation.

The rest of the session is devoted to an explanation of how to write a policy. Basically, this means that you will tell trainees what format in which to write the policy and what kinds of grammatical structures to use.

This mode of instruction is like the longer lecture in that you are operating from a premise that you have information that they need, that your information is correct, and that they stand to gain from what you have to say. It is essentially a one-way, instructor-to-student, instructional technique. It is also lecture-like in that you expect minimal trainee give and take, although you will get some trainees involved during general question and answer. Basically, you are *talking to* a group, not with individuals.

Remember that the best we know about adult learning theory suggests that adults prefer to control their own learning, they learn well from peers, and they don't like to be "talked to." For all these reasons, keep lectures and lecture-type methods to an absolute minimum in all kinds of training, and when you must use lecture format, intersperse it with some interaction.

For the balance of this session on how to write a managing diversity policy, your objective as an instructor is to present the format for writing policy and to provide trainees with some examples of how to say it. Do this most effectively by asking trainees to suggest to you—call out—their ideas, category by category. Write their words in your format on the flipchart or directly on the overhead. Conclude the session by handing out a blank "Policy for Managing Diversity" form and wishing trainees good luck as they write their own policies.

TIME REQUIRED TO DELIVER THIS TRAINING

1½ hours: 45 minutes panel (3 or 4 panelists); 45 minutes policy writing during a self-selected small group session at a training conference.

TRAINEE LEVEL

This group will probably represent a wide range of persons. It can be expected to attract managers and supervisors who know nothing about policy development as well as those who are in various stages of writing policy. The session will attract some who are primarily interested in hearing panelists, some who are more interested in the general subject of managing diversity than in the particulars of diversity policy, and some who are interested in the "how to write" part of the session.

TRAINING OBJECTIVES

- To facilitate a panel discussion of "how to get started in writing a managing diversity policy" with four panelists at no more than 10 minutes each
- To lead a five-minute question-and-answer period between panelists and the trainee audience
- To introduce the policy format to trainees
- To show trainees how to develop a managing diversity policy within this format

LEARNING OBJECTIVES FOR THE TRAINEE

- To see and hear a panel discussion on how to get started in writing a managing diversity policy
- To ask questions of the panel as interest indicates
- To receive the blank form, "Policy for Managing Diversity"
- To participate in the group exercise of working through the form, giving examples of ways in which to fill out each section

METHODS TO EVALUATE THE TRAINEE'S PROGRESS

As you carefully read the learning objectives for the trainee, you'll see that they are all very weak, requiring little effort on the part of the trainee. There are no requirements for problem solving or high-level decision making. This is especially true of the first three learning objectives—to see and hear, to ask, and to receive. These objectives taken in the aggregate could be seen as preparatory objectives, designed to create an awareness at some basic level for a skill that will be developed later. Any skills developed here are simply at the most elementary level of both the cognitive and the psychomotor skill continuum. (Refer to *Trainer's Worksheet 3.1* to find out about differentiated skills.)

These are typical of the learning expectations inherent in lecture-type training methods. They foster the kinds of training experiences that cause trainees to say training is a waste of time, yet so much of what is called training still relies on the lecture. By taking the time to create training plans, such as the ones in this book, you will see clearly just exactly what kinds of learning experiences you are building into your instruction.

Lectures have their place in teaching adults, but don't fool yourself into thinking that high-level skill development will occur because of them. At most, a well-designed lecture will *set the stage for* skill development—it can build readiness.

Only the last objective, "to participate...giving examples," requires the trainee to engage in active learning. (The second objective, to ask questions, is optional for trainees, although it does require a low level of critical thinking for those who choose to ask a question.)

Evaluation of these low-level objectives amounts to your observation that all trainees can in fact see and hear the panel and that they did see and hear the panel, that interested persons did ask questions, that all trainees received the form, and that they gave examples of ways in which to fill it out. Again, know what you're about when you evaluate low-level objectives; you are evaluating *readiness*, not whether or not trainees have learned to write policy.

It is so tempting when teaching adults to get blinded by the lofty nature of the topic that you lose sight of exactly what you are evaluating. This blinding effect is also why it is difficult to learn anything about the quality of your instruction and the quality of learning from standard "smiles sheets" that often are dispensed at the end of a course in the name of an evaluation form. Very often, all these smiles sheets evaluate is the ambience of the training room and the personality of the instructor.

TRAINING TIPS	*EXERCISES*
1. Prior to their going on stage, be sure all panelists have a list of the major points to consider during their presentations.	1. Hand to each panelist a cue card with key topics as a reminder to stay on track. These are examples: How to Get Started in Writing a Managing Diversity Policy • Key Players • Real Business Objectives • Good Words • Obstacles
2. Introduce the topic and each panelist.	2. Keep it focused and simple. Give business addresses of panelists, either as a handout, in the program, or on a flipchart. Relate the individual panelist to the topic in a personal way.
3. Set the timer; be ready to interrupt any panelist who is getting off track or is too wordy.	3. Stick to the 10-minute limit per panelist. The point of the panel is to create interest among your trainees, not to hear a lengthy chronology of how this person did the job of creating policy. Interest is probably created better by having trainees see and hear a variety of presenters, not by one person's going into great depth.
4. Conduct a 5-minute question-and-answer session between trainees and panelists.	4. Make this a no-pressure exercise, calling on only those trainees who obviously have burning questions.

5. Summarize briefly the presentations as a whole, thank and excuse the panelists.

5. Use this summary and thank you as a transition to the policy-writing lesson that comes next.

6. Take control of the focus of learning. Trainees will be scattered in their thinking because of the stimulus of the range of ideas and personalities of the panel.

6. Do something physical and obvious; for example:

- move a flipchart to the center of the room
- turn out the lights and turn on a projector
- bring the focus literally to yourself in the center of the room

7. Present the blank form for a managing diversity policy. (*Trainee Handout 2.4*)

7. Talk about managing diversity while trainees are looking at the blank form. Give the big picture of policy development by asking the group some rhetorical questions or comments such as:

- "Think about what our management practices will look like"
- "How will we get from where we are to where we want to be?"
- "In what ways will managing diversity well benefit your organization and the business as a whole?"
- "Who is responsible for what?"

8. Give trainees the general ground rules for stating policy.

8. As you point to each of the five categories, suggest these ground rules:

- Use first person,
  "We are committed to . . .
  We believe that . . .
  It is therefore our policy to . . .
  We challenge . . .
  We accept responsibility to. . . ."
  and to
- Choose action words that can be measured and evaluated when listing things that should be done: *provide, prepare, build, create, include, identify, promote,* and *monitor.*

9. At this point, hand out a blank form to each trainee. If you've been using an overhead projector in subdued lighting, turn on the lights to signal a change. Make it rather obvious that you want them to participate in the next exercise. Tell them that you are interested in seeing how they'll meet the challenge of creating a policy. Let trainees use the blank forms as their focus rather than the overhead.	9. Ask for suggestions of commitment statements. Write on the overhead or flipchart a list of several commitment statements; go on to the belief section of the form and do the same. Stop here to contrast commitment and belief, emphasizing the importance of each. Continue on to the policy statement itself, suggesting that they relate it to an overarching business purpose. List several trainees' comments. Try for variety and stimulation here, not for creation of the perfect policy. (If this were a workshop for learning higher-level decision-making skills, you might go for the perfect policy. It is, however, a workshop at the lowest skill level, readiness and awareness; match the techniques to the true objectives, and don't be fooled by the importance or gravity of the topic.) Continue in the same fashion through the form sections on challenge and organizational responsibilities.
10. Conclude the session with a statement of challenge to trainees to take these ideas back to their own organizations and write their own policy for managing diversity.	

Trainee Handout 2.4

FORM FOR WRITING A MANAGING DIVERSITY POLICY
Use this form as a worksheet for creating an organizational or company policy regarding managing diversity.

Statement of Commitment:
Statement of Belief:
Succinct Policy Statement:
Challenge to Employees:
Organizational Responsibilities:

adapted from *Training Program Workbook and Kit* by Carolyn Nilson, Englewood Cliffs, NJ: Prentice-Hall, a division of Simon & Schuster, 1989, p. 297.

TRAINING PLAN 2.5

How to Prepare a Manager's Personal Action Plan for Managing Diversity

This training plan is an outline of the key elements, methods, and procedures required to train managers and supervisors to *create their own individual management plan using planning software* for dealing effectively with a diverse workforce. Unlike the policy workshop session detailed in the previous training plan, this workshop session is aimed at teaching high-level skills. It is more interactive, continuously evaluative, and leads the trainee on an individual basis through guided practice to producing a product—the Personal Action Plan for Managing Diversity. This session is based on mid-level and high-level cognitive and psychomotor skills.

OVERVIEW OF TRAINING METHODOLOGY

This training methodology makes use of several important characteristics of adult learners—characteristics that research in adult learning styles and adult learning motivation consistently reveals. These are that:

- Adults prefer to be active during learning
- Adults like to learn from peers whom they respect
- Adults at work insist on learning that's related to the challenges of their own jobs
- Adults learn effectively when they can relate new knowledge and skills to the knowledge and skills they already have experienced; adult learning must be experience-based for maximum effectiveness
- Adults need to see the payoff for them personally in order to expend personal resources in training
- Adults like to be in charge of their own learning; they don't like to be told how to learn

From this base of adult learning styles and preferences, we superimpose the educational psychology of learning taxonomies in cognitive and psychomotor studies to provide the educational structure for this workshop session. By far, the most well-known taxonomy-builder is Benjamin Bloom, professor at the University of Chicago, who, in 1954 published his first book on the taxonomy of educational objectives in the cognitive domain. Most of his professional life has been devoted to numerous studies and major research projects in cognition and learning; he has spawned thousands of followers and has written hundreds of articles and papers on the subject over the decades since his first publications in the 1950s.

Bloom's taxonomy[1] categorizes cognitive objectives from low-level of "knowledge" and "comprehension" objectives to high-level objectives of "synthesis" and "evaluation," and some mid-level objectives in between. In any cognitive training, Bloom has shown through his research that low-level objectives must be met before high-level ones can be attempted. Bloom's taxonomy of educational objectives in the cognitive domain include:

[1]from *Taxonomy of Educational Objectives: The Classification of Educational Goals: Handbook I: Cognitive Domain* by Benjamin S. Bloom, et al. Copyright © 1956, 1984 by Longman Publishing Group. Reprinted with permission.

1. *Knowledge:* facts, terminology, classifications, sequences, categories, principles, methods, and the skills of identifying, defining, recalling, naming, stating, reciting, labeling, and listing.
2. *Comprehension:* basic level reception of communication without understanding of fullest implications and relationships, including such skills as translating, illustrating, representing, restating, and explaining.
3. *Application:* use of abstractions in concrete situations, including skills of applying, generalizing, relating, developing, computing, producing.
4. *Analysis:* revealing the parts by breaking down the whole, including skills of differentiating, contrasting, categorizing, classifying, arranging, summarizing.
5. *Synthesis:* combining elements to form a new whole, including skills of hypothesizing, composing, writing, formulating, strategizing, planning, creating.
6. *Evaluation:* judging the value of something for a stated purpose, including skills of standardizing, appraising, criticizing, concluding, assessing, evaluating.

In a training session such as this, in which trainees perform the task of producing a product (that is, a personal action plan), the trainer is alerted to the need for design and instruction in Bloom's categories 3, 4, and 5. Trainees will have to apply certain abstractions about diversity and corporate values to the very tangible action plan required of the training. They will also have to identify and clarify the many interacting parts of organizational life and their own abilities that must figure into the completed plan, and they will have to create a workable plan out of the many disparate pieces. By asking the question, "what will trainees have to do during this training?" the trainer can see clearly that the major tasks of the training are mid- to high-level cognitive tasks.

In addition to the application, analysis, and synthesis objectives of this training, there are some fine-motor skills in writing, using a computer, following a format, and producing a document that are required in this workshop. Because there is a tangible product involved in this instruction, the trainer must teach not only to facilitate new thinking, but also to facilitate the production of an acceptable end product.

Trainers must be aware, whenever there is a product at the end of training, that trainees need adequate preparation and guidance for working towards a production standard. In this situation, they need to understand the format in which they are expected to produce their plans, they need to know how to use the typewriter, keyboard, or software system they are expected to use, and they need guided, instructed practice with the brain-hand (psychomotor) tasks of their assignments. In this kind of product-oriented training, it is not enough to deliver information or give a motivating pep talk about the virtues of the task: trainers must teach successively more difficult cognitive and psychomotor skills.

In addition, this session is one at which trainees are expected to use a personal computer (or terminal to a mainframe) and printer, as well as planning software, during training. For this session, we make the assumption that the planning software has tutorials and help screens built into it.

This workshop session combines the instructional design elements of cognitive and psychomotor level consideration with learning process preferences such as active trainee involvement at mid- and high-cognitive levels, peer feedback, use of actual work challenges, and an end product of importance to individuals as they deal with a difficult management problem.

TIME REQUIRED TO DELIVER THIS TRAINING

2 hours, during the conference; probably towards the end of the conference to take advantage of the information and stimulation of previous sessions, keynote addresses, and personal networking.

Trainees will each be seated at a personal computer or terminal.

TRAINEE LEVEL

Any manager or supervisor who must produce a Personal Action Plan for Managing Diversity.

TRAINING OBJECTIVE

- To facilitate the creation of a Personal Action Plan for Managing Diversity by each trainee, using the management-approved format and planning software.

LEARNING OBJECTIVE FOR THE TRAINEE

- To create a Personal Action Plan for Managing Diversity using the management-approved format and planning software.

METHODS TO EVALUATE THE TRAINEE'S PROGRESS

The evaluation of this session is on two levels: the summative, end-of-process evaluation of whether or not each trainee produced a Personal Action Plan for Managing Diversity, and the constant, in-process evaluation, support, and feedback of peer review that is going on all during the workshop, especially as trainees pair off for mutual support during use of the computers. Of course, you, the facilitator, will also be giving in-process feedback to trainees all during the workshop session, but this training, in fact, depends primarily on peer evaluation during the creation of the action plans.

TRAINING TIPS	*EXERCISES*
1. Introduce the session by working backwards from the expected outcome, that is, the Personal Action Plan. The assumption is that trainees are prepared for this workshop session, have bought into the idea that these Personal Action Plans are necessary, and are motivated by the various preceding communications from top management to be at this workshop. Let trainees begin to imagine what their finished Plan might look like.	1. Briefly describe the workforce demographics predicted for the next five years and their effects on your business. Comment on as many areas or functions of the business as your trainees represent (for example, sales, marketing, customer service, accounting, engineering, research, operations, transportation, personnel, and so on.) Be very sensitive to exactly who is in your trainee audience, giving credibility to the good work that has been done in the recent past by these people. Send the message that you value the experience base represented by your trainees. State the broad corporate goals for managing diversity, within the five-year context. Write these on a whiteboard or flipchart to remain visible throughout the training session.
2. Show trainees the Plan format and describe the software that has been agreed upon by top management. At this point, you have introduced both learning streams, the cognitive and the psychomotor.	2. Use an overhead transparency or slide, and give each trainee a template such as that on *Trainee Handout 2.5.*
3. Remind trainees that the reason they are together here is to create their own Personal Action Plans for Managing Diversity. Build the sense of value represented by the collective experience in this training room, and the expectation that each trainee will be available to other trainees to share experiences and to offer help during the process of plan development.	3. One effective way to engage trainees' thinking about the need to and value of cooperating during development is to ask questions designed to bring forth differing points of view and meant to highlight unique contributions of various trainees. For example, you might ask "What do you think will be the key section of your plan?" or "In what significant way do you expect that your plan will help the company?"

4. Elaborate on the ways in which to write plans that integrate the corporate goals into the work of each trainee's organization.

   Use trainees' experiences here to expand the group's thinking.

4. Begin by giving examples such as writing plans for:
   - pay analysis and adjustment actions
   - a Black managers' support group
   - a standards-setting exercise with suppliers
   - a mentoring program for Asian engineers
   - a revision of days off policy for home care-giving workers
   - new recruiting methods

   Ask trainees to tell you about any planning efforts they have already begun, and what they're hoping to institute.

5. Ask if there are any questions about what the end product is supposed to look like. Answer all questions with examples, if possible. Be sure that they understand the format.

5. Try to get trainees themselves to answer questions raised by their peers. Build in the "learning from each other" early in this workshop.

6. Ask trainees to focus on the three or four areas of their organization which will be most affected by implementation of managing diversity plans.

   Call attention to the variety of effects, thereby highlighting the differences —and the range of expertise—among the trainee audience.

6. Call on individual trainees to give you their areas. Make a running list of these; add to the list as trainees respond to you. Try for a list of at least 10 different items.

7. Now concentrate trainees' attention on the computer. Begin at logon or loading the planning software. Wait until all trainees are at the main menu of the program. Encourage trainee-to-trainee interaction. Expect the rest of the class to be somewhat noisy as trainees talk with each other, lean over to help each other, and look at each other's work.

   Be sure that everyone knows how to print the file. The ideal situation is a PC plus printer at each trainee station. If you must use a terminal environment with a single printer networked to all terminals, rely on a training specialist to manage the printing, doing the running back and forth for trainees (so they are free to help each other while they wait for printouts).

7. Suggest that trainees pair off with a partner to work through computer access and command problems.

   Be available to circulate around the room, guiding trainees who need help making the computer into the tool they need.

8. When you are sure that all trainees are into the program which they'll need to use to create their plans, challenge them to take approximately the next hour to create their own Personal Action Plan for Managing Diversity, following the tutorials and procedures embedded in the software according to the template.

8. Challenge trainees to analyze their own strengths as they analyze their organizations according to the template (*Trainee Handout 2.5*).

   Suggest that they spend at least 15 minutes of quiet time to organize their thoughts, once they've gotten into the tutorial on-line, after which encourage them to share ideas with other trainees, both giving and receiving information.

9. Let trainees know that the hour is up, but don't necessarily try to tidy things up by having trainees read their plans to the group. That kind of summarizing *by you* is not part of the objectives for the session.

9. In this kind of training, you are the facilitator of their activities. Your job is to carefully set up the learning environment so that *they* do the creating and develop both the product that's called for and the confidence to use it.

Trainee Handout 2.5

MANAGER'S PERSONAL ACTION PLAN FOR MANAGING DIVERSITY (TEMPLATE)

(Add duplicate pages according to your needs.)

Corporate goal:

Related organizational objective: ______________________________

____

____

	due date	person responsible
Action item: ______________________________		
Action item: ______________________________		

Related organizational objective: ______________________________

____

____

	due date	person responsible
Action item: ______________________________		
Action item: ______________________________		

TRAINING PLAN 2.6

Closing the Conference Evaluation Loop

This training plan does not follow the other training plan formats because it is really a description of how the instructional systems design (ISD) concept works for the training event known as the "conference." It is important that the reader view the conference as an instructional event, set within the ISD framework. There will come a time when you'll be called upon to repeat the conference planning process next quarter or next year, and you'll want to be able to refer to documentation from this conference in order to do the good things again, and know how to correct any problems with your first conference so you don't repeat them.

This is the instructional system design model, as it applies to creation of a course or a conference:

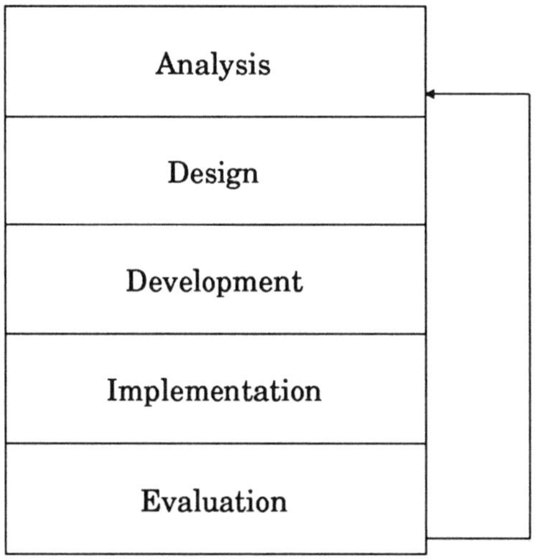

An instructional designer follows these processes in order, when designing a one-hour course or a three-day conference, using the evaluation process to feedback into the analysis process to keep the system going.

The following worksheets are various kinds of tools to use in evaluating a conference on managing diversity. The ideas presented in these four worksheets, obviously, can be readily adapted to a conference on any topic you choose. They are included here because they treat the conference as a whole as an instructional event and they contribute to the quality planning of similar instructional events in conference format.

These four additional worksheets are:

2.6-A **Civil Rights /Equal Employment Opportunity (EEO) Checklist for Trainers**—a checklist to be used during conference planning as sessions, vendors, speakers, and handout materials are taking shape.

2.6-B **Small Group Session Feedback Form**—to be completed by attendees at each small group session and returned to the conference chairperson; distributed at the start of each small group session.

2.6-C and D **Conference Feedback Form**—to be completed by all conference attendees; usually included in the trainee's registration folder, and collected as attendees exit the conference.

2.6-E **Guidelines for Reporting to Management**—an outline form for attendees to report to their bosses what they learned at the conference; especially important for first-time conference-goers; ideally handed to the trainee at the time of registration confirmation by the trainee's supervisor or manager; an excellent device to get the conference attendee thinking as an evaluator and therefore contributor to the ongoing quality development of such training formats.

Trainer's Worksheet 2.6-A

CIVIL RIGHTS/EQUAL EMPLOYMENT OPPORTUNITY (EEO) CHECKLIST FOR TRAINERS

To be used by the conference chairperson or designee during conference planning. This checklist applies to conference planners and staff at every level, speakers, exhibitors, and attendees. Use this checklist yourself, delegate its use to some responsible staff member, and circulate it to persons outside your company who will be involved in the conference. Its use is especially helpful when dealing with a culturally diverse workforce.

Face-to-Face Communication

____ 1. Take the time to attend to others. Watch for clues in body language, facial expressions, eye contact, personal distance.

____ 2. Show respect and caring for intellectual or commitment risks that another person is taking. Step back and listen; don't "bulldoze."

____ 3. Give people a chance to explain. When you seek information, ask open-ended questions. A person of "difference" might need some time to clarify a position.

____ 4. Verify the messages you receive. Be sure that the other person understands that you understand. Paraphrase, reflect your feelings, check assumptions, use examples.

____ 5. Protect your own self-worth as well as that of others. Explain your own cultural point of view as well as ask the other person to explain his or hers. If you don't understand, say so, and ask the other person to help you understand.

____ 6. Be aware of feelings. If something bothers you, tell the other person how you feel; and be open to the possibility that you might hurt someone else's feelings. Feelings and beliefs are powerful motivators at work and should not be denied.

____ 7. Make sensitive decisions. Develop options and assess their consequences. Consider differences in norms and try to minimize conflicts in values. Involve others in decision-making.

____ 8. Correct information deficits.

____ 9. Remove barriers to contribution.

Written Communication

____10. Examine conference materials for evidence that no discriminatory language exists regarding race, ethnicity, religion, gender, age, or disability. Look at these kinds of materials:

- ____ • slides and overhead transparencies
- ____ • films, videotapes, and audiotapes
- ____ • computer software, programs, CBT lessons
- ____ • textbooks

Trainer's Worksheet 2.6-A (continued)

____ • student manuals, instructor manuals
____ • articles, pamphlets, and other handout material
____ • promotional materials from vendors and exhibitors
____ • the conference registration form, confirmation forms, and all pre-conference publicity
____ • artwork (posters, cartoons, graphic slides, etc.—be especially careful about gender and racial stereotypes)

Accessibility

____11. Establish procedures for persons to report violations of equal employment opportunity.

____12. Establish procedures to discipline persons who violate protections of equal employment opportunity.

____13. Advertise the conference equally to all persons whose jobs can benefit from it.

____14. Make sure classrooms, libraries, laboratories, conference areas, and all other learning areas are accessible to handicapped persons.

____15. Make sure rest rooms, eating rooms, and lounges are accessible to handicapped persons.

Evaluation and Testing

____16. Solicit conference evaluations and session evaluations and make sure you receive one from each attendee. Also, process them equally to give each attendee an equal voice in feedback to improve training.

____17. Make sure testing done to indicate mastery or achievement is directly related to the job.

____18. Review tests to ensure they are free of bias in design as well as in language.

____19. Validate tests and make sure they are reliable.

____20. Make sure tests are administered fairly by competent test administrators.

____21. Make sure test takers are given opportunities to remediate poor testing performance.

____22. Explore alternatives to testing thoroughly before embarking on a testing program in a course, seminar session, or any training event.

Note: Training is considered by many people to be an "opportunity of employment." Every training event that you sponsor must be governed by principles of access and equity according to Federal law—and this includes conferences.

Trainer's Worksheet 2.6-B

SMALL GROUP SESSION FEEDBACK FORM

A stack of feedback forms should be available at each small group session, handed out at the beginning of each session with instructions about to whom to return the completed forms.

Many conferences have a feedback collection team whose job is to go from room to room collecting these completed forms—often the speakers or workshop leaders are tied up with trainees who hang around for individual attention right after the session, and they forget to collect the feedback forms. If you're really serious about the usefulness of feedback, you might want to consider assigning the job of collecting the forms to a collection team.

There are many ways to create a feedback form. The most common and least effective is to ask trainees to use a rating scale of 1-5 to indicate their feelings about the instructor, the seminar facilities, and the training materials. Such forms will contain items such as "instructor's knowledge of the subject," "instructor's presentation," "seminar materials," "seminar facilities." Feedback from such forms does not give you much to go on to correct problems or improve the session before it's given again at another conference.

When you create a feedback form, decide what you are evaluating. At a small group session, the best kind of feedback form will include specific references to the content of the speaker's or instructor's presentation, that is, the form will contain many items referring to the major topics of the instructor's outline or teaching points in the training plan.

Some items from a course on how to create a spreadsheet using your personal computer might be:

commands

functions

macro routines

rules of thumb

Ask trainees to indicate their rating of each item in terms of its value to them. Give them space on the feedback form in which to write comments about how each item could be improved or made more useful or of greater value. Give them a 4-point rating scale, so that they won't be tempted to choose the mid point. The point is to get specific about content, especially in the small group session feedback. If you ask trainees for their opinions, give them the assurance that you are evaluating significant things, not the elements of the conference that are peripheral.

If you are in fact trying to get feedback about the facilities or the instructor's personality, be honest about this and tell trainees what you're after. Don't try to tell trainees that you're looking for their help with the program content and usefulness if you, in fact, are doing something else.

If you are serious about using trainee feedback to make improvements, take the time to develop customized small group session feedback forms. It will pay off in the long run.

Trainer's Worksheet 2.6-C

DESIGNING A CONFERENCE FEEDBACK FORM

This is the appropriate form on which to ask trainees for their general impressions of the conference—the program, the keynote speakers whom everyone hears, the facility, the overall conference management. This kind of feedback is what is affectionately called "the smiles test" because it indicates conferees' general satisfaction level with the conference as a whole. It is a measure of conference management, not of instructional content. The results will not tell you whether or not anyone has learned anything, and have only marginal value in helping you redesign instruction for the next time. It is a worthwhile exercise because the results will give you a range of "customer" opinion about overall value of your approach and will help you decide whether or not to offer the same type of conference at another time.

When you design your conference feedback form, build in a four-point rating scale corresponding to terms such as "unsatisfactory, poor, good, and excellent." List each conference element down the left side of the form, with a range line after each.

Allow some space for trainees to elaborate in narrative fashion on any aspect of the conference. Provide minimal structure to this part of the form. The accompanying *Trainee Handout 2.6-D* provides a sample conference feedback form.

Trainee Handout 2.6-D

CONFERENCE FEEDBACK FORM

Please rate the conference in each of the following areas:

	1	2	3	4
1 overall quality				
2 overall usefulness to your job				
3 facilities				
4 refreshments				
5 materials, handouts				
6 schedule				
7 publicity				
8 registration				
9 keynote speaker(s) (add names)				
10 choice/range of topics (general sessions)				
11 choice/range of topics (small group sessions)				

Key:
1 unsatisfactory
2 poor
3 good
4 excellent

Please give us your suggestions for improvement: ______________________

____

____

____

Which parts of the conference did you find most useful? ________________

____

____

____

Trainee Handout 2.6-E

GUIDELINES FOR REPORTING TO MANAGEMENT

Use this outline as a guide to preparing a report for your own management, that is, the person whose budget your registration fee came from. Use this either as a guide to a written report or to an oral report.

1. **Identification**
   Seminar title, speaker, sponsoring organization, date and site.
2. **Purpose**
   Briefly indicate your reasons for attending. What instruction, information, assistance or problem-solving guidance was sought?
3. **Overall Evaluation**
   A. Presentation:
   ❑ Excellent ❑ Good ❑ Fair ❑ Poor
   - Was the speaker qualified — by training and experience?
   - Was the program leader effective in delivering instruction?
   - Did the speaker hold audience attention?
   - Were explanations clear, questions encouraged — and answered?

   B. Program content:
   ❑ Excellent ❑ Good ❑ Fair ❑ Poor
   - Was subject matter valid, realistic, down-to-earth?
   - What principal points were addressed?
   - Was the instruction geared to your specific needs?
   - What solutions for current problems were offered?
   - Which of your current practices were confirmed/reinforced?
   - What new ideas or techniques were introduced?
   - What is the reference value of the seminar workbook?

   C. Audience:
   - What was the general make-up of the group (titles, functions)?
   - How did the group respond, interact with the seminar leader?
   - What worthwhile contacts were made with others in your function, what experiences shared?
4. **Applications and Action**
   - What was learned that will improve your daily operations?
   - How will your activity — and the organization — benefit?
   - What further steps should be taken to capitalize on the instruction?
   - What additional instruction (if any) should be undertaken?
   - Would you recommend this program for others within the organization?

Source: Reprinted with permission, The Dun & Bradstreet Corporation Foundation, Business Education Services.

Chapter 3

Training Techniques to Help Managers and Supervisors Ensure Employee Accountability

Probably the key function and the most encompassing one of managers and supervisors is to ensure accountability within the workforce. Managers and supervisors are entrusted with translating the company's values and ways of doing business into employees who want to and can do the work. Training for some of these basic skills is the subject of this chapter.

The fundamental problems of managing people and managing work are complicated today by changing values about what management really is and by the changing face of the workforce that reflects society's demands for new kinds of benefits and opportunity. On the operational front, managers and supervisors have the following pressures:

- to drive up the quality of processes, products, and services
- to share control of operations and decision making with employee teams
- to increase productivity by expending fewer resources
- to always work for better return on investment

On the human resources front, managers and supervisors are forced to deal equitably, sensitively, and creatively with a diverse workforce with greater differences among groups than in the recent past; moreover, new forms of benefits and concerns about job security challenge managers and supervisors to constantly redefine the limits of accountability. Managers and supervisors are increasingly called upon to demonstrate their concern and their employees' concern about the environment, the community, the schools and colleges, and charitable giving. It's tough these days to know what the dimensions of employee accountability are and how to go about managing and supervising among these changes and challenges.

The premise in developing management and supervisory training that works in this area of accountability is that the tugs and pulls on managers are great and sometimes disorienting—that the traditional choices regarding how to sail the ship are blurred by the new organizational and human resources demands. It is difficult for managers and supervisors to know to what or to whom to be accountable themselves, and how, in turn, to ensure that employees get the same message.

This chapter, therefore, deals with the ordinary functions of a manager's or supervisor's job that have an impact on employee accountability, the functions of accounting for one's time, operating legally and fairly, and protecting the company's intellectual property. These areas of detail are often taken for granted, but often also make the difference between a superior manager or supervisor and one who just gets by.

These and other accountability issues are discussed in the framework of today's disparate requirements for a less controlling supervisory style, more participative management, empowered employees, greater ROI, and higher quality. Being on the front lines of responsibility for today's bottom line demands flexibility, versatility, and sensitivity within a grounding in the security of standards, limits, constraints, measures, and procedures. Managers and supervisors need to know how to deal with the seemingly shifting priorities of employee accountability.

BEING SURE OF WHAT'S RIGHT AND KNOWING HOW TO DO IT

Trainers can help. You can help first by knowing when training is not required, that is, when a memo, a manual, or a breakfast meeting might be a better vehicle for communication. When training is needed, you can help by choosing the delivery method to fit the specific persons who need to be trained. That is, if you have only two or three managers or supervisors to be trained, a conference room or table in your office is a better choice of location than a classroom. If the manager or supervisor's job is heavy in vendor contracting and light in supervising employees, you'll need to develop the contracting section of your training more thoroughly than the lessons on accounting for employee time. Trainers can save time and resources by designing and presenting training around the needs of individuals. Trainers need to be flexible and accountable too.

The rest of this chapter suggests training methodologies for teaching managers and supervisors how to ensure employee accountability. Three traditional management functions are discussed:

- accounting for employees' time
- operating legally and fairly
- protecting intellectual property

These three functions have been chosen because they illustrate many of the complex issues today's more flexible managers and supervisors must cope with.

This instruction is set within a management employee orientation program, and it encompasses many training techniques which are especially useful during orientation training.

TRAINING PLANS

Three training plans provide a comprehensive sample of training techniques for teaching managers and supervisors to ensure employee accountability through the three building blocks of good management.

Where appropriate, worksheets are appended to each training plan. Each training plan with its appendices is intended to give you, the trainer, the instructional design and presentation guidelines that you need. In these training plans, we do the conceptual work for you—you need only to flesh out the plans with your own company jargon, names, and specific data.

Training Plans for Chapter 3 include:

management issues	*training techniques*
3.1 Accounting for employees' time	How to teach procedures
3.2 Accountability, rights, and benefits	Creating and using job aids
3.3 Protecting intellectual property	Using case study in a classroom setting

TRAINING PLAN 3.1

Training Managers and Supervisors to Ensure Employees' Accountability Regarding Time

This training plan is an outline of the key elements, methods, and procedures required to train managers and supervisors by *training them how to teach procedures.* This training plan, then, becomes both a "train the trainer" plan, with the manager or supervisor as trainer, and a plan for the instructional technique of teaching procedures.

The subject or content to which this technique is applied is employee time accountability, a topic of increasing concern to managers and supervisors as spans of control expand, employee work teams are proliferating, quality initiatives supersede normal production deadlines, flextime and working at home are entering the work schedule, remedial classes in reading, writing, math, and critical thinking are part of daily business, old forms of motivation are no longer accepted, and empowerment is the word of the decade. Many other topics in management training could have been chosen as applications for the technique of teaching procedures.

A training plan begins with objectives for training itself as well as objectives for the learner, and with evaluation methods tied to the learning objectives. Teaching points related to the content of a manager's or supervisor's area of responsibility provide the foundation for topics covered during training. Sample exercises suggest ways to deliver this kind of instruction. Helpful worksheets follow the training plan.

OVERVIEW OF TRAINING METHODOLOGY

The trick in teaching procedures is to distinguish between the areas of no flexibility and those where flexibility is essential. Trainers must learn steps in order, yet sometimes that order can be changed. They need to see cause and effect where that is important. Today's managers and supervisors who are eager to empower employees need to know where to build in opportunities for the employees' greater control over resources, greater control over scheduling, and greater authority over communication processes surrounding their work. Effective procedures have a relationship to all of these concerns.

In addition, those who are learning new procedures or who are trying to get back on track procedures that have gotten in a rut need to learn in a certain way, with a differentiated skill set so that the procedure becomes second nature.

Here are some dimensions of this differentiated skill set:

1. Skills are generally organized into the following categories:
   - cognitive (mental, thinking) skills
   - psychomotor (hands-on, body movement) skills
   - skills associated with values and attitudes (affective skills)

   Learning procedures usually involves both cognitive skills and psychomotor skills. Therefore, teaching procedures means teaching both kinds of skills. (See *Trainer's Worksheet 3.1-A.*)
2. Skills are further broken down into high-level (advanced) skills, mid-level skills, and low-level skills. Learning procedures generally involves low- and mid-level skills. Learning occurs best when low-level skills are mastered before higher-level

skills are introduced. Instruction in learning procedures must be designed with this in mind. See *Trainer's Worksheet 3.1-A.*

3. Skills must be practiced to be adopted. During training and after training skills must be demonstrated and reinforced. This means that you have to build into your instruction the opportunity for trainees to practice both the cognitive skills and the psychomotor skills and to demonstrate to you and to themselves that they have learned them. After training, back on the job, trainees' demonstration of learned skills must be reinforced by recognition from peers and superiors and by systems that support the exercise of the new skills. New procedures cannot live in an inhospitable environment. Managers and supervisors need to be aware of the organizational supports which they influence and control, so that change can be made if necessary. The job of getting a new procedure instituted requires both organization development and training.
4. Adult learners like assurance and security, especially when it comes to having to learn a long list of new steps or differentiated skills. They relate well to checklists, competency lists, and items they can check off as they complete what's required of them as students.
5. When teaching procedures, be very clear about steps—what comes first, next, and so on. If there's ever any question, draw a flowchart of the procedure before you begin to design instruction. When testing trainees on whether they have learned the procedure, know where you are in the sequence of steps, give cues to trainees if they need them, and help trainees get the steps in the right order. If they need mnemonics or memory tricks to remember, give them these too. Be patient with adult learners; they want to get it right. Remember, in testing for mastery of procedures your goal is to facilitate 100 percent accuracy and to acknowledge achievement, not to intimidate those who learn more slowly. Be clear, be logical, and be helpful.

Designing Effective Procedures

Another fundamental element in instruction in procedures is the design of the procedure itself. Prior to meeting employees in a teacher-student relationship be sure that the procedure is correct, that is, correct in content as well as correct in the processes required to accomplish it. If it is a new procedure, verify it with those who will be affected by it or by those who must initiate it; do a dry run of the procedure itself before you attempt to teach it. Here are some characteristics of procedures that should be evident in design; review these before you create instruction:

1. Numbering, display, and format conventions are consistent.
2. Related material is grouped together.
3. Conditional or contingency information has been sorted out and presented in its proper place, that is, before decisions are required and in clear "IF...THEN" or "IF...AND...THEN" statements and decision tables.
4. Sequences written down are analogous to real work sequences.
5. Operational statements requiring action are stated simply with few or no modifiers.
6. Overviews are used to show the scope, variety, and interrelatedness of actions.
7. Key words and terms are defined before they are used.
8. Sentences are short, follow the "subject-verb-object" format, and are in active (not passive) voice.

9. Admonishments such as "danger," "caution," "warning" always precede operational statements to which they refer.
10. Support information such as "Notes" and "Comments" are placed correctly either before or after the operational statement.
11. References are realistic, that is, they are related to available documents and persons.
12. Job aids are available to assist trained employees with implementation of learned procedures.

As we apply this methodology to the situation of accounting for employees' time, we make some assumptions about work and the workforce in order to develop an example for illustration. These assumptions are that:

1. The managers and supervisors in the training program are responsible for a group of employees, their productivity, and the quality of the service or product that is their output
2. Within the manager's or supervisor's direct reports, there is a variety of work schedules, e.g., different shifts, some work at home or flextime arrangements, some billable or project work, and some non-billable or overhead work
3. Those who report to the managers and supervisors have work objectives and standards to guide their efforts and know by what measures they are evaluated
4. Managers and supervisors want to develop self-responsibility in their employees and are willing to help their employees take charge of their own work lives
5. Managers and supervisors believe in their employees

This training plan, then, is aimed at the manager or supervisor who believes that teaching employees the procedures for accountability regarding their time will have a payoff in employees' productivity and quality, self-responsibility, and satisfaction with work.

TIME REQUIRED TO DELIVER THIS TRAINING

1 hour
This training can stand alone or be part of a management and supervisory orientation program.

TRAINEE LEVEL

This training is aimed at the manager or supervisor who has people reporting to him or her. It is also aimed at the manager or supervisor who must function as the teacher of the procedure. This training plan is designed for either new managers and supervisors or new procedures.

TRAINING OBJECTIVES

- To teach managers and supervisors how to teach procedures to help their employees account for their time.
- To model effective training techniques through a "lesson" in teaching procedures embedded in this hour of training.

LEARNING OBJECTIVE FOR THE TRAINEE

- To teach the procedures involved in helping employees account for their time.

  Note: Teaching is a high-level skill involving mastery of many lower-level skills before being able to teach. The objective here is expressed as the high-level skill, making the assumption that the lower-level skills have been mastered first.

METHODS TO EVALUATE THE TRAINEE'S PROGRESS

Evaluating trainees' progress is best done at many times during the delivery of training, and in a friendly and somewhat informal way. This is called "formative evaluation" because it is evaluation that helps to form or shape instruction.

In this one hour of training, the primary form of evaluation is formative evaluation. However, during the section of the instruction containing a lesson on how to write procedures there is an example of "summative evaluation," or evaluation at the end of a learning process.

TRAINING TIPS	*EXERCISES*
1. You need a way to find out what your trainees' problems are regarding their people's use of time, so you'll have to ask them at the beginning of class. They will also need the opportunity to "spout off" a little about their difficulties within the supportive atmosphere of this training. Expect some variety in the concerns. Look for time problems regarding shifts, concerns over flextime, concerns about overruns and miscalculations, and concerns over nonbillable hours. Expect some concern about standards, especially quality standards which to some managers seem to conflict with productivity goals. Write down their exact words.	1. There are two basic ways to conduct this kind of "opener" fact-finding investigation: by leading trainees into an expression of their concerns as statements of "what I want to get out of this training," and by your writing down their concerns in a list on the whiteboard or flipchart. If you phrase your questions in terms of what they want to get out of the training, you'll have a succinct checklist to use as a wrap-up exercise at the end of training. To do this, simply take a few minutes at the end of class to go down the list and ask trainees if your training satisfied each of the trainees' wants.

2. Teach to the concerns your trainees raise. Be sure to acknowledge the personal responsibility and anguish of managers and supervisors but prod trainees into extracting the larger issue or the big picture reflected by their comments (e.g., profit targets are unrealistic, workers need more remedial math, quality incentives are getting in the way of accurate schedule forecasting).	2. Allow discussion to go on no longer than 10 minutes including your interventions and synthesizing commentary. Bring the discussion around to the need for teaching your employees effective procedures to follow regarding accounting for their time. Set yourself up for presenting training in how to do the procedures within the larger concerns of the company, articulated by your managers and supervisors. Keep your trainees' list of what they want to get out of the training very visible and refer to it point by point as you address each concern through the procedures that you are teaching—that is, relate how a good procedure can help prevent some of their problems from arising. Your constant referral back to their individual concerns and their feedback to you will be your formative evaluation that drives your teaching forward.
3. Teach trainees how to do the procedure. Suggest that they pay attention to both what you say and how you say it, that is, to the content as well as the instructional techniques that you demonstrate. From this point on, you are **modeling** the behavior that you want them to demonstrate when they become instructors (i.e., points 4 through 7).	3. Use a model employee time sheet from your company or one like *Trainee Handout 3.1-B*. Have several copies available for each trainee so that they can make notes in the margins. Make this model into an overhead transparency so that you can point out key sections of it to the class.
4. Show the transparency of the employee time sheet, (*Trainee Handout 3.1-B*, pages 98-99) focusing trainees' attention on the "task code" key at the bottom left of the form. This is the first attempt to define terms—a low-level skill.	4. Ask trainees to take a minute to review this list of codes and add any to it, reflecting their particular concerns. Add these in washable marker to the transparency. Refer to their lists of "wants" to be sure they've translated all of their concerns into task codes.

5. Next, focus trainees' attention on the "Work Codes" section of the form. Point out the specificity of information that you'll receive in the three columns. Point out that accounting for time in this kind of detail gives the company and the employee a monitoring tool, a pricing and budgeting tool, and a planning tool.	5. Lead trainees in a "naming" exercise, another low-level skill, asking them to first identify some typical charge code numbers or list some typical clients. Code them in some way for purposes of illustration. Repeat this exercise for the "Project Identification" column. You'll note that the other large space on the time sheet is where the hours get assigned to days of the week. Since this is self-explanatory, you can omit a detailed scrutiny at this point, and allow trainees to stretch a bit and grasp this for themselves. Chances are that if anyone has a question, it will be asked.
6. Show the other half of *Trainee Handout 3.1-B*, with the completed sample time sheet. By now, you will have presented the "overview" of the time sheet procedure. If you had been asked to write the procedure down, you would have written overviews to step 4 and step 5 using examples of various task codes, project identification, and charge/client numbers. Trainees should respond positively to this summarizing device without your having to go into a lengthy defense of the procedure.	6. When trainees see the completed sample, they might be encouraged to think about specifics of their own scheduling and record-keeping practices (mid-level skill, application). If they don't, ask one or two trainees specifically when they distribute time sheets and who collects them, are they done in ink or pencil, and any other detail that will help direct the flow of training towards the final exercise of having trainees fill out their own sample time sheet.
7. As a "summative" or end-of-process evaluation, have trainees fill out their own sample time sheet, using their own last three days of work as data. Ask them to remember as much detail as they can, that is, give educated estimates.	7. As they are doing this, wander around the room looking over shoulders to be sure everyone is doing the exercise. Identify as possible errors anyone who assigns 100 percent of his or her time to the same number. Encourage more careful analysis, which should result in a more varied and spread timesheet. Suggest that the more analytical approach to accountability yields more useful business information, making accountability record-keeping a strategic planning tool rather than just an audit function.

8. Encourage trainees to develop with their staffs the steps and requirements for completing such a form in their organizations. When all have agreed, encourage them to write down the steps and distribute them to all concerned as well as post them liberally around common areas where employees gather.

9. Make a copy of the model items in tips 4 through 7 (in box), for the trainees to use during their preparation to train their employees. Hand this out to trainees before they leave class.

10. In the last five minutes of the training session, refer back to the list of "what I want to get out of this training" and go over it point by point to verify that in fact you met your trainees' needs. If you haven't, plan follow up within the next two days to those who require more attention.

8. Suggest that they take back with them the list of 12 items that characterize the design of written procedures, found on pages 91 and 92 of this chapter.

Trainer's Worksheet 3.1-A

DIFFERENTIATED SKILL SETS

Common skills are listed here in alphabetical order in columns of low-, mid-, and high-level skills. Low-level skills must be learned and taught before mid-level and high-level skills. It is important that all training be designed this way. Teaching procedures this way is especially helpful to the learner.

Low-level skills	Mid-level skills	High-level skills
	COGNITIVE	
define	ask	classify
describe	compute	conclude
identify	explain	differentiate
label	generalize	extrapolate
list	illustrate	formulate
name	relate	judge
recall	rephrase	plan
recognize	translate	summarize
	PSYCHOMOTOR	
feel	connect	build
hear	cut	calibrate
place	depress	demonstrate
see	insert	isolate
sit	lift	modify
smell	mark	operate
stand	remove	reconstruct
wait	straighten	simulate

Trainee Handout 3.1-B

TRAINING TIME SHEET BLANK AND SAMPLE

Work Codes			Mon	Tues	Wed	Thurs	Fri	Sat	Sun
Task Code	Project Identi-fication	Client/ Charge number	(Enter hours (1.0) and half hours (0.5) only)						

Use the following task code:

-
-
-
-
-
-
-
-

Source: adapted from Carolyn Nilson, *Training Program Workbook & Kit*, Englewood Cliffs, NJ: Prentice Hall, a division of Simon & Schuster, 1989, pp. 404-405.

Trainee Handout 3.1-B (continued)

TRAINING TIME SHEET
SAMPLE

Work Codes			Mon	Tues	Wed	Thurs	Fri	Sat	Sun
Task Code	Project Identi-fication	Client/ Charge number	(Enter hours (1.0) and half hours (0.5) only)						
W	4456	CL05	3.0	1.0			8.0		
F	4459	CL15	5.0	2.5					
—	X	SICK		4.0		1.0			
M	4953	Z100		1.5	5.0				
F	4646	Z100			3.0	7.0			

Use the following task code:

- R = Research
- W = Writing
- P = Project management
- N = Negotiation
- S = Sales
- F = Financial analysis/documentation
- M = Marketing
- D = Production

TRAINING PLAN 3.2

Using Job Aids to Teach Managers and Supervisors How to Maintain Employee Accountability Regarding Rights and Benefits

This training plan is an outline of the key elements, methods, and procedures required to train managers and supervisors *using job aids instead of instructor-led training.* Like training plan 3.1, this training plan is one that can be modeled by managers and supervisors when they must train the people who report to them.

Job aids can be used in many training situations. In most cases, they are designed to replace instructors. As such, job aids are often seen as money- and time-saving devices. Their use is encouraged, with the cautions that they should be designed by trainers (not by marketers and promoters) and they should be readily available in every place that they are required. (Sometimes folks get carried away with the saving money mentality and scrimp on the quantity of job aids that are produced, leaving some employees who need them out in the cold.)

The subject to which this training technique is applied is the subject of employee accountability regarding rights and benefits. This subject is dear to the hearts of managers and employees alike. It has complex, evolving content as well as communication dimensions to it. It has a strong requirement for managers and employees alike to follow correct procedures.

Good management and supervision in accountability regarding rights and benefits is a basic challenge of human resources management today. Job aids can help train employees and managers to follow correct procedures, to know what their responsibilities are, and to gain the maximum opportunities from being at work as they are accountable for their jobs and their personal conduct in the workplace.

This training plan begins with objectives for training itself as well as objectives for the learner, and with evaluation methods tied to the learning objectives. Teaching points related to the content of the job aid provide the foundation for topics to cover during the use or application of the job aid. Sample exercises suggest ways to deliver instruction through a job aid. Helpful worksheets follow the training plan.

OVERVIEW OF TRAINING METHODOLOGY

The reason that an instructor or instructional designer should design job aids is that the purpose of using the job aid method of *instruction* is helping the student to continuously be able to apply the knowledge or skill represented by the job aid. That is, a job aid has a learning purpose, not simply an information purpose. Learning is accelerated by the example, the cueing, the associations, and the procedures portrayed by the job aid; and because the job aid is always accessible to the learner/performer, the critical elements of the learning task are resident in the job aid itself, thus freeing the learner from having to memorize and recall those critical elements at the point of application. By its design, the job aid replaces the instructor and should therefore be created by someone who understands teaching and learning.

Job aids follow the "stimulus-response" line of educational psychology. One would choose a job aid instead of instruction when using a job aid would reduce the response time after the stimulus in a complex mental or physical operation, thereby promoting the accuracy and increasing the cost-effectiveness of training. That is, using a job aid instead of a day spent in a classroom with an instructor results in a better and less expensive way to assure getting the job done. In other words, the response time in a complicated operation is shortened because of the job aid, and precious time and money have been saved. This is especially significant in learning tasks of high complexity and low frequency, as in many kinds of personnel tasks.

As in other forms of stimulus-response learning, job aids must provide stimulus signals (cues, verbal instructions, audio or visual signals) to the learner regarding *when to act* in a certain way, and must provide response directions regarding *how to act* and what performance *results to expect*. The instruction inherent in a job aid addresses both the stimulus context and the response context.

Common examples of job aids are:

- food recipes
- IRS forms
- flowcharts
- rules of grammar
- map keys
- working models
- help screens
- if-then tables
- checklists
- stick-on instruction panels
- troubleshooting guidelines

Often, job aids include a decision dimension ("if this is true, then ...") as well as an instruction to follow a certain procedure ("...then turn the frame over onto its left side"). The trick in designing the job aid is to differentiate in your own mind the various kinds of mental tasks you are asking the trainee to do, and to then design the job aid to enable the trainee to do each task in the quickest and surest way possible. That is, give the trainee all of the cues and parameters of the decision tasks as well as all of the steps and instructions to facilitate implementation behaviors.

Often the effective use of a job aid is enhanced by a face-to- face explanation of it by an instructor who demonstrates its use. This is done either in a classroom setting with a group of job aid users, at a meeting in a manager's or supervisor's office, or in one-on-one instruction setting either peer to peer or manager/supervisor to employee. In the example chosen for this chapter, the training setting is the manager's or supervisor's office where several new employees are gathered to find out about rights and benefits.

Two basic cautions about choosing a job aid over regular instructor-led learning are mostly of a practical nature. First, be sure that the employee can in fact use the job aid—for example, an airline pilot during take off probably is too busy to consult a job aid, or a salesperson in the middle of a sale probably couldn't stop to consult a procedure chart on how to close a sale. Second, be sure that the employee is motivated to use a job aid, and not embarrassed by using it. The best candidates for job aids are complex procedures that must be performed rather infrequently; that is, job tasks that are critical to do correctly and that are especially subject to retention loss because of having to do them only infrequently.

Trainer's Worksheet 3.2-A contains a chart of the options in job aid design. *Trainee Handout 3.2-B* contains an example of a job aid to use in this lesson, "How to Assure a Drug-Free Workplace," one of many lessons regarding employee responsibilities, rights, and benefits. This approach would be suitable for the areas of sexual harassment, theft, violence, age discrimination, AIDS management, and discipline and discharge—all complex areas of a manager's or supervisor's job that have to be dealt with accurately but hopefully infrequently. Lengthy classroom training in any of these areas is probably a waste of time because most trainees will have forgotten the procedures by the time they have to use them. As in the example, a job aid just might be the answer to these kinds of training challenges.

TIME REQUIRED TO DELIVER THIS TRAINING

15 minutes
This training uses a job aid and is delivered by using that job aid in a small group meeting (3 - 5 persons) in a manager's or supervisor's office. Continuous learning and transfer of learned tasks to the job are expected to be facilitated by the trainee's use of the job aid back on the job.

This training could also be done as part of a management employee orientation program for large companies with a classroom full of new managers. In this situation, breakout groups of 3 - 5 managers would meet simultaneously for 15 minutes.

TRAINEE LEVEL

This training is for managers or supervisors who must teach the people who report to them how to use the company's rights/benefits—responsibilities ratio to their own personal advantage for the ultimate good of the company. Most people requiring this training will probably be new hires or existing employees recently promoted to management or supervisory positions.

TRAINING OBJECTIVES

- To use a job aid to teach managers and supervisors about employee responsibilities, rights and benefits
- To show managers and supervisors how to use a job aid as an instructional technique with their employees

LEARNING OBJECTIVES FOR THE TRAINEE

- To use a job aid to learn about employee responsibilities, rights and benefits
- To teach employees about their responsibilities, rights and benefits by using a job aid

METHODS TO EVALUATE THE TRAINEE'S PROGRESS

Evaluating trainees' progress is best done at many times during training, even in training of such short duration as 15 minutes. This kind of evaluation is known as "formative evaluation" because it is evaluation that helps to form or shape instruction. Realistically, when job aids are in use, the formative evaluation consists mostly of immediate feedback and comment on the specific steps or outcomes of the procedures suggested by the job aid. Very often, evaluation is made easy by the synthesized and organized nature of the job aid, and evaluative questions and comments easily relate to specific sections or features of the job aid.

Evaluation activities during training of short duration such as these 15 minutes in your office (or breakout room) will be brief, targeted, and personal. They could include providing simulated situations requiring the trainee to use the job aid to arrive at a solution to a hypothetical problem that you present.

TRAINING TIPS	***EXERCISES***
1. Review when to use this job aid.	1. Discuss the federal "Drug-Free Workplace Act of 1989" and this company's Employee Assistance Programs (EAPs).
2. Show trainees how to use this job aid.	2. Go through the job aid, line by line. Focus on consequences or outcomes.

Trainer's Worksheet 3.2-A

OPTIONS IN JOB AID DESIGN

Job aids are the training delivery method of choice when complex tasks have many subtasks that can be facilitated by having the job aid at hand for reference and instruction at the time the tasks must be done.

Here are some of the options for job aid design:

TYPE	ATTRIBUTES	TYPICAL FORMATS	WHEN TO USE
Example	Illustrates responses required to complete a task	Forms filled in with correct information or sample of document (letter, etc.)	When format or location of information is important
Cueing	Signals a specific action without providing step-by-step directions. Also, directs attention to specific characteristics of objects, procedures, situations or information.	Checklists, worksheets, using photodiagrams, arrows, underlining or circles, task lists	When each step in a several-step procedure is relatively simple, but an error will result if a step is out of sequence. Also, with lengthy or seldom-used procedures
Association	Relates unknown information to existing or already known conditions or information	Conversion tables, graphs, code books, reference documents	When information must be transformed for use in predictably different environments or when the conversion process is not important
Proceduralized	Provides pictures and text in a programmed sequence that both illustrates and describes each step in a procedure	Do-it-yourself repair books for cars, bikes, appliances and so on	When training for skills in the manipulation of objects, materials or equipment
Analog	Provides information that cannot be presented directly	Schematic drawings, organization charts, flowcharts, formulas, equations and symbolic logic	When correct job performance requires knowledge of organization, structure, relationship or flow

Source: Rakow, J. "Performance Aids: How to make the most of them." Reprinted with permission from the September 1981 issue of *Training* Magazine. Copyright 1981, Lakewood Publications, Inc., Minneapolis, MN (612) 333-0471.

Trainee Handout 3.2-B

HOW TO ASSURE A DRUG-FREE WORKPLACE (JOB AID)

The problem of dealing fairly with drug abusers at work is one that nearly all managers and supervisors face. Drug abuse is climbing at a rapid rate, three times as many workers are involved now as there were in 1985[1] and multiple addictions plague more and more people.

Lost productivity, absenteeism, accidents, impaired judgment, and illegal activity are just some of the negative spinoffs of this workplace problem. There is no doubt that the issues are complex and the human resources development responsibilities in this area are falling squarely on the shoulders of managers and supervisors.

This simplified "IF...THEN" chart can help a manager or supervisor "tick off" the important considerations in drug abuse prevention by using this job aid. Obviously, IF...THEN charts can be created in great detail, items can be sequenced and prioritized, and procedures can be presented either generally, as in this example, or in considerable detail.

IF...THEN charts are especially adaptable to human resources issues because of the multiple decisions generally required to solve problems in this field. Often, all a manager or supervisor needs is a memory-jogger or mental organizer to help him or her get started in the problem-solving process, and this is exactly what a good job aid will do.

If the trainee: (manager or supervisor)	Then do this:
• Has not seen the *Drug-Free Workplace Act* (March 1989) and the company's Employee Assistance Program regarding drug abuse	• Hand out copies and highlight key provisions
• Is not familiar with the company's drug policy	• Hand out a copy and check off the provisions prohibiting these actions in the workplace: —illegal manufacture —distribution —dispensation —possession —use of a controlled substance

[1]Milt Freudenheim, "More Aid for Addicts on the Job?. *The New York Times,* November 13, 1989, p. D1.

Trainee Handout 3.2-B (continued)

If the trainee: (manager or supervisor)	Then do this:
• Cannot list suitable objectives for a drug abuse prevention program	• Suggest: —To provide a safe working environment —To protect employees' health —To protect customers and stockholders —To promote productive work —To assure quality —To protect company assets, tangible and human resources
• Must invoke disciplinary procedures because of drug abuse	• Communicate policy and performance standards • Monitor and measure equitably • Keep records confidential • Confront employee in private • Be sure that the employee acknowledges that he/she has a problem • Offer assistance options • Develop an individual assistance plan with the employee and get his/her agreement to an implementation timetable

TRAINING PLAN 3.3

Using a Case Study in a Classroom Setting to Teach Managers and Supervisors About Protecting Intellectual Property

This training plan is an outline of the key elements, methods, and procedures required to train managers and supervisors *using the case study during a class.* To illustrate this training method, the subject of intellectual property was chosen as an example of a complex employee accountability issue and the sort of training challenge that the case study method of instruction addresses well.

Case study requires a good bit of investment of preparation time on the part of the instructor. In order to develop the most effective kind of case study, trainers should choose an actual current business challenge and adapt it for case study. Some large companies temporarily assign writers in the marketing department or technical writers to the training organization to work with instructional designers or instructors to create case studies for use in training. If you are not an experienced writer, you might want to consider finding someone in your company who is and can help you write a well-constructed case study.

The subject of ensuring employee accountability regarding protection of the company's intellectual property is one of the most far-reaching and comprehensive responsibilities of management. It stretches across the board from entry level to the executive suite and involves every employee, vendor, supplier, consultant, and temporary worker who is privy to the company's unique ways of doing business or who has access to the company's files.

Protection of intellectual property, too, has become more important in recent years because of changes in the workforce and work itself, and of competitive challenges at home and from abroad. Less able entry-level workers primarily made up of large numbers of untrained and minimally educated minorities, immigrants, and women comprise the worker pool, yet only about 4 percent of new jobs in the U.S. can be filled by these low-skilled persons, and more than half of all current jobs require education beyond high school.[2] A company's intellectual property in the form of highly educated and skilled employees is increasing in value because of its scarcity.

The study by ASTD also indicates that massive doses of training and retraining of the existing workforce are necessary each year in this decade to increase productivity by as little as 3 percent, and that more than a third of Americans at work say that they both received no formal preparation for their jobs and received no skill upgrading on the job. Our intellectual property is becoming a nonrenewable resource, and therefore more in need of protection on all sides.

On the competitive front, the ASTD study notes that 20 percent of American adults, both at home and in the workplace, are considered functionally illiterate, as contrasted to just 5 percent of Japanese adults. It takes the American auto manufacturer 60 months to bring a new car to market from design to dealership, whereas in Japan, the same process takes only 40 months. American working adults seem to lack the higher-level intellectual skills that foster the competitive edge—skills required in problem solving, creative thinking, goal setting, teamwork, interpersonal relations, negotiation, and leadership.

---

[2]Reprinted from Anthony Carnevale, "Training America: Learning to Work for the 21st Century." Copyright 1990, the American Society for Training and Development. Reprinted with permission. All rights reserved.

As a society we are largely neglecting the building of a foundation of cognitive strength, and whatever intellectual property we have left in our corporate mind simply must be preserved and enhanced in order for our country's businesses to be able to make a contribution to the world economy. The common practice of recent years of "dumbing down the jobs" to fit the lowest paid slot on the organization chart, with the expectation that computers and automated machines would fill in the production gaps, has absolutely backfired on the corporate bottom line. We seem to have lost sight of the fact that in an information-intensive, globally connected marketplace it is a country's collective intelligence that gives value to its businesses, products, and services both in the at-home market and throughout the world.

Thus, the protection of intellectual property is a critical responsibility of today's managers and supervisors. Most managers and supervisors are familiar with confidentiality statements or nondisclosure agreements which employees sign upon hiring on with a company. These signed agreements are legal documents subjecting the employee to fine or other punishment if they are broken. Breach of trust in these matters is generally cause for dismissal. In most cases, the hiring manager represents the company and signs the agreement too, thus becoming formally and contractually responsible for the employee's action regarding intellectual property.

It is wise for managers and supervisors to take this responsibility seriously as the workplace changes, employees at lower and middle levels job-hop from company to company, and work becomes more information-based. Many employees don't even think about what is and what is not intellectual property; many assume that all companies work "this way"; many are so familiar with company records that they can't imagine anyone would want to steal such "common" information. Open communication within company walls and a pleasant working environment can lead employees to want to share information about the company with friends and persons outside the company. It's not that employees are devious—it's that they just don't think about consequences in the same way that a manager or supervisor should think about them.

If your company has no formal structures to protect its intellectual property, consider developing some. Take a hard look at information access and flow throughout the company: voice, data, research, marketing, applications development, production support, media support—who initiates, who receives, who monitors, who inhibits information flow, who is accountable, and where does information go. Take a look at your corporate mission and strategy statements to find words such as "provide the technology base," "enter the global market," and "develop services," "design systems." Focus on the operations and information that make your particular corporate approach unique, and create the accountability structures that protect them. *Trainee Handout 3.3* at the end of this training plan lists some of the dimensions of intellectual property. Use this list to spark your imagination about the kinds of information, business processes, products, systems, procedures, standards, guidelines, finances, customers, suppliers, vendors, consultants to include under the intellectual property umbrella. Develop confidentiality and nondisclosure agreements for employees to sign, and initiate procedures and documentation to assure security and an accountability trail for privileged information.

The training plan for using the case study method to train managers and supervisors to protect the company's intellectual property is an example of a training methods approach—and not everything they need to know about intellectual property. The training plan begins with objectives for training itself as well as objectives for the learner, and with evaluation methods tied to the learning objectives. Teaching points related to the content of the case study and sample exercises suggesting ways to deliver this kind of instruction are also detailed. Helpful worksheets follow the training plan.

OVERVIEW OF TRAINING METHODOLOGY

Choose to use case study as the best delivery method when you want your trainees to practice good judgment when dealing with complicated personnel issues, like the issues involved in the protection of intellectual property. During case study, trainees must analyze a situation identifying correctly the factors that affect certain outcomes; they must synthesize information; and they must evaluate various plans of action.

In a classroom setting, they must interact with their peers in a way that could expose their biases, managerial shortcomings, lack of flexibility, or lack of intellectual depth. In case study, trainees often are required to see analogies and make quick and accurate translations from the fictionalized elements of the case to the actual problems they face on their jobs. Case study is not for the timid or insecure manager or supervisor.

Using a case study requires considerable preparation on the part of the trainer. You must be thoroughly familiar with all of the details of the case and with the nuances of decision effects. The best kind of case to use is a customized case and one that clearly illustrates a range of decision points (some easy, some difficult, some clear, some ambiguous, some with low consequence, some with high financial, legal, or personnel consequence, and so on). It is best to limit the case to one major issue, such as "How would you discharge your responsibilities regarding protection of the bank's unique software system for accessing investors' buy decisions?" Your trainees will rise to the challenge of devising a plan of action when they can see the real implications to their own work in the case you've chosen. It should be an easy-to-define situation but with a good, solid challenge to critical thinking and evaluation at many levels.

If you create your own case for use in training, or if you supervise a writer to create the case, here are some guidelines for development:

- Assemble organizational information about the persons or work groups (e.g., organization charts, job titles within work groups) around whom the case is set.
- Get job descriptions for all relevant persons in the case.
- Get actual performance data (systems performance, sales performance, personal productivity performance, and so on) and camouflage it for use in the case study. Make the numbers real.
- Assemble any quality standards for products and services, jobs, and processes that are featured in the case.
- Prepare a glossary of terms used in the case.
- List historical events and dates that are relevant to the case but not necessarily in the case as written. Provide background information.
- Use a clear writing style in simple "subject-verb-object" order. Follow standard rules for good technical writing. Stay focused on the key issue.

You might find *Trainee Handout 3.3* helpful if you have to create a case study on some aspect of protection of intellectual property. You might also find this approach useful to design a case study on any topic. The design process begins by simply making a list of all the dimensions of the topic that you can think of, and by grouping these into sets that make some sense. Other kinds of cases in the area of legal rights and responsibilities could begin the same way—areas such as sexual harassment, union concessions and givebacks, merit pay and perqs, copyright and patent infringement, and so on.

When you use a case study during training, here are some techniques to help you encourage your trainees' best thinking:

A. Prepare or choose a case to fit your need, your trainee audience, and the time allotted for training
   1. Be sure it is not overly complex
   2. Be sure it illustrates precisely the problems you face
   3. Be sure to allow enough time for problem analysis: the current situation, the desired situation, and the actions necessary to reach resolution
   4. Tell trainees why you chose this case; state learner objectives
B. Provide each trainee with the narrative of the case
   1. Lead trainees into the case with a brief description of your own
   2. Give them time to read and analyze the narrative—overnight, if necessary
C. Provide each trainee with case analysis guidelines
   1. Be sure all trainees know what problem has to be discussed; if there is more than one obvious problem, be sure each one is differentiated from the others
   2. Provide character descriptions
   3. List major events in the case
   4. Point out how this case relates to their work
   5. Provide study guidelines such as "look at relationships; uncover motivations; define feelings...."
D. Lead the discussion of the case in a "brainstorming" fashion, setting an informal, non-judgmental, accepting, and creative tone
   1. Accept all comments as valid
   2. Involve all trainees in discussion
   3. Steer discussion toward conclusions only after all trainees have contributed ideas several times—new ideas grow from old ideas
   4. Close the training session by asking trainers to relate what they learned from case analysis to their own jobs

Source: From Nilson, C. *Training Program Workbook & Kit*, Englewood Cliffs, NJ: Prentice Hall, a division of Simon & Schuster, 1989, p. 209.

TIME REQUIRED TO DELIVER THIS TRAINING

2 hours
Trainees will need time to read, organize their thoughts, and interact with each other in some depth. If this session is used as part of an orientation program, be sure that it is scheduled after trainees have had a chance to "warm up" to each other; that is, put this case study session near the end of the orientation program so that much of the getting acquainted business is finished before you require the in-depth kind of analysis and response that a case study entails.

This case study to be accomplished in two hours should not be more than four pages long. Peripheral material may be handed out on separate sheets, e.g., organization charts, glossaries, specifications.

TRAINEE LEVEL

Any level manager or supervisor who is responsible for protecting the company's intellectual property. Various organizational levels can be represented in a classroom of managers—it's the issue or the case that's the important thing, not the trainee's level within the company.

TRAINING OBJECTIVES

- To present a customized case study to a classroom of managers and supervisors for analysis and discussion
- To facilitate critical thinking, evaluation, and judgment by trainees
- To guide trainees to make good decisions within a range of decision points illustrated by the case
- To encourage the transfer of learning by giving trainees maximum opportunity to practice issue analysis and problem solving, and by providing reinforcing feedback at key learning points during case study

LEARNING OBJECTIVES FOR THE TRAINEE

- To read the case analytically, breaking it down into its key elements
- To identify the decision points in the case
- To prioritize or assign weight to each decision in terms of each decision's effect on business health
- To answer questions raised by the case, drawing on personal experience, corporate law, company policy, and acceptable practice
- To discuss one's own interpretation of the case with fellow trainees in large group and small group sessions
- To begin to plan a program of protection of intellectual property for employees

METHODS TO EVALUATE THE TRAINEE'S PROGRESS

Evaluating trainees' progress is best done at many times during the delivery of training, and in a friendly and somewhat informal way. This is called *formative evaluation* because it is evaluation that helps to form or shape instruction. It is also known as "in-process" evaluation, contrasted to "end-of-process" evaluation. Formative evaluation is developed in relationship to a specific learning objective, thus contributing to the effective accumulation of understanding and skill during a lesson.

In this kind of lesson in which you strive for increasingly higher levels of skill, it is important that you give trainees plenty of feedback about the depth of their understanding at many stages during the analysis of the case. For example, when they begin to break down the case into its key elements right after they've finished reading it, correct them if their analyses are shallow, if they've overlooked an important factor, or if they have not been able to see certain cause-and-effect relationships. Give plenty of positive feedback if they are right on target with their analyses and have identified particularly important relationships among the various factors in the case.

Ask for lists of decision points. Lead trainees either in small groups or as a large group to prioritize the decisions. When they've done it, thank them, or tell them that their work was good. If they have trouble doing this, tell them that they are not quite correct; give them cues about how to see the correct way of doing things. Set them straight early in the exercise; keep on them; don't let trainees go forward to the next task without mastering the one at hand. Remember that higher-level skills are built upon a foundation of lower-level skills. Use evaluation and feedback to drive instruction onward.

Finish your evaluation with an examination of your trainees' ability to synthesize the lessons of the case into a plan for their own employees. Give each trainee or small group of trainees specific feedback on their plans. Suggest your own follow-up involvement if this seems appropriate, either as facilitator or monitor. Keep before your trainees the concept of formative evaluation, even when they get back on the job, because it is formative evaluation that keeps learning happening. Teaching should be balanced in roughly this proportion:

- 50% instruction or explaining
- 35% practice and exercise of newly learned skills
- 15% evaluation and feedback

Expert instructors engaging in formative evaluation will exhibit this balance during each 10-minute segment of the class.

TRAINING TIPS	***EXERCISES***
1. Review the context of the case. State why the company thinks the issue(s) exemplified by this case are important to business.	1. Distribute a 2- to 4-page case study and all related handouts (organization chart, quality guidelines, payroll information, job descriptions, and so on) to the class. Point out important sections and any highlighted questions.
2. Give trainees time to read the case. (You could have assigned the reading for homework, but generally, adults will not do homework in spite of their best intentions!) Instruct trainees to read analytically, with the aim of identifying the key elements of this case.	2. While they're reading, begin cueing them to look for important points. Do this by writing key words on the whiteboard or flipchart—words such as standards, records, margin, unique, and customer. See *Trainee Handout 3.3* for ideas. Do this silently, making no comments. Choose key words from several of the categories on the worksheet to suggest a range of points.
3. Lead trainees in a general group discussion of the case, perhaps beginning with who they saw as the key players, leading into identifying the decision points in the case.	3. Keep the discussion open and expanding during the general discussion to allow all points of view to be aired. A variety of viewpoints will help clarify identification of the decision points.
4. Ask trainees to prioritize or give weight to each decision.	4. Attempt to get consensus from the group on these priorities or weights.

5. Break into small groups to deal with the case in greater depth.	5. Group trainees according to some organization plan that's tied to their jobs, their interests, or stake in the issue—for example, by type of customer, by investment strategy, by industry type, by bank organization, and so on.
6. Structure the small group sessions around key questions that lead trainees into relating the decisions in the case to their own jobs. Allow about 30 minutes to work in small groups.	6. Use bold type or highlights on the case itself or hand out a separate sheet of paper with questions on it. Appoint a group leader and recorder for each small group.
7. Reconvene the large group for general discussion of a company-wide program for protection of intellectual property.	7. Ask one representative from each small group to share his/her group's insights with the large group, steering the discussion to what can be done in this company.

Trainee Handout 3.3

DIMENSIONS OF INTELLECTUAL PROPERTY

Use this worksheet to design a program for protecting your company's intellectual property and to design a training case study involving a specific example of a protection issue.

A. People Who May Work with Intellectual Property

employee
customer
supplier
vendor firm
consultant
installer
construction worker
maintenance contractor

C. Characteristics of Intellectual Property

valuable
special
unique
secret
confidential
proprietary

E. Protective Procedures

accountability form
authorized user list
monitoring procedure
security procedure
loss procedure
destruction procedure

B. Intellectual Properties

data
information
documentation
software
records
organization charts
formulas
computer systems
production systems
specifications
standards
payroll
sales
margins

D. Format of Intellectual Property

written
oral
coded
programmed
graphic
photographed
filmed
taped
copied

Chapter 4

Training Managers and Supervisors to Protect Employee Health and Safety

The complexity of modern life drives individuals to seek protection of their most basic needs for safety in both their private lives and their social lives, including their lives at work. Employers are becoming increasingly responsive to employees' concerns, willingly as well as because of legislation and judicial decision, and managers and supervisors find themselves on the front lines of a sometimes aggressive implementation program to make sure that the workplace is a good and safe place to engage in business. Health and safety issues are so numerous these days that they cannot be left to the human resources department to deal with; managers and supervisors have to know what to do and how to do it.

Threats to personal health and safety are unfortunately a part of living and working in a technology-rich society. Modern chemicals, lasers, radiation, high-speed machines, new viruses all present enormous challenges to employers who used to have to be concerned with only fire prevention, first aid, and noise barriers. Employees today are aware that toxic levels in their working environments can occur quickly, that unharnessed technology and improperly shielded instruments can cause swift and permanent personal harm, and that complicated medical problems on the rise such as cancers and AIDS have a deep and lasting effect on workers and the work that must be done. Making the workplace a viable place is harder today than it ever was.

Examples abound:

- AT&T announced on August 1, 1989 that by 1994 it would end all use of chemicals that deplete the earth's ozone layer, no small task for the company which uses three million pounds of chlorofluorocarbons (CFCs) per year in the manufacture of computer chips and circuit boards.[1]
- A small wallpaper manufacturer in New York mounted an aggressive advertising campaign citing its competitors—who still produce vinyl- and polypropylene-based wall coverings—for potential violation of New York City's building code for minimum toxicity. They said that the popular vinyl wall coverings produced dangerous levels of toxic smoke when exposed to flames or high temperatures such as those common in high-rise building fires.[2]
- Farm workers in Florida won the right through the 11th United States Circuit Court of Appeals to be compensated for pain and suffering from being in a highway accident in an employer's vehicle on the way to work. These damages were in addition to the typical medical and lost wages reimbursement of workers compensation provisions.[3] The newspaper indicated that the employer was appealing the

decision, arguing that such rulings would only make the cost of insurance sky-rocket and probably inhibit employment of such workers in the long run.

- In another court case, the 7th United States Circuit Court of Appeals upheld the right of a Milwaukee company to bar all fertile women from working in jobs where they are at risk to unborn fetuses—in this case, a job whose working environment contained high concentrations of lead.[4] To cries of sex discrimination from the National Organization of Women and the American Civil Liberties Union, the company stood by its claim of concern for worker safety.
- In New Jersey, all new employees at one division of Merck & Company (pharmaceuticals)—some 150 per year—receive a safety training program in proper handling of hazardous chemicals as soon as they report for work, through interactive videodisc training.[5]
- Various recent updates to OSHA regulations include stiffer standards for protective gear, including helmets, face guards, eyeglasses, and safety shoes. The original OSHA legislation in 1970 mandated safety shoes for men, but not for women, and these new standards were meant to reflect the realities of today's workplace.[6] In addition, the National Safety Council estimates that eye, head, face, and foot injuries represented about 14 percent of disabling work injuries in 1987, the most recent data available.
- And from New York to San Francisco, companies are complying with local legislation designed to protect workers from "non-toxic illnesses" such as back problems and carpal tunnel syndrome associated with repeated motion over long periods such as that of data entry at a computer or checking out groceries at a supermarket. At least 13 different states and localities during the past two years have introduced legislation specifically aimed at employers of office workers who work at computers.[7] Known as "VDT (video display terminals) legislation," its purpose is to protect workers by requiring employers to provide ergonomically sound offices with proper chairs, lighting, desks, and rest time for employees who use computer keyboards for their jobs. Employers estimate that compliance could cost several thousands of dollars per work station. The Labor Department's annual accounting report of occupational illnesses and injuries for 1988 showed that repetitive motion disorders accounted for 48 percent of all workplace illnesses, up ten percent over 1987.[8]

Managers and supervisors, obviously, are involved in cases such as those reported above, and will continue to be called upon to make wise decisions for their companies and the employees who report to them. Guaranteeing employee health and safety are monumental tasks in today's complex working environment.

Also, the spinoffs of a complex lifestyle are even with employees, and, of course, their managers and supervisors. Workers seeking relief from stress often turn to alcohol or drugs. Substance abuse is costing employers more than $100 billion a year; and that during that year alone, three times as many workers took advantage of employee assistance programs than did in the previous five years combined.[9] The good news is that employers are taking action, not only in dealing with a problem but also in helping to prevent that problem from occurring.

Other areas of lifestyle stress management are also being addressed by employers. Outdoor fitness trails, indoor fitness centers, weight control and nutrition programs, aerobics, quit smoking programs, and mental health support groups of all sorts are commonplace. Travel groups, hobby groups, volunteer aid organizations, sports teams, and theatre groups often round out the recreational opportunities an employer provides employees to help make their lives more interesting and less stressful. Like it or not, managers and supervisors do get involved in administering and reaping the benefits of such employee activities, and often the quality of that benefit depends upon the manager's or supervisor's ability to manage the health and safety concerns well.

Aetna insurance company in their brochure, "Fighting Substance Abuse at Work," outlines eight key elements of an alcohol and drug awareness program; these key elements could be the foundation of many kinds of health and safety protection programs. They are:

- Management commitment to maintain a workplace free from the effects of alcohol and drugs,
- Written policy and procedures,
- Employee assistance program (EAP),
- Education and training of employees and supervisors,
- Program promotion,
- Program administration,
- Recordkeeping, and
- Program monitoring.[10]

(This brochure is available free of charge by writing to Aetna, P.O. Box 303, Hartford, CT 06141.) Managers and supervisors must be ready to be involved in each of these key elements, and management trainers must have effective teaching strategies to help management with the prevention, reporting, and direct intervention tasks that go along with their responsibilities in the area of employee health and safety.

SPECIAL TRAINING CONSIDERATIONS FOR PERSONAL RISK SITUATIONS

For many people, the added dimension of being at personal risk for not having learned is a powerful incentive to learning.

This phenomenon is common in safety training at the physical risk level, and in training such as first aid/CPR training that results in recognition such as certification or getting a passing grade on a test. Both physical risk (being unsafe or unhealthy) and emotional risk (being embarrassed or perceived as a failure) are powerful motivators to learning lessons well, and both risks commonly motivate managers and supervisors to learn the tasks well for guaranteeing employee health and safety. Additional objectives such as complying with contract obligations, local, state, and federal laws, and protection of company and community property help to provide a trainee population that's ready to learn. Negative citations, hits, and penalties historically have been strong motivators for positive preventive action, and management training programs often have been seen as part of the positive side of that equation.

No workplace is exempt from the requirement to provide for employee health and safety. Offices, factories, warehouses, stores, nursing homes, schools, restaurants, and a host of other business places are governed by a web of compliance laws under legislation such as those of the Occupational Safety and Health Administration (OSHA), the Drugfree Workplace Act, and the Ombudsman Reconciliation Act (OBRA) for nursing homes—to name only a few. *Government* is concerned that employees be protected from noise, heat, dust, fumes; that work areas are consistently safe and nonhazardous; that specific safety and health-promoting procedures are followed; and that both preventive and compensatory actions are implemented. *Management* should be no less concerned.

TRAINING TECHNIQUES TO FACILITATE SAFETY TRAINING

All of these challenges, pressures, and motivations are somewhat different from the drivers for other kinds of management training. In an attempt to recognize these differences, this chapter focuses on two major instructional delivery techniques and several other techniques that in this context comprise the major techniques. These are:

- Demonstration, comprised of
  —using videotapes
  —videotaped feedback
  —hands-on training
  —cross-training
- Effective use of reference materials, comprised of
  —documentation and reporting
  —testing

There are some guidelines for instruction in the generic technique of demonstration. Elementary school children know this as show and tell, and it's a teaching technique that's been around for a long time. Through the first two training plans, this chapter elaborates on these basics of demonstration:

- Demonstration generally leads to emulated action in which the trainee follows the example of the trainer.
- The demonstrated example generally becomes the performance criterion against which the trainee's action is measured.
- Measurement of the trainee's action is generally done on the spot during training with the trainer as evaluator.
- Successful demonstrations require training that helps set the trainee's mental frame of mind for psychomotor or physical movement that follows (it's *show* and tell):
  —color, sound, smell, and tactile cues are important
  —pattern recognition is important
  —giving discrimination and association hints is important
  —providing clear step-by-step instructions is important
- Demonstrations generally involve a person's mechanical, spatial, and practical intellectual structures in addition to one's verbal ability.
- As the trainee begins to follow the trainer's lead, it's important for the trainer to give guided practice to the trainee.

The training plans that follow in the next section elaborate on this list of characteristics of demonstrations.

No instructional techniques book would be complete without some discussion of "the final exam," so this is considered in the next section of this chapter in the context of safety certification. Here are some basic guidelines for summative (end-of-process) testing:

- Each item on the test is independent of every other item.
- Each item is relevant and important to work.
- The difficulty of a test item is based on the difficulty of the problem involved, not on the difficulty of the language used in the item.
- Words used on the test are unambiguous; they have only one meaning.

- The difficulty of the test is appropriate for the intended use of the score.
- The test is based on the instruction provided and the content that was covered during training.
- The test is free of cultural bias.
- The test has been pilot tested and troublesome items removed or revised.
- The test gives each test taker equal opportunity to succeed or to fail.
- The test is administered fairly and consistently.

Endnotes

[1]Philip Shabecoff, "AT&T Barring Chemicals Depleting the Earth's Ozone," *The New York Times*, August 2, 1989, p. A12.

[2]Ann Hagadorn, "Turning Safety into a Competitive Issue," *The Wall Street Journal*, July 25, 1989, p. B1.

[3]Linda Greenhouse, "Court Refuses to Hear Occupational Safety Appeal," *The New York Times*, October 3, 1989.

[4]William E. Schmidt, "Risk to Fetus as Barring Women from Jobs," *The New York Times*, October 3, 1989.

[5]"Ideas and Trends," *Lotus*, March 1990, pp. 15-16.

[6]Albert R. Karr, "OSHA Proposes Stiffer Standards for Protective Gear," *The Wall Street Journal*, August 17, 1989. p. A7.

[7]Larry Reynolds, "Ergonomic Concerns Stiffen Rules Regarding VDT Use," *Personnel*, April 1991, v. 68, no. 4, pp. 1-2.

[8]Peter T. Kilborn, "Rise in Worker Injuries Is Laid to the Computer," *The New York Times*, November 16, 1989, p. A24.

[9]Milt Freudenheim, "More Aid for Addicts on the Job," *The New York Times*, November 13, 1989, p. D1.

[10]Copyright 1991, The Aetna Casualty and Surety Company. Reproduced with permission.

TRAINING PLANS

Three training plans combine the different instructional elements presented in this chapter:

- 4.1 addresses both videotapes and videotaped feedback
- 4.2 deals with both hands-on training and cross-training
- 4.3 outlines the kind of training that results in preparation for testing and third-party (for example, state, federal, or professional) certification

Several worksheets are appended to these training plans to provide supplementary material that might be helpful in designing or delivering training to help managers and supervisors guarantee employee health and safety. Training plans are selected to represent examples from among the many topics in the employee health and safety area. Many others could have been chosen; these simply illustrate the range of both content and methods.

Training Plans for Chapter 4 include:

management issues	*training techniques*
4.1 Video Display Terminals (VDTs) and Ergonomics	Teaching with videotapes
4.2 Fire and First Aid	Hands-on competency through cross-training
4.3 Operator Certification	Computer simulation training

TRAINING PLAN 4.1

Using Videotapes to Teach Managers and Supervisors to Protect Employees Against Occupational Illness from Video Display Terminals (VDTs)

This training plan is an outline of the key elements, methods, and procedures required to train managers and supervisors *using conventional videotapes.* The last decade has spawned a great proliferation of training videotapes, a large majority of which are not training at all, but are simply entertainment or information. Trainers who use them frequently report that trainees viewing them often assume a couch potato mentality in a classroom when the video is about to begin.

The following discussion of correct use of videotapes is set within the learning context of the demonstration. The subject of ergonomics and employee health and safety in front of computer screens (VDTs) provides the challenge to managers and supervisors within this management training technique challenge to trainers. This training plan is somewhat different from others in that it details the use of two kinds of videotapes, one that has been created by a vendor or corporate video staff and shown to trainees, and the other that is made on the spot of the trainee doing a demonstration and then played back for the trainee's self assessment during the class. This plan gives you two valid uses for conventional videotapes during training.

A training plan begins with objectives for training itself as well as objectives for the learner, and with evaluation methods tied to the learning objectives. Teaching points related to the content provide the foundation for topics covered during training. Sample exercises suggest ways to deliver this kind of instruction and how to ensure that it doesn't slip into simply entertainment.

OVERVIEW OF TRAINING METHODOLOGY

Videotape methodology is discussed in two sections: Viewing a prepared tape and then recording and playing back the trainee's actions. This training plan uses both applications of conventional videotape for a lesson in VDT safety. The videotape is first shown to the manager or supervisor; then, in this same training session, the manager or supervisor is videotaped demonstrating the correct safe behavior. The goal is for both tapes to be shown to employees at a later date.

Viewing a Prepared Tape

As with instructor-led training, training through videotape can be more or less involving for the trainee. For example, if a classroom full of trainees seated theatre style view a 40-minute videotape, it's probably a passive endeavor. On the other hand, if that same tape is given to a trainee to use with a portable VCR/monitor in his or her office with an accompanying study guide, it could be the set up for an active learning experience.

Personal Computing magazine, November 1989, ran an article by Adams and Huff about their experience using videotapes for word processing training in a bank. They found that videotape instruction was most effective at the introductory level, and that basic concepts could be learned as well through video instruction as with an instructor.

However, as the material became more complex conceptually, an instructor was needed to work with trainees. Use of videotapes for introduction of formats and commands saved their trainers time as they then concentrated on advanced work in other instructor-led courses, and it was a convenient and economical way to introduce the word processing system to trainees at remote branch locations.

How to Get the Most Out of Training Videotapes

In general, videotaped instruction should be more than a speaker in motion on tape. At minimum, the tape should be divided into distinct lessons giving the viewer a chance to pause and process thoughts. Instructions for doing this should be given on the tape itself or through a coordinated study guide. In addition, give your viewers some pre-viewing guidance in effective listening. Such guidance could include these points:

- Pay attention to the speaker's logic; try to anticipate the speaker's next point based on what's previously been said.
- Use the media-rich context of images and motion to "frame" the logic; that is, allow yourself to be aware of more than the words, and don't be distracted by color or sound in isolation.
- Try to keep a mental tally of main points and supporting information; try to identify the parts and embrace the whole chunk of related material.
- Periodically summarize what's been presented, about every five minutes is a good rule of thumb. People assimilate meaning at a much faster rate than we recognize speech; using this lag time to summarize helps organize information in a useful form in one's memory.
- Mentally jump from the videotape images to images of your own work situation in an attempt to relate the instruction to your needs.

Effective listening is sometimes a trainee's only tool for learning through videotapes. Trainers have a responsibility to give trainees at least this much guidance before they show a videotape.

Because videotape is a visual representation in motion, it is an especially good vehicle for giving a demonstration. Video is good at teaching people to discriminate among kinds of motion, such as speed, interactions of parts, and characteristics of patterns. A camera's ability to zero in on edges and shapes and to see an object from different angles makes it a superb vehicle for presenting definition and discrimination exercises to learners.

Video is also an excellent medium for modeling various movements, for example, keystrokes at a computer keyboard in slow motion focusing on the wrist, or the effects of a day's worth of improper sitting on the lower back using fast forward photography and replay. Modeling correct behavior is also done very well in video format, and can have extra punch for the trainee if the model is someone important to that trainee's success—like the company president, for example.

Video is good at showing both what shouldn't be done and what should be done, and people learn easily through comparison and contrast. Photography and playback techniques such as compression and extension of time and split screen images can add to the interest and help the training message come across more effectively.

Here are several ways to encourage active learning when videotapes are shown in class:[11]

---

[11]Lookatch, R. P., "How to Talk to a Talking Head," *Training & Development Journal,* September 1990, pp. 63-65. Reprinted with permission from the *Training & Development Journal.* Copyright September 1990, the American Society for Training and Development. All rights reserved.

- include a question-and-answer period following the tape
- encourage advance questions before showing the tape, suggesting what trainees should look for in the tape and what will be expected of them following the tape
- make sure case studies are built into the tape of people or situations trainees know
- search and skip through the tape to highlight only what's important to that particular class
- print materials listing objectives for the training, the content outline of the videotape, study questions and workbook space for the trainee to answer the questions

Many of these considerations for facilitating learning through the medium of videotape apply equally to trainees in a classroom situation and to those who engage in independent study by viewing a tape in their offices, libraries, or homes. For independent learners, trainers have the additional responsibility to be sure that the equipment and the tape itself are in good working order and that the trainee knows how to make the equipment work. At minimum, equipment instructions should be packaged with the tape and equipment as it travels from individual to individual. Do not make the assumption that everybody knows how to work a VCR; and don't just drop the stuff and run—let the trainee know that you, the trainer, care about how the training goes:

- spend a few minutes either in person or on the telephone with the trainee before he or she gets started
- point out key sections in the study guide
- be sure that the trainee knows the quirks of that particular VCR
- confirm that the trainee in fact has the time to view the tape
- suggest when the new skills or information will have to be used

Recording and Playing Back the Trainee's Actions During Training

This is the second most common use of videotape for instruction. Companies have used this for many kinds of instruction for managers, as an objective and nonjudgmental feedback instrument especially when managerial behavior is being learned (e.g., presentation techniques, how to appear in court, effective interviewing, how to terminate employees, and so on). This application of video technology is also very good for showing a manager his or her strengths and weaknesses in demonstrating good actions to others—as in proper seating before a VDT, proper use of safety protective gear, proper bending and lifting, proper packaging, and disposal of chemicals.

Most people need some advance information before they are videotaped. They want to be photographed at their best, and will want to know about what colors to wear, and which side of their faces and what kind of lighting look best. You'll need an experienced videocamera person to set managers and supervisors at ease when they are due to be videotaped.

As in other kinds of training, you'll want to be sure the person being taped understands the objectives of the taping session; for example, to demonstrate correct posture and hand position during data entry. In addition, for this playback application of video instructional technology, your trainee will need to know the objectives of the playback part of the training; for example, to use a scoring checksheet on my own demonstration of correct posture and hand position to rate myself, and to identify and correct errors in my demonstration until I get an acceptable training tape that can be shown to my employees. In this sort of training, the structure of a checklist or other feedback form will keep the trainee focused on tasks at hand—it's easy for trainees to get confused, angry, or embarrassed when they see themselves "performing" on the tape. Video feedback sessions require a trainer close at hand to keep the learning going.

TIME REQUIRED TO DELIVER THIS TRAINING

60 minutes per trainee: 10 minutes of prepared videotape, 10 minutes of videotaping, 30 minutes of tape feedback, and 10 minutes for set up and paperwork. This training could be done in small groups (three or four persons) to share viewing of the prepared videotape. If the training is run as a small class, three or four persons could be accommodated during a half-day period.

LEVEL OF TRAINEE

Manager or supervisor.

TRAINING OBJECTIVES

- To show managers and supervisors a 10-minute videotape demonstrating the importance of protecting the health and safety of employees who work at VDTs
- To train managers and supervisors to model the correct behavior and posture for VDT operators
- To videotape managers and supervisors modeling the correct behavior and posture during a 10-minute taping segment
- To playback the videotape to the trainees so that they can self-critique their demonstration, using a VDT operator's checklist. To facilitate the feedback and self-evaluation
- To correct any problems with the demonstration, setting individual retaping sessions for managers who need them prior to their incorporating their videotapes in training for their employees

LEARNING OBJECTIVES FOR THE TRAINEE

- To view the VDT safety videotape with guidance from the prepared study guide. To complete any exercises in the study guide
- To recognize safe and unsafe behavior and posture
- To use the checklist as a guide to my own safe behavior
- To be videotaped modeling safe behavior and posture using the training workstation
- To view myself on the videotape and, using the checklist and instructor feedback, critique myself
- To correct any errors and set up a remake of the videotape if necessary

METHODS TO EVALUATE THE TRAINEE'S PROGRESS

Trainees are evaluated in two different ways during this training session. First, the completed study guide as the prepared videotape is being viewed is evidence of the trainee's engaging in learning at some level. Of course the ultimate success of the message of the videotape is whether or not that manager or supervisor takes action to protect the health and safety of employees who work at VDTs.

Second, trainees evaluate themselves by using a checklist as they view their demonstration of safe behavior and posture. Trainers also can add constructive evaluation based on the same checklist. *Trainee Handout 4.1* is an example of this kind of evaluation checklist.

After the videotape has been made according to safety and health standards, the objectives for this training have been accomplished. When the manager or supervisor then uses this videotape as part of the instructional package for his or her employees, a new training plan for employees' training must be developed.

TRAINING TIPS	***EXERCISES***
1. Show the 10-minute prepared videotape on VDT safety.	1. As the tape is showing, guide trainees in following the study guide, suggesting that they answer the questions posed in the guide. (Questions might be fill-in-the-blank type questions or multiple choice questions based on either the trainees' prior knowledge about VDT safety or on what they just saw in the tape.)
2. Review the VDT operator safety checklist, *Trainee Handout 4.1.*	2. Tell trainees that they will use this in two ways during this training: to serve as a guide to viewing and noting the correct behaviors being demonstrated by the actors on the tape, and to rate their own demonstrations of safe behaviors and postures during the videotaping of them.
3. Videotape each manager or supervisor demonstrating safe VDT operation.	3. Distribute a 10-minute pre-written script for each manager or supervisor to follow during the taped demonstration. Be sure that the trainee saw this several days ahead of the taping session so that he or she doesn't stumble over words while trying to concentrate on demonstrating correct behaviors. Practice reading the script ahead of time in class if you think that's necessary to allay nervousness.
4. Playback the videotape for trainees to critique themselves using the checklist.	4. Hold back and let the trainees handle the critique themselves if possible. Intervene only if they are missing important safety precautions or are not following the checklist. This is learning by doing, and the more they can do themselves, the better they'll learn.

Trainee Handout 4.1

VDT OPERATOR'S SAFETY CHECKLIST

____1. Adjust your chair so that your feet rest firmly on the floor or a footrest, supporting your legs at a 90-degree angle.

____2. Place the VDT (computer screen) two feet away at 20 degrees below eye level, or at a comfortable viewing place considering your eyeglasses.

____3. Place the keyboard two to four inches below the standard desktop, so that arms and hands are parallel to the floor while typing.

____4. Position the VDT screen to avoid reflections.

____5. Adjust the VDT screen contrast and brightness to a comfortable level.

____6. Place document holder at approximately the same distance from your eyes as the VDT screen.

____7. Position your desk lamp to illuminate source documents but not the VDT screen.

____8. Change position whenever you are tired, or take a 15-minute break every two hours.

____9. Rest your eyes occasionally by focusing on a distant point.

TRAINING PLAN 4.2

Using Hands-on Competency-based Cross-training to Train Managers and Supervisors in Fire Safety and First Aid

This training plan is an outline of the key elements, methods, and procedures required to teach managers and supervisors about fire safety and first aid. In this plan, *three specialized training techniques* are featured and combined. The fundamental principles of *hands-on training* are discussed with the added dimension of *competency-based standards.* These two traditional training techniques are then set within the newer technique of *cross-training,* popular in many companies today that are committed to empowerment and team efforts.

The drive for safer workplaces is accelerated by new materials and more advanced technologies. Updates and improvements in OSHA guidelines provide incentives for employers to prevent accidents from happening. Managers and supervisors need to know at a "get-your-hands-dirty" level how to prevent accidents and what to do in case of fire or bodily injury. Management trainers must provide such training.

The New York Times, November 16, 1989, p. A24, reported that the most hazardous jobs are in construction, and lumber, steel, food, stone and glass, and automobile manufacturing.[12] The same article reported that during 1988, 4 percent of all full-time workers suffered illness or injury on the job, the highest level since 1980. Repeated trauma injuries in hands, wrists, and fingers and respiratory illness associated with toxic agents top the list. Infection control in our burgeoning healthcare establishments, hospitals, nursing homes, clinics, and labs is a major management challenge in those workplaces. Fire disasters such as Chernobyl, Bhopol, and the poultry processing plant in North Carolina are grim reminders that management has an ever-widening scope of responsibility regarding worker safety in our contemporary workplace.

In the book *Human Resources Director's Handbook,*[13] Mary Cook reported OSHA's ten most common violations:

1. No posting of the OSHA notice of employer obligations.
2. No grounding of electrical equipment connected by cord and plug.
3. No machinery guards at point of operation.
4. No guards for pulleys.
5. No guards for live parts of electrical equipment.
6. No enclosures for blades of fans in use less than 7 feet above floor of working level.
7. No guards for belt, rope, and chain drives.
8. Disorderliness in aisles and passageways.
9. No guards for vertical and inclined belts.
10. Not maintaining a log and summary of job injuries and illnesses.

[12]Peter T. Kilborn, "Rise in Worker Injuries Is Laid to the Computer," *The New York Times,* November 16, 1989, p. A24.

[13]Mary F. Cook, *Human Resource Director's Handbook,* © 1984. Reprinted by permission of the publisher, Prentice-Hall, a division of Simon & Schuster, Englewood Cliffs, NJ.

OSHA guidelines are specific and clear. Abiding by them might not just be a matter of carelessness on the part of employers; managers and supervisors might not, in fact, know what to do and how to do it—that is, compliance might be a matter of knowledge and skill deficiency, the classic discrepancy situation for which training is the solution of choice. The director of OSHA was quoted as saying, "We seem to be asking people to do their jobs faster and in smaller, more finely defined tasks."[14] Better-designed tools and better-designed workplaces seem to be in order.

In safety training, managers and supervisors are asked to do something to an employee's work station. Objects are involved, tangible devices must be manipulated, and correct actions must be performed. A different kind of training methodology seems appropriate for this kind of performance need.

OVERVIEW OF TRAINING METHODOLOGY

Hands-on training for managers is not commonplace. For years, management trainers have focused on the planning and decision-making aspects of a manager's or supervisor's job. But then the "management by walking around" idea began to take hold, and effective managers moved out from behind their printouts and mahogany desks. They got dirty, they worked out product improvements at quality seminars with their employees, they scaled rocks and walked blindfolded through the woods with their employees, and they worked shoulder to shoulder on all sorts of teams with those who reported to them. The principles and applications of hands-on training are due for a revival!

Hands-on training received a great deal of attention in the 1940s when a huge workforce was required to manufacture, process, package, warehouse, and distribute wartime and defense items. Training programs in shop skills proliferated, and the industrial model of assembly line productivity pervaded our approach to quality management and to workplace learning well into the 1960s. Because hands-on training was a methodology that focused on tangible objects and movement, it served well in the heyday of American manufacturing.

In safety training today, there is also a need for a focus on objects—and for managers and supervisors, not just workers themselves, to be involved. For a variety of reasons associated with workplace culture changes as well as organizational changes, today's managers and supervisors are simply closer to work. A review of the fundamentals of hands-on training is worth doing.

Hands-on training first of all requires a stimulus and a response—an environmental event followed by sensory perception and intentional action. Managers and supervisors, and employees too, do not automatically know how to be good at stimulus-response learning. People often are "lopsided" when it comes to sensory abilities—for example, one person's hearing might be superb but his or her tactile sense might need a lot of training; one's eyesight might be poor, but one's sense of taste particularly acute. A group of managers might be quite deficient in their ability to distinguish gradations of smell, often indicators of trouble. Managers and supervisors who sit in their offices and plan don't need this kind of training; managers and supervisors who manage by walking around probably do.

Hands-on training also has the basic tenet that patterned action is the behavioral goal for all of the steps of training leading up to it; that competent performance means doing it right the first time, the hundredth time, the thousandth time, and so on. Mastering physical motor skills and repeatedly following procedures are essential. All of these are very different kinds of learning than what's been offered in the typical management development curriculum of the recent past. Yet safety training *for man-*

[14]Kilborn, op cit, *The New York Times*

agers and supervisors requires that those in charge act perceptively, quickly and correctly, and consistently according to patterned competent performance standards. If people are expected to behave this way, then they must be taught these behavioral skills—not the skills of intellectually manipulating information. It's not good enough to know where the first aid manual is located.

Basic Steps in Hands-On Training

Craftspeople, apprentices, and students in vocational-technical schools have long known the following steps to hands-on training:

1. *Sharpen your skills of perception.* This means that you focus on stretching the capacity of whatever senses are required for you to be aware of that stimulus—for example, variation in color or odor, intensity of heat or cold, the character of sound, the feel of a surface. Accurate perception means that you will enhance the quality of your learning, and ultimately of your performance.
2. *Be prepared.* This is a complex step that involves being able to lay your hands on everything you need to respond correctly to the environmental stimulus. It means that you know the steps to follow in procedures associated with each possible stimulus, and that you know which course of action to follow. It means that you can identify and distinguish cues and prioritize probable actions. Preparation training involves cognitive skills associated with categorizing information and with remembering and retrieving information. It also means that all relevant workplace objects (for example, materials, windows, doors, security cameras, and so on) are ready to be used correctly—of particular concern in safe evacuation of buildings during fires and toxic leaks.
3. *Respond correctly with coaching.* The third step in the hands-on methodology is to train someone to respond correctly, given the right cues. Many kinds of computer-based training are very good at this step. The American Heart Association's first-aid CPR course is also very good at this step of training.
4. *Practice patterned actions.* Practice enough in a controlled training situation so that you habitually and reliably perform the correct action whenever it is required. Often overlearning, or going beyond the mastery level for a skill, is an approach to teaching patterned actions. This step goes beyond guided response, resulting in predictable action made possible because of practice. Emergency Medical Technicians and volunteer fire fighters are generally good at this step; they know that patterned actions require practice.
5. *Perform consistently and reliably over time.* Each of these steps in hands-on training requires lessons designed carefully by management trainers. The first three steps, especially, are ones that deserve a great deal of attention, as managers and supervisors make their presence felt in the places where the action of working occurs. Hands-on training means that trainees get their hands on the reasons for the training and the objects they need to succeed.

TIME REQUIRED TO DELIVER THIS TRAINING

20 hours, during the first two weeks of each fiscal quarter (January, April, July, October)

LEVEL OF TRAINEE

Manager or supervisor.

TRAINING OBJECTIVES

- To develop a cross-training program for first aid and safety training for all managers and supervisors. To include training in each manager's or supervisor's unique area of risk and responsibility so that the entire management staff can perform all first aid tasks commonly required in this company. Include areas such as: wounds, toxic fumes, burns, injuries to muscles/bones/joints, eye injuries. First aid tasks common to all managers such as Cardiopulmonary Resuscitation (CPR) and First Aid for Choking (Heimlich Maneuver) are handled through regular classroom training sponsored by the clinical field service staff of the local hospital.
- To cross-train all managers and supervisors during the first two weeks of each fiscal quarter for a period of 20 hours any time during those two weeks.
- To brief each manager cross-trainer on basics of how to be a peer trainer (see *Trainer's Worksheet 4.2*).

LEARNING OBJECTIVES FOR THE TRAINEE

Note: The following sections extract just one example of cross-training, the area of "wounds," in order to show the reader how hands-on, competency-based training is presented.

- To master the techniques of first aid regarding wounds: to protect the wound from contamination and to control bleeding
- To demonstrate proper wound prevention actions

METHODS TO EVALUATE THE TRAINEE'S PROGRESS

Many of today's managers and supervisors have grown up with an evaluation system which they remember as being characterized by grades, percentiles, and the normal curve. These are all features of "norm-referenced" measurement, and are familiarly applied in school and college tests of achievement and in the broad scale tests for admission to higher education and professional programs (SATs, LSATs, MCATs, and GREs, to name a few). This model of measurement is not usually appropriate in measuring hands-on learning.

Measurement that's better suited to hands-on training is "criterion-referenced" measurement, sometimes more commonly referred to as competency-based. What this means is that scores, or success, in achievement are reported as "against a standard" rather than as one's place along the distribution of a normal curve. This, of course, means that those standards, or criteria, must be established for each action that's measured.

In competency-based training, the trainee is evaluated on whether or not he/she met the standard. The checklist is the simplest form of evaluation documentation for this kind of training. Check marks in a "yes" column generally mean that the standard or criterion was met; check marks in a "no" column generally mean that the standard or criterion was not met. When a criterion has not been met, more training is generally indicated—training to standard is usually the rule.

Criterion-referenced tasks abound in safety training. Refresh your memory by reviewing OSHA's ten most common violations (on page 128). Look at violations number 2 and 3: correct action is implied as performing according to the criterion of ". . . *any* equipment *connected by cord and plug*" and ". . . guards *at point of operation*." Or, look at violation number 6: ". . . in use *less than 7 feet above floor* of working level." Such guidelines for success, or correct action, are object-oriented, very tangible, very clear to understand. They are criterion-referenced items, measurable by criterion-referenced tests or exercises in which trainees demonstrate their competence at meeting those criteria. Management trainers who design hands-on training need also to design criterion-referenced tests or evaluation exercises to go along with it.

These two basics of safety training—hands-on and criterion-referenced—can work very well in a cross-training program for managers and supervisors. Cross-training is a kind of training that is characterized by people learning what other people do—"walking in their moccasins." Applied to safety training, cross-training would involve managers and supervisors learning what safety actions were required in each other's jobs. At the employee level, cross-training would mean that each employee would know the safety actions required of other employees who report to the same manager or supervisor.

These are some characteristics of cross-training:

- Someone from the training organization who's in charge
- A specified number of hours in which cross-training occurs (for example, the first 40 hours on the job, 2 hours every Wednesday afternoon)
- An appointed trainer from the host organization, for example, a manager, supervisor, or peer of the person to be cross-trained
- Instructions or train-the-trainer training for the host trainer from the training organization
- A competency-based checklist of training tasks to be accomplished during cross-training; copies of this for both the host trainer and the person to be cross-trained
- Columns on the checklist for recording time: the date and time when each task is scheduled to be trained, and columns for both the trainer and the trainee to check when each task was completed
- A page following the checklist on which both trainer and trainee can comment on the training in a narrative way
- An accountability trail, indicating to whom to report the conclusion of training—this could be simply posting the checklist somewhere in a commonly visible place, giving the checklist to one's manager, notifying the training organization, or each party, trainer and trainee keeping a copy in their files; places for the names of trainer, trainee, and person who reviews the completed checklist

The training that is detailed in the following section uses one small sample from the wide range of safety training that could be done through hands-on, competency-based, cross-training.

TRAINING TIPS	*EXERCISES*
1. Define the four types of wounds by letting the trainee handle the equipment that typically causes each type: —abrasions —incisions —lacerations —punctures	1. Take the trainee to the place where the equipment is typically used. Coach the trainee in correct positioning of the equipment for use. Point out the dangerous part of the equipment itself and the dangerous steps in the process of set-up and use. Let the trainee position each piece of equipment for safe use.

2. Tell the trainee what to look for and listen for as the equipment is activated and as it runs safely.	2. Separate these two preparation tasks; use checklists for each, and relate the cues on the checklists to the actual part of the equipment of concern in safe operation (for example, let the trainee hear the correct RPMs when the machine is operating safely. Play an audiotape of unsafe RPMs so the trainee can hear the difference. Show the trainee why slower or faster RPMs can cause the possibility for abrasions, incisions, and lacerations.)
3. Move beyond the safety lessons to the wound itself.	3. Show photographs or slides of types of wounds that could be caused by improper operation of this equipment. Relate back to the part of the equipment that caused the wound in the picture and to relevant items on the checklist.
4. Discuss contamination with the trainee.	4. Ask the trainee to inspect the immediate workplace surrounding the equipment to identify possible contaminants for each type of wound that might result from faulty operation of that equipment. Correct any errors the trainee might make in judgment or omission.
5. Discuss infection control. Point out which medicines are most useful for each type of wound. Point out parts of the body where wounds are especially dangerous.	5. Open your first aid kit to show the trainee various kinds of medicines to help prevent infection. Let the trainee hold the containers and smell the medicines.
6. Coach the trainee in applying a dressing to each type of wound that could result from improper use of this equipment.	6. Refer back to the pictures one at a time. Give the first aid kit to the trainee along with the instructions step-by-step for dressing each type of wound. Simulate a wound on yourself with a washable marker and let the trainee practice dressing it.
7. Coach the trainee in stopping bleeding in the type of wound that could result from improper use of this equipment.	7. (Follow a similar procedure as in number 6 above.) Instruct the trainee in applying direct pressure and a pressure dressing to a wound. Instruct the trainee in finding pressure points in arms and groin.

8. Test the trainee on each dressing and bleeding situation. Record evaluations on the checklist.	8. Enlist the help of another employee who could simulate a wound, or repeat the process yourself using different areas (leg instead of arm, for example) for practice. Let the trainee do it him/herself, without coaching from you.
9. Suggest that the trainee take a complete first aid course sponsored by the American Red Cross for complete first aid training.	

Trainer's Worksheet 4.2

TRAINING THE TRAINER: GENERAL GUIDELINES FOR PEER TRAINERS

Cross-training is often a situation in which employees of similar responsibility levels become instructors and students. There are different interpersonal dynamics at work in peer training than there are when a "real instructor" from the training organization or a vendor is in the position of training authority. Often in cross-training—and in any situation where non-trainers are put in the position of being instructors—you'll need to run a train-the-trainer program. Here are some things peer trainers can do to make their job of instructor a little easier and make learning more effective:

1. Describe the "big picture" of how your work and the trainee's work both contribute to company goals. Establish yourselves as co-equals both working for the good of the company.
2. Tell the trainee that you value the work he or she is doing.
3. Take the time to understand the trainee's emotional relationship to the tasks at hand—fears, anxieties, misunderstandings, biases, hopes, enthusiasm, and so on. View these problems as opportunities for focused training.
4. Show and tell. Demonstrate correct procedures, set up experiments, show how things work; tell the trainee why certain approaches work or don't work.
5. Talk out loud. Talk to the trainee when you set about a task; let the trainee "read your mind" as you troubleshoot problems, analyze risks, or critique the trainee's performance of training tasks. Stop frequently to emphasize key decision factors.
6. Let the trainee show you that he or she has "gotten it." In peer training especially, it's important to recognize the peer relationship. Too, teaching is a good way of encouraging people to structure their thinking correctly. Give your trainee the opportunity to do this.
7. Allow the trainee to learn from mistakes, within the bounds of safety, of course. Allow a mistake to continue only long enough so that the trainee can see the consequences of it. Tell the trainee the precise point at which he or she went wrong, and guide the trainee through corrective action immediately.
8. Encourage questions; answer them with "what" and "why."
9. Give the trainee the chance to accumulate small successes. Separate the training tasks into small parts that can be described clearly and acted upon independently.
10. Schedule peer training at a time that's convenient to the trainee and adjust your own work so that you can do a good job of training.
11. Have a clear end to peer training and re-establish your relationship as co-workers.
12. Be available to your trainee after training as a coach if the trainee needs review or a little confidence-building when the new skills must be applied on the job.

TRAINING PLAN 4.3

Certification Training Via Computer Simulation

This training plan is an outline of the key elements, methods, and procedures required in the kind of operations training that leads to certification. This training is delivered *by a computer simulation* of the problem-solving challenges of an operating environment. This is a generic training plan, applicable to many kinds of process operations in which chemicals are used or in which physical relationships (heat, cold, force, combustion, speed, and so on) present potential risks to employee health and safety.

The world of the 1990s is a curious enterprise, pushing extremes of investigation—far reaches of beyond the solar system and inside viruses. People who engage in such investigation for their work are confronted with a wide range of decisions in terms of materials and processes as well as in terms of the importance of those decisions to society. In addition, government is involved both in the guarantee of competence and the protection of individuals through various laws, regulations, and certification requirements. The nature of technological work demands technical training equal to the challenges.

Many companies have dual tracks to responsibility and high pay, the management track and the technical track. High-level technical employees at places like AT&T, Bell Laboratories, DuPont, IBM, Kodak, or Corning enjoy the same prestige and opportunities of employment as do high-level managers. In smaller technology-based companies, high-level technical employees often are the high-level managers. The point is that in many companies today, management training must meet the needs of high-level technical employees too. It is especially appropriate in certified operator training. This training plan suggests one example of this kind of training.

OVERVIEW OF TRAINING METHODOLOGY

Computer simulators have been used in training for several decades in industries such as plastics, fertilizers, ammonia, gas, oil, refineries, ceramics, pharmaceuticals, and in nuclear power plants, in flight training, and in space and defense applications. Through simulator training, operators can experience an equivalent number of years of in-plant training in only weeks on the simulator; they can live through a broad and complex range of operating events equivalent to years of on-the-job experience. All of the tests for safety can be presented to a trainee in a safe environment, yet with decision-making and problem-solving requirements equal to those in a risk situation.

Good simulation training will reproduce the control room environment of the trainee's workplace, using the same control devices (handles, buttons, levers, gauges, displays) as the trainee is required to use on the job. Process simulations will be activated through that familiar control interface. An instructor station is generally linked to the trainee station, or an expert system for instruction and a monitoring and feedback system are built into the training.

When simulation training is tied to certification, use of reference materials either hard copy or on-line is built into the training, and documentation of the trainee's progress during training is essential. Criterion-reference tests and competency exercises are usually part of the simulation instruction.

Standard content features of process simulation training are: effective use of controls both to perform tasks and to access information, normal operations, process upsets and instrument malfunctions, effects of variable changes, optimization, and problem analysis. Guided practice is an essential component of all lessons. Pre-tests, post-tests, and follow-up tests can all be part of simulation training, especially if the simulation training is essentially self-study, that is, through on-line expert system instruction, not controlled by an actual person.

The design of simulation training should take into consideration the specific plant and job of the particular individual trainee. In managerial-level certification situations, training must be geared to the individual who will be applying for certification. Simulation training is very good at this because of the features of computer speed, branching, and memory capacities.

In designing simulation training, variables such as temperature, level, pressure, and flow are represented by mathematical equations. The working of valves, pumps, fans, and compressors likewise is reduced to numerical values and grouped together in logical units to represent operations. Control functions such as on/off, signaling, and looping; instrument, utility, and equipment failures all are represented logically or mathematically. Actions by the trainee operating the simulated controls in a variety of situations show up on the simulator screen in the same way as they would on monitors back at the work site. In simulation training, the trainee is free to examine cause and effect actions with no fear of disaster. Limits can be pushed, and standards can be tweaked in experiments with no risk to health or safety.

Certification requirements such as these are designed into the training:

- Knowledge of operating characteristics and process performance
- Knowledge of all safety rules
- Ability to follow all procedures of safe operation
- Ability to diagnose and correct operating problems
- Ability to startup and shutdown a process
- Ability to handle an emergency

These knowledge and skill areas often form the content of certification tests; in addition, certification may require performance tests on simulators to demonstrate certain skills. Simulation training is the training method of choice for this kind of learning requirement.

TIME TO DELIVER THIS TRAINING

6 hours of simulator time; probably spread over two days of training. One to two hours on the simulator is about all the average trainee can do at one sitting.

LEVEL OF TRAINEE

Manager or supervisor with high-level technical responsibility for safe operation of process equipment.

TRAINING OBJECTIVES

Note: For the rest of this training plan, only one lesson is presented in detail, to plainly show the relationships among certification requirements, documentation, use of data bases, and operator training using the simulator. This one lesson might take 15 minutes.

- To let the trainee experience how a boiler responds to changes in steam drum pressure, through pre-programmed exercises and instructor input.
- To guide the trainee in use of data bases for pressure, temperature, and flow ranges and indicators, and in operator safety regulations and certification requirements.
- To show the trainee how to benefit from the system's monitoring, documentation, and feedback features.

LEARNING OBJECTIVES FOR THE TRAINEE

- To operate the boiler safely.
- To see how pressure changes affect boiler operation.
- To analyze the causes of pressure changes by studying malfunctions, remote functions, process ranges, and instrumentation.
- To use results of documentation and feedback to operate more efficiently and optimally, that is, achieving maximum design effects at minimum cost.

METHODS TO EVALUATE THE TRAINEE'S PROGRESS

A performance printout is generated at the end of each lesson. That is, the trainee's problem-solving logic is evaluated against an expert standard, the trainee's speed of response is indicated against various time criteria, and the trainee's numbers of false starts and decision errors are enumerated. Particular attention is paid to errors leading to safety risk and violation of safety regulations. These errors are highlighted and reported separately. The performance printout is criterion-referenced. Topics for remediation or further training are cross-referenced to each documented error so that the trainee can quickly bring himself or herself up to 100 percent competency through additional targeted individualized training. This performance printout is continuous and cumulative, and can be accessed at any point during the lesson.

Certification testing is typically a pencil-and-paper test created by the national certifying board. It is a test that focuses on "what if" situations, problem solving, and decision-making for optimization. In addition, the certification test has 40 percent of its questions on regulations, legislation, and standards for operator safety. It is a norm-referenced test, with scores reported for the industry nationwide on a normal curve, letting the test taker know how he or she stands relative to the norm of all persons taking the test. The assumption for this test is that certification is based on attaining a score of 75 percent or more on the test. *Trainee Handouts 4.3-A* and *4.3-B* provide information about rating scales and the administration of such tests.

This particular lesson would probably be addressed by only one or two items on the operator certification test.

TRAINING TIPS	*EXERCISES*
1. Select normal operating conditions.	1. Initialize all parameters to normal. Call up the tables for pressure, temperature, and flow. Look up the configuration of all related blowers, burners, heat exchangers, fans, and pumps in normal operating modes.

2. Review safety regulations.	2. Find the on-line safety regulations file. Go to the specific regulations on the steam drum. Look up this same section in the safety manual on the shelf.
3. Select steam pressure controllers, fuel gas controller, and air flow controllers to change.	3. Refer to the engineering drawing of boiler operation and locate all relevant controllers. Anticipate the effects of changes in each.
4. Increase steam pressure by small increments.	4. Monitor fuel gas flow and oxygen ratio; adjust all instruments to continue safe operation within the changed environment.
5. Decrease steam pressure by small increments.	5. Monitor and adjust, as in step 4.
6. Increase and decrease steam pressure by larger increments up to the limits of safe operation.	6. Monitor and note the limits of acceptable performance. Identify actions to compensate for errors.
7. Introduce malfunctions in equipment and problems with remote functions.	7. Monitor and note the effects on all processes of faulty equipment. Figure out what steps to take to compensate for faults and failures.
8. Get the criterion-referenced evaluation printout for this lesson.	8. Check all work and specify additional training to correct errors and gaps.

Trainee Handout 4.3-A

GUIDELINES FOR RATING SCALES

In large-scale testing such as certification testing, the rating scale is usually based on numbers 1 to 100. Scores are often reported as percents or percentiles. This kind of scale is illustrated along with several other types of scales. Here are the guidelines for creating scales:

1. *Logic.* Present respondents with a scale that is logically differentiated. Some examples are:

   - . ______ . ______ . ______ .
1 2 3 4
   - never sometimes often
   - completely dissatisfied / unhappy / pleased / completely satisfied
   - F______D______C______B______A
(51-60) (61-70) (71-80) (81-90) (91-100)

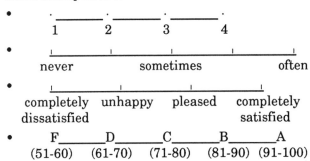

   In the same measurement session, present scales that "read" in the same direction, that is, low to high, left to right. Be careful not to unwittingly affect results by a confusing or illogical way of asking a question or presenting a scale. Check your form for consistency.
2. *Choices.* Present no fewer than four choices and no more than seven choices on a scale. Don't invite respondents to always choose the midpoint.
3. *Weighting.* Be sure each item on a test or questionnaire is equally and accurately weighted, so that responses on a scale have equivalent meaning during data analysis.
4. *Freedom.* Always include a space for free response, elaboration, or explanation with any scale. People sometimes cannot fit their responses into your mold. Allow them the freedom to add narrative comments.
   Additional comments: ______________________________

   ____

Source: Nilson, C. *Training Program Workbook & Kit,* Englewood Cliffs, NJ: Prentice Hall, a division of Simon & Schuster, 1989, p. 142.

Trainee Handout 4.3-B

TEST ADMINISTRATION CHECKLIST

Occasionally an employer gets involved in the administration of a large-scale test such as a certification test in which a roomful of people sit down and take the same test. Most people get nervous before a test. Never administer a test in a haphazard or casual way. Be sure everyone understands testing instructions. Use this checklist as you prepare to administer any kind of the test. A rule of thumb as you face your trainees is "Equal and All" — that is, equal instructions are given to all persons taking a test; all persons have an equal opportunity to succeed or fail during testing.

- ☐ Review the test and its scoring key for accuracy (typographical errors, clarity of language, correspondence between each item and the correct answer). Make corrections if necessary.
- ☐ Regulate the test environment for access, light, heat, chairs, tables, and space. Be sure each person to be tested has an equivalent test environment.
- ☐ Be sure the test site is near a clock, drinking water, and rest rooms.
- ☐ Post no smoking signs and don't allow smoking during testing.
- ☐ Get a list of persons to be tested. Prior to the test, notify each person on the list at the same time that testing will be done, when it will be done, and where it will be done.
- ☐ Prior to the test, tell persons to be tested how test results will be used.
- ☐ Prepare testing instructions. Ask several colleagues to check the instructions for clarity and usefulness.
- ☐ Assemble all testing materials at the test site: e.g., videotapes, terminals, disks, audio tapes, cameras, pencils, paper, simulation props, job-related equipment, and so on. Secure the test site if materials have to be left overnight.
- ☐ Administer the test equally to all test takers.
- ☐ Be sure each test has a place on it for identification of the test taker. Be sure test instructions include instruction to fill in the identification information. (Test takers often forget this in their haste to get on with the test.)
- ☐ Collect all testing materials and answer sheets (disks, etc.) from test takers immediately after the test.
- ☐ Formally solicit, document, and report feedback on the test design, environment, and administration from test takers to those who designed the test.
- ☐ Keep testing materials and scores in a locked storage place.

Source: Nilson, C. *Training Program Workbook & Kit,* Englewood Cliffs, NJ: Prentice Hall, a division of Simon & Schuster, 1989, p. 154.

Chapter 5

Training Managers and Supervisors to Hire and Keep Competent Employees

The marketplace for workers has changed. Managers and supervisors are now challenged with an employee pool that's vastly different from their own group of peers and with workplace conditions dissimilar to the work environments in which most of them began their careers.

The American workplace is more diverse, less populated across departments, leaner in terms of levels of management, more global in outreach, more information-based, and more service-oriented. The employee pool of available workers in the mid-1990s is smaller at all levels, less educated at the bottom, more Hispanic and Asian, more female, and older.

The design of jobs, the requirements for training, the mix of benefits, perks, and hiring enticements likewise are changing to reflect these realities. Motivations and expectations of this workforce and potential workforce are quite different from those of the workforce most current managers and supervisors know from their experience. Today's managers and supervisors need to know how to deal with these workplace changes at the hiring end of their responsibility in order to maximize the opportunities inherent in the current workplace profile for the benefit of both the individual employee and the company.

TRAINING THAT DEALS WITH SHRINKING PERSONNEL RESOURCES

An important aspect of this training is the necessity for trainers to understand that the manager will be generally tempted to make comments like: "Things just aren't the way they used to be; our choices are so limited now; we'll need to spend a fortune on training." Trainers will have to be ready to respond with compassion—and with good solid training techniques—to managers and supervisors who will long for "the good old days."

Trainers will have to be prepared to help managers accomplish the following:

- redefine entry-level standards
- work through problems of language and literacy
- recognize the value in diversity and develop viable management skills for enhancing the benefits of a broader range of differences
- design jobs and create job descriptions that truly reflect the current nature of work

- envision employee development programs that tap the potential and encourage the growth of individuals

Today's trainers will have to show managers how to hire talent and how to maintain a competent workforce in the midst of shrinking and changing personnel resources.

TRAINING PLANS

Four different training plans provide a comprehensive sample of management training techniques for use in training to help managers and supervisors hire and keep competent employees. Where appropriate, worksheets are appended to each training plan. Each training plan with its appendices is intended to give you, the trainer, the training design and presentation guidelines that you need.

In these training plans, we do the conceptual work for you—you need only to flesh out the plans with your own company jargon, names, and specific data.

Training plans for training managers and supervisors to hire and keep competent employees include:

management issues	*training techniques*
5.1 Hiring Panels	Briefing/debriefing
5.2 Batched versus Single Applications	How to effectively present "dry" material
5.3 Employee Development	How to use performance technology and performance support systems
5.4 Employment Opportunities	Interactive videodisc

TRAINING PLAN 5.1

Briefing and Debriefing Techniques to Train Managers and Supervisors How to Use Hiring Panels

This training plan is an outline of the key elements, methods, and procedures required to train managers and supervisors using a minimalist approach to training known as *the briefing and the debriefing*. This outline is structured to enable the trainer to create lesson plans, an instructor guide, or a course outline from it.

A training plan begins with objectives for training itself as well as objectives for the learner, and with evaluation methods tied to the learning objectives. Teaching points related to the content of a manager's or supervisor's area of responsibility provide the foundation for topics covered during training. Sample exercises suggest ways to deliver this kind of instruction. Helpful worksheets follow the training plan.

OVERVIEW OF TRAINING METHODOLOGY

Using hiring panels to secure the best job candidate is a highly professional endeavor. Such panels are generally made up of managers and other key employees who represent the company and know the work of the organization in which the candidate is seeking employment.

A hiring panel can meet together to do the interview or can work independently, one after another, to interview the candidate. If the group approach is used, try to have five interviewers per candidate in order to increase the reliability of interview data.

Panel members will want to do a good job of interviewing, will not want to waste time or unconsciously bias the interview, and will want to be able to efficiently arrive at consensus about the candidate.

Training these kinds of managers for this situation requires a high-level, efficient training methodology that recognizes the expertise of individual panel members yet encourages a kind of "group think" in order to progress to an effective conclusion of the interview process. Of concern is the issue of inter-rater reliability, an issue of consistency in evaluation methodology used during interviews, of fairness to the candidate, and of decision quality for the company.

Using briefing and debriefing techniques allows the trainer to deliver very targeted, very high level, and very spare training. These training techniques are extremely cost-effective.

TIME REQUIRED TO DELIVER THIS TRAINING

2 hours:
1 hour for briefing and 1 hour for debriefing

TRAINEE LEVEL

This training plan is for any person who must be part of a hiring panel.

Because the delivery methods are focused on the documented results of the interview process, it is fairly easy to address differences among trainees regarding experience levels and comfort levels with the interview process. The burden is on you as a trainer to be very attentive to individual responses of your trainees as you step your way through the content checklists and recommended interview procedures.

By the end of the briefing session, you will want to be sure that all trainees are at the same level in terms of understanding what results you're looking for. Frequent pauses for evaluation, careful listening, and individualized feedback are your best techniques for getting your trainees to that level of confidence and understanding.

TRAINING OBJECTIVES

- To provide each panel member with a content checklist to cover during the interview
- To annotate the content checklist during group discussion at the briefing
- To describe and explain correct interview procedures to assure reliability
- To facilitate role play or other demonstration of trainee ability to apply correct procedures
- To achieve consensus at the debriefing session regarding the chosen candidate

LEARNING OBJECTIVES FOR THE TRAINEE

- To cover all itemized content during the interview
- To apply standardized interview procedures during the interview
- To gather information leading to effective hiring decision making

METHODS TO EVALUATE THE TRAINEE'S PROGRESS

Evaluating trainees' progress is best done at many times during the delivery of training, and in a friendly and somewhat informal way. This is called "formative" evaluation, because it is evaluation that helps to form or shape instruction. It is also known as "in-process" evaluation, contrasted to "end-of-process" evaluation. Formative evaluation is developed in relationship to a specific learning objective, thus contributing to the effective accumulation of understanding and skill during a lesson.

In this kind of two-part training separated by days or even weeks, that is, *briefing and debriefing,* it is more important than ever to engage in formative evaluation. Because the time for each training session is only about one hour, this "on the spot" evaluation must be built into about each 8-10 minutes of instruction throughout the hour.

Here are some ways to quickly and effectively evaluate trainees during briefing and debriefing:

- At the end of the briefing, send home with each trainee a checklist of items to cover during interviewing. Instruct trainees to complete the checklist during or immediately after the interview. At the start of the debriefing, have trainees read their ratings and comments as you record them on a flipchart. Continuously ask the trainees for "additional comments" as you record each item. By doing this, you should be able to tell whether in fact the content has been covered and whether standard procedures were followed.

  If content or procedures were not complete—thus leading to lack of reliability of the results of interviewing and possibly the wrong choice of candidate— it will be up to the group to compensate for the lack before choosing the winning candidate. You can facilitate this decision making by being sure that the group sees what the problem is and addresses only the problem, in order for the reliability of the result to get back into balance.

- During the briefing, pause after describing several checklist items and ask the group "Is this clear?" and then "Give me an example of what you'd expect the candidate to say in response to this question." Your trainees' responses will give you a pretty good idea of their understanding of how to get the most out of each interview question.

  If their comprehension is shallow or incomplete, it's up to you to do a better job of instruction, perhaps through using examples or of suggesting how several different kinds of candidates might respond.

  Remember, your goal is for the trainee to be ready to apply this checklist to ultimately get the best candidate to accept your job offer.

- The final test of this training will be at the debriefing session when all trainees have had a chance to report the results of their interviewing. As this happens, your job will be to encourage full participation and make an on-the-spot assessment that the interview was conducted fairly and thoroughly. Before concluding the debriefing, look at each trainee and give him or her specific feedback about how you believe that person performed during the interview.

  If you feel that the person lacked some skill or understanding, tell the person exactly where he or she performed poorly so that the next time around, that person can correct the problem. It's your job as evaluator to specifically indicate to your individual trainees exactly what they must do better. When each trainee reports to the group, it's a good idea for you to keep a log of problems as each person reports. In formative evaluation, problems are good things. Most people will try to correct behavioral problems if they know what they are. Managers especially relate well to "to do" lists!

TRAINING TIPS *During Briefing:*	***EXERCISES*** *During Briefing:*
1. Read aloud the interview checklist, (*Trainee Handout 5.1-A*) soliciting comments and changes from trainees.	1. Hand out "draft" triple-spaced copies of the interview checklist; ask trainees to mark up their copies as you read.
2. Get consensus from trainees regarding content.	2. Record trainees' changes on flipchart or whiteboard as they give them to you; ask for show of hands as to whether or not to include the changes. Make the changes yourself and distribute final interview checklists to your trainees within two days.
3. Be a facilitator for a trainee brainstorming session about effective interviewing techniques.	3. Borrow a key member of the personnel department to act as brainstorm leader/recorder and agree to let this person "throw out" the leading questions to your trainees, and allow you to focus on the quality of each person's response.

Pay attention to the depth of each trainee's contributions and questions. Prod each trainee to "tell why" this is important, or to "elaborate" on a certain point.

Ask those trainees who seem to have the best understanding of effective interview processes to demonstrate the right way to do it using the brainstorm leader or yourself as the candidate; that is, get the trainees to show you (and their peers) exactly what to do and what not to do on specific process techniques. Distribute handouts on "Inter-rater Reliability Guidelines" (*Trainee Handout 5.1-B*) and "Common Mistakes Interviewers Make" (*Trainee Handout 5.1-C*) at the appropriate times during the brainstorming session.

By focusing on specific techniques, you'll have a much better chance of having all interviewers do it the same way. Build quality in by concentrating on fine-tuning each small and specific technique of interviewing.

4. Show an overhead transparency of the "Interview Summary and Rating Form" (*Trainee Handout 5.1-D*).

4. Run this form through a copy machine on the correct type of acetate for your machine to make an overhead transparency. Showing a form as "an overhead" is a quick way to focus the attention of a group on the big picture and to enable you to point out the potential problem areas to the entire group at once.

Ask the group if there are any other potential problems with this form, and tell them that it was designed with provision for their individual interpretations. Instruct them to record their particular points of view in the "Comments" section, and to bring all of their results to the debriefing session (specify the date).

5. Instruct trainees to pick up their copy of the "Interview Summary and Rating Form" as they leave the briefing session today.	

During Debriefing:

6. Ask trainees to sit at a table wide enough to spread out the interview checklists (*Trainee Handout 5.1-A*) and the "Interview Summary and Rating Form" (*Trainee Handout 5.1-D*) side by side in front of them. Focus on the information on the "Interview Summary and Rating Form," using the interview checklist for reference. Solicit responses from the group on each item for each candidate.	6. Use a whiteboard to record tally marks and comments on a "master form," that is, an enlarged copy of the "Interview Summary and Rating Form" matrixed with candidates' names. Be sure that the tally is not visible to casual passersby. Be sure to erase the tally marks and names before you leave the debriefing.
7. Review the guidelines for inter-rater reliability (*Trainee Handout 5.1-B*), either by reading them aloud yourself or enlisting the help of one of your trainees as reader.	7. After each guideline is read, facilitate discussion on that one item so that all trainees describe or explain their attempt to follow this guideline. Get group consensus either that the process worked consistently for all candidates or that certain actions must be taken to compensate any candidate who got shortchanged by a flaw in the process.
8. Arrive at consensus about who is the best candidate, referring back to the matrixed tally on the whiteboard. Use the final ten minutes of the debriefing session to demonstrate to the trainees that in fact they learned to conduct a hiring interview as a "panel," and that in a brief two hours they were able to make a good business decision.	8. As a final instructional activity, point to each candidate's name on the whiteboard as you encourage consensus. Suggest that trainees check back to their interview checklists. Focusing on the persons by name should help bring about the decision regarding whom to hire.

Trainee Handout 5.1-A

INTERVIEW CHECKLIST FOR USE BY A HIRING PANEL

____1. A job opening exists.

____2. All paperwork has been submitted by and about the candidate (for example, resumé, references, application, testing results, class rank).

____3. Your attorney has told you what questions are illegal to ask (for example, marital status, sexual orientation, age, religion).

____4. You have scheduled a comfortable interview location.

____5. You have freed your schedule so that you will have no interruptions during the interview.

____6. Your standards are set in the following areas:

- experience
- capability
- education/skills
- goals and ambition

____7. You know what other contingencies or requirements are peculiar to this job (for example, relocation is likely in six months, second shift opening only to start, department operates as work teams).

____8. You understand the dimensions of the rating scale.

Trainee Handout 5.1-B

INTER-RATER RELIABILITY GUIDELINES

1. Agree on the "traits" or specific items on the interview questionnaire. That is, agree on the definitions, paying special attention to parameters, limitations, cut off points, standards. Strive to establish an immovable baseline for investigation.
2. Use consistent language. Agree not to use certain confusing or possibly misleading terms.
3. Agree on ways to expand, clarify, and probe. Develop a list of acceptable phrases to use.
4. Strive for uniformity in documentation. Agree on the format for writing things down, for example, phrases beginning with action verbs, complete sentences, key words.
5. Agree on a rating scale; agree on its differentiation points, for example, numbers, points on a line, percents.
6. Agree on what kinds of experiences and work behaviors constitute value.
7. Agree on when to use tallies, checkmarks, percents, words.
8. Pay attention to time:
   - establish a schedule to allow each interviewer to be fresh, alert, uncompromised by other work pressures
   - set guidelines about time allotments for each question and response
   - be on time for your interview; pass on the candidate to the next interviewer on time
9. Take time after the interview to synthesize information about the candidate. Set guidelines for how much time—for example, 20-30 minutes for synthesizing. Avoid belaboring the task or giving it too short a time for adequate reflection.
10. Keep results of interviewing confidential. Wait until debriefing or a summary meeting of all interviewers to discuss your interview, the candidate, or the results.
11. Agree that each member of the panel of interviewers has an equal stake in the outcome of the interview process—that is, the choice of candidate is equally important to all interviewers.
12. Agree on which documents you must review before conducting the interview.

Trainee Handout 5.1-C

COMMON MISTAKES INTERVIEWERS MAKE

1. Does not plan the interview; goes in "cold."
2. Has a poorly conceived or shallow interview questionnaire.
3. Doesn't take the time to practice using the interview questionnaire; makes false assumptions about flow, clarity, and timing.
4. Forgets to safeguard against interviewer bias (gender, ethnic, racial, age, and so on).
5. Is confounded by the "halo effect" whereby one excellent trait tends to sway all ratings to higher than they should be.
6. Fails to separate each interview response; lacks ability to differentiate responses.
7. Fails to focus on reliability; fails to conduct all interviews equally.
8. Plays "I gotcha"—asks for information that the candidate cannot be expected to have.
9. Uses jargon or company-specific language to intimidate.
10. Loads questions with one's own value system.
11. Asks irrelevant questions.
12. Asks questions that have already been answered in previously submitted paperwork.
13. Fails to stick to the agreed-upon probes, leading to lack of comparability among interviewers' documented comments.
14. Tends to favor writing down negative information.

Trainee Handout 5.1-D

INTERVIEW SUMMARY AND RATING FORM

Position ______________________ Name of Applicant ______________________ Yes ___ No ___

This rating form will become a part of the candidate's permanent record which will be made available to governmental compliance agencies upon request.

DO NOT FILL OUT IN PRESENCE OF APPLICANT Consider the overview of the candidate in all categories below and comment on each rating in Section V.	Outstanding	Above Average	Below Average	Average	Inadequate
I. EXPERIENCE—How does previous experience relate to current position opening? Consider communications and other skills such as knowledge, information and technical competence based on previous training.					
II. CAPABILITY—Verbal ability, judgement, analytical, logical, decisive, resourceful, imaginative.					
III. EDUCATION/SKILLS—Degrees(s), professional licenses, registrations, certifications, data processing, languages and equipment.					
IV. GOALS AND AMBITION—Initiative, persistence, drive, goals are well defined (as they relate to predicting success on the job).					

V. OTHER FACTORS—Geographical preference, management potential, current salary, etc.

____

____

____

____

Comments: ______________________

____

____

____

For Additional Comments Use Back

Overall Appraisal:

Outstanding ______ Above Average ______ Average ______ Below Average ______ Unacceptable ______

Recommend employment for current position opening: Yes ______ No ______

Future Consideration: Yes ______ No ______ If Yes, for ______________________
Position Title

Recommendation Based Upon: Resume/Application Review ☐ Interview ☐ Telephone Contact ☐

______________________ Signature of Interviewer

______________________ Date Completed

Source: Mary F. Cook, *Human Resource Director's Handbook*. Prentice Hall, a division of Simon & Schuster, Englewood Cliffs, NJ: 1984. Used by permission of the publisher.

TRAINING PLAN 5.2

How to Effectively Present "Dry" Material

This training plan is an outline of the key elements, methods, and procedures required to train managers and supervisors in *something they need to know in order to make good hiring and placement decisions, yet which they consider boring information.* This training plan gives you all of the conceptual elements of how to make those seemingly dull topics in management and supervisory training a bit more interesting.

One of the most common problems in management training is that managers and supervisors by nature are doers, energized by production or service crises and challenged by the dynamic interactions of the people around them. They generally do not like to stay in one place (for example, a classroom) very long, and it's often difficult to get them to commit to coming to a class or workshop.

How to present dry material in an interesting way is a frequently expressed problem of the management trainer, and this example from the area of personnel responsibilities can be adapted to similar type material from any other responsibility area. The example chosen here is that of deciding whether to use the single job application or batches of job applications when hiring. (*Trainee Handout 5.2-D* explains the advantages of reviewing batches of job applications.)

A training plan begins with objectives for training and for the learner, and with evaluation methods tied to the learning objectives. Teaching points related to the content of a manager's or supervisor's area of responsibility provide the foundation for topics covered during training. Sample exercises suggest ways to deliver this kind of instruction. Helpful worksheets follow the training plan.

OVERVIEW OF TRAINING METHODOLOGY

The parameters of the training challenge include:

- making the training experience itself attractive enough to get managers and supervisors to come to class
- making the end result of training, that is, the decision which way to go regarding type of application process, be seen as an event with major implications for achieving overall management success
- devising an instructional delivery technique that will be viewed by managers and supervisors as right on target, all they need to know and nothing more
- choosing an instructor with a great deal of credibility in the area of personnel practices, particularly in the area of interviewing and selection; don't make the mistake of assigning a mediocre instructor to an unpopular topic—it's these kinds of topics that demand the most credible and most skilled instructors

Using a traditional classroom with handouts is a cost-effective way to provide trainees with the materials they'll need to make an effective decision. The classroom setting provides the peer contact and support in a sheltered and structured way which can facilitate the decision making if networking among peers is encouraged by the trainer. Busy managers and supervisors will probably not balk at attending just one hour of training if it is made convenient and conducted superbly well.

TIME REQUIRED TO DELIVER THIS TRAINING

1 hour
This hour can stand alone, for example, after a luncheon meeting, or between 4 P.M. and 5 P.M.; or can be part of a full day of training in various personnel practices.

TRAINEE LEVEL

Every manager or supervisor who is ultimately faced with decision making about the operational costs, equity, and procedural validity of the interviewing process should have this training. Just as managers and supervisors vary in their capacity for decision making in other areas of personnel relations, they will vary as learners in this kind of training situation.

You can expect some trainees to relate better than others to forms and paperwork—some will grasp details quickly; others will hate to deal with details. Most managers and supervisors will learn procedures well and will want to learn them well, so be sure that you are very accurate and clear in teaching them what to do, step by step towards making the decision. Keep your focus on the quality of the decision, and don't get buried in the excruciating details of the forms themselves.

Expect your trainees to be at the same readiness level for wanting to make a good economic decision regarding interviewing. Especially in changing times when the applicant pool looks different from that of a decade ago, decision makers will be looking for procedures that help them hire competent workers who will be on the job for a good long time.

Expect differences among trainees in managerial style when it comes to dealing with paperwork.

TRAINING OBJECTIVES

- To list and discuss economic issues of interviewing and selection
- To engage trainees in helping to create the list of issues
- To guide trainees into prioritizing the economic issues
- To set the trainees up for being able to establish standards for applicant quality in whatever jobs those particular managers and supervisors have open
- To present new information about applicant batching and processing batched applications

LEARNING OBJECTIVES FOR THE TRAINEE

- To list the economic issues of interviewing and selection
- To discuss the economic issues of interviewing and selection
- To prioritize the economic issues of interviewing and selection
- To articulate one's own department's economic motivation regarding staffing
- To establish standards for applicant quality using a representative sample of the company's standard job descriptions
- To compare and contrast two interviewing approaches: single applications versus batched applications

METHODS TO EVALUATE THE TRAINEE'S PROGRESS

Evaluating trainees' progress is best done at many times during the delivery of training, and in a friendly and somewhat informal way. This is called "formative evaluation" because it is evaluation that helps to form or shape instruction. It is also known as "in-process" evaluation, contrasted to "end-of-process" evaluation. Formative evaluation is developed in relationship to a specific learning objective, thus contributing to the effective accumulation of understanding and skill during a lesson.

In this kind of *important but boring subject,* you'll want to be sure that the trainees' potential annoyance at having to be in class doesn't get in the way of their learning. You'll want to be sure to pose small, distinct learning challenges and to measure the success of trainees as they respond to these individual challenges. In this kind of training, plenty of feedback to the trainees is important as they accumulate learning successes in response to these challenges.

Here are some specific ways to use formative evaluation creatively to counter a potential attitude problem in this kind of training:

- Focus on getting each trainee to participate actively, that is, to speak up and contribute ideas, to come up in the front of the class and help you record responses, to organize a small group session, to be a small group recorder or reporter. Encourage each individual who participates or volunteers ideas, as each person speaks up—don't wait until the end of the lesson to thank everyone generally. Enthusiasm and energy builds as individuals feel that they are valued for their experience and ideas. Let it be known that you think highly of the process of participation and of those who engage in it during this hour of class. Your encouragement and feedback to individuals and the resulting energy that these create will help to "form" the dynamic context for the entire class, helping to increase the motivation for staying there.
- After trainees have come up with the list of economic issues and prioritized them, read the entire list aloud to the class so that trainees get a chance both to see and hear the finished consensus list. Simply ask the class, "Is this list complete, now?" They will then evaluate their own choices, thus helping themselves to solidify their own individual positions.
- Ask for each department's statement of economic motivation regarding staffing. Your evaluation goal is not to say one is better than the other, but rather to get each trainee to state a position. Some trainees might not be able to think clearly within a group of peers, and you quite possibly will have to allow some slower or more shy trainees to put their positions in writing. If this is the case, physically move over to a trainee who needs to write it down first in order to nudge that person into writing something down. Your "policing" action sends the message that this task is important and that this trainee needs some catching up.
- In the group exercise on quality standards based on sample job descriptions, strive for at least three quality improvements per job description. When you get at least three, praise the group for their contributions and tell them that you have three good improvements and that there are probably more improvements lurking between the lines.
- Devise some structure through which to compare and contrast the two application processes, single versus batched. Make it clear to the group that there are pros and cons associated with each process. If you want to take this one evaluative step further, do a Force Field Analysis of the pros and cons. (See *Trainer's Worksheet 5.2-A* and *Trainee Handout 5.2-B*.)

TRAINING TIPS	*EXERCISES*
1. Make the point that, as times have changed, the applicant pool has changed.	1. Refer to the "Six Challenges" at the end of the book, *Workforce 2000*. (*Trainee Handout 5.2-B*) Turn this into an overhead transparency, a handout, or read from the worksheet.
2. Suggest that there are three important motives for interviewing and selection based on this employee pool: 1) efficiency and economy of the interview process itself, 2) being able to spot quality and competence, and 3) fairness to applicants.	2. Either make these points yourself by writing them on a flipchart and talk about each as you write it, or encourage trainees to come up with the important motives. If trainees don't identify these three, add them to the trainees' list and highlight them, subgrouping the trainees' responses, and of course acknowledging them.
3. Bring discussion down to a practical level now by focusing on the economic, or dollars and cents issues, of interviewing and selection.	3. If general question-and-answer format doesn't produce an adequate list of issues, break into small groups of three persons, thus forcing most trainees to offer ideas. After 10-15 minutes, reconvene the large group and record each group's ideas on a flipchart or "write on" overhead transparency. If you need to, take the time to do the small group work in order for a rather large quantity of ideas to be brought to the fore. Quality of ideation often comes with discussion and revision of quantity of ideation.
4. Guide trainees in prioritizing the economic issues.	4. Strive for an animated discussion, playing the devil's advocate role if you need to in order for trainees to reinforce and solidify their own thinking.

5. Set the trainees up for being able to establish standards for applicant quality in whatever jobs those particular managers and supervisors have open.	5. Do this by examining several typical job descriptions, for example, sales representative, administrative assistant, accountant, or project manager. Hand out to all trainees a copy of each job description and focus on the problems with each job description as written. Revise them so that each line reflects a quality upgrade. Make revisions that the group agrees upon on your own copy of the job description blown up as an overhead transparency so that all can see the changes as trainees call them out to you. Use a fine point nonpermanent marker. Have a tissue at hand to use as an eraser on the transparency.
6. Present some new information about applicant batching and processing batched applications.	6. Get consensus among the group about the pros and cons of interviewing by seeing batches of applications. Use *Trainee Handout 5.2-D* as a conceptual framework, filling in company-specific data. In this exercise, be sure to get your points across, even if it means limiting discussion. This is a time for your trainees to listen. Because the single application approach is probably the standard approach, your group will learn more by focusing on the batched process, or the nonstandard option. Use this approach to training to save time; your group will subconsciously use the standard process as the baseline from which to compare both processes, thus reviewing the strengths and weaknesses of both approaches by taking the time to concentrate on only the alternative. They'll also come away from training with the feeling that they learned something new, and that they didn't waste time on what they already know.

Trainer's Worksheet 5.2-A

FORCE FIELD ANALYSIS

In this situation analysis technique, decision makers list and weight the forces that make a decision easier or harder. They do this by describing the three possibilities—ideal, current, and worst case—that define the parameters of the decision, or the boundaries of the situation. After the group gets agreement on the situation definitions, they identify the forces that either drive them away from staying mired in the worst case (upward-driving field of forces) or that prevent them from achieving the ideal situation and tend to perpetuate the status-quo (the downward-pushing field of forces). All forces are weighted according to some evaluation scheme, such as 1 = low, 2 = medium, and 3 = high, or by a rough dollar affect, such as a $5,000 force, a $50,000 force, or a $100,000 force. By being so highly structured at the analysis level, decision makers can often see more clearly the reality and possible effect of their deciding one way or the other. The Force Field Analysis technique often takes a circular discussion and channels it in the right direction.

The accompanying *Trainee Handout 5.2-B* is a representation of a Force Field Analysis that uses information from a lesson on interviewing techniques, for example, deciding to use single or batched job applications.

Trainee Handout 5.2-B

SAMPLE FORCE FIELD ANALYSIS

1 = low force
2 = medium force
3 = high force

Ideal Situation:
We were able to hire new employees who were competent and enthusiastic workers to fill all of our open positions.

	(2)	(1)	(1)	(3)
Restraining Forces	We've always done it one at a time ↓	We don't know how to define competence ↓	We tend to want to hire people who look like us ↓	Our managers are overworked because of tremendous business growth—interviewing time is scarce ↓

Current Situation:
We need to find competent new hires from the current diverse employee pool.

Driving Forces	↑ This labor market region is full of potential, especially at entry- and R&D levels	↑ Batched applications show us a range of competency	↑ New workers are moving into our region who have been highly educated at foreign universities	↑ Reviewing batches takes less time than reviewing single applications
	(3)	(3)	(3)	(3)

Worst Situation:
We hired incompetent people because we had no system in place for fair and effective interviewing.

Trainee Handout 5.2-C

SIX CHALLENGES FOR THE YEAR 2000 FROM *WORKFORCE 2000,* HUDSON INSTITUTE, 1987

- *Stimulating Balanced World Growth:* The U.S. must pay less attention to its share of world trade and more to the growth of the economies of the other nations of the world, including those nations in Europe, Latin America, and Asia with whom the U.S. competes.
- *Accelerating Productivity Increases in Service Industries:* Prosperity will depend much more on how fast ouput per worker increases in health care, education, retailing, government, and other services, than on gains in manufacturing.
- *Maintaining the Dynamism of an Aging Workforce:* As the average age of American workers climbs toward 40, the nation must insure that its workforce does not lose its adaptability and willingness to learn.
- *Reconciling the Conflicting Needs of Women, Work, and Families:* Despite the huge increases in the numbers of women in the workforce, many of the policies and institutions that cover pay, fringe benefits, time away from work, pensions, welfare, and other issues have not yet been adjusted to the new realities.
- *Integrating Black and Hispanic Workers Fully Into the Economy:* The shrinking numbers of young people, the rapid pace of industrial change, and the rising skill requirements of the emerging economy make the task of fully utilizing minority workers particularly urgent between now and 2000.
- *Improving the Education and Skills of All Workers:* Human capital—knowledge, skills, organization, and leadership—is the key to economic growth and competitiveness.

Trainee Handout 5.2-D

IDEAS TO GENERATE DISCUSSION AND UNDERSTANDING ABOUT BATCHED APPLICATIONS

1. A group of applications for the same job points out the range of talent out there.
2. Viewing a group of applications at once helps us focus on preparation and experience gaps across the board.
3. Gaps across the board could indicate that we are unrealistic about the employee pool.
4. Gaps in skills and knowledge in the applicant pool suggest training development commitments we might need to make.
5. Batching applications helps us verify our advertising; a group of responses indicates how effectively we communicate our message and where our strengths and weaknesses are.
6. Reviewing a batch of applications at once takes less time overall than reviewing single applications.
7. Batching is a safeguard against bias regarding a changing employee pool (seeing a single "different" applicant tends to reinforce bias). Batching has a norming quality about it.

TRAINING PLAN 5.3

How to Use Performance Technology and Performance Support Systems (PSS) in Employee Development

This training plan is an outline of the key elements, methods, and procedures required to teach managers and supervisors about employee development by *using an electronic performance support system (PSS)*. This training plan is in fact a model of the kinds of performance support systems that can lead all employees into truly self-directed, on-the-job training exactly at the time when training is needed. Through this training plan, management trainers unfamiliar with PSSs will see how such a performance improvement system can work.

Gloria Gery, editor, author, and consultant in computer-based training, defines a Performance Support System this way: "It is an integrated electronic environment that is available to and easily accessible by each employee and is structured to provide immediate, individualized on-line access to the full range of information, software, guidance, advice and assistance, data, images, tools, and assessment and monitoring systems to permit the employee to perform his or her job with a minimum of support and intervention by others." She suggests nine ways in which a PSS derives power and impact. These are:

1. Number of on-line support functions,
2. Quality, completeness, and relevance of the functions,
3. Quality and degree of internal and external integration,
4. Degree of intelligence built into the system,
5. User interface and access to functions,
6. Context sensitivity,
7. Number of forms of information,
8. System levels and qualifiers, and
9. Overall power of the system.[1]

In its basic form, the PSS contains a large information base, tools such as expert systems or other structured logic approaches to performing tasks, and practice and feedback of the various tasks in relationship to the information base. Obviously, constructing such a system requires the collaboration of training designers, evaluation technicians, organization development and human resources development specialists, systems analysts, computer graphics specialists, subject matter expert practitioners, documentation specialists, and adult training specialists under the direction of management who understands the complexity of the PSS development job, and who can envision and enable the payoff of widespread employee use of such a system.

Supporters of performance support systems point to their application for organizational leverage in training a less experienced and educated workforce, as the power of the PSS is unharnessed equally by all yet for each individually. Supporters claim it is a tool made to order for the American worker.

[1]Gery, Gloria, "Electronic Performance Support Systems," *CBT Directions,* June 1989, pp. 12-15. Reprinted with permission.

That businesses are not organized to make such a system happen easily is part of the challenge for management in the 1990s, and especially for trainers and human resources management. That some companies such as Aetna, AT&T, Federal Express, and IBM are devoting time and money in key places to develop and use performance support systems is encouraging.

As in other more traditional training plans, this one, too, begins with objectives for training itself as well as objectives for the learner, and with evaluation methods tied to the learning objectives. Training tips related to the content of employee development provide the foundation for topics covered during training. Sample exercises suggest training principles and methods built into the electronic delivery system.

OVERVIEW OF TRAINING METHODOLOGY

The training methodology chosen to illustrate performance support systems is more than a training methodology; it is an information management and decision-making tool also. The best way for managers and supervisors to learn to use it for employee development is to use it themselves, by themselves in the same kind of learning mode that they expect their employees to engage in during their use of the performance support system. This training plan, therefore, suggests an approach to a manager's or supervisor's self-directed learning, with corporate training guidance.

One of the most important attitude adjustments facing most managers and supervisors when it comes to "training" employees through a performance support system is they must believe that all adult learners are competent learners, and with the right tools will become efficient learners and better at learning. Adults' competencies come from experience, and their skills vary, their information bases vary, and their problem-solving capacities vary. Their jobs require many levels of decision making in many diverse situations and at many different times. It's the principle of valuing individual differences that, at the most fundamental level, makes performance support systems work.

Performance technology, the conceptual framework that spawned electronic performance support systems, accounts for these many variables in human performance. The National Society for Performance and Instruction (NSPI) says that "human performance technology is a set of methods and processes for solving problems—or realizing opportunities—related to the performance of people. It may be applied to individuals, small groups, or large organizations." According to the NSPI approach, solving performance problems means looking at the workplace, the work itself, and the worker to find causes for discrepancies between "what is" and "what should be," between actuals and optimals.

Identifying Elements of Employee Performance

Solutions to identified problems often involve training, but often they do not. Performance technologists like to talk about the "M's" of performance technology—materials, money, manpower and womanpower, machinery, methods, and motivation—mnemonic simplifications of the performance technology matrix developed by Tom Gilbert, considered to be the "father" of performance technology. This is Gilbert's matrix, which in 1978 he called "the behavior engineering model."[2]

[2]T.F. Gilbert, *Human Competence, Engineering Worthy Performance* (1978) © Copyright, McGraw-Hill. Reproduced with permission of McGraw-Hill, Inc.

	Information	***Instrumentation***	***Motivation***
Environmental supports	Data ① 1.1 Relevant and frequent feedback about the adequacy of performance 1.2 Descriptions of what is expected of performance 1.3 Clear and relevant guides to adequate performance	Instruments ② 2.1 Tools and materials of work designed scientifically to match human factors	Incentives ③ 3.1 Adequate financial incentives made contingent upon performance 3.2 Nonmonetary incentives made available 3.3 Career-development opportunities
Person's repertory of behavior	Knowledge ④ 4.1 Scientifically designed training that matches the requirements of exemplary performance 4.2 Placement	Capacity ⑤ 5.1 Flexible scheduling of performance to match peak capacity 5.2 Prothesis 5.3 Physical shaping 5.4 Adaptation 5.5 Selection	Motives ⑥ 6.1 Assessment of people's motives to work 6.2 Recruitment of people to match the realities of the situation

Gilbert's point is that there are elements other than the employee's ability and motivation (or lack of same) that affect a person's work performance. Training is generally reserved as a solution for only the first item in matrix cell 4, item 4.1; other, often less expensive, solutions to performance problems can be found in all of the other cells, items 1.1 through 6.2, and it's this total search for what can be changed that performance technologists pursue.

The enormous power of the computer in database management, organizing, graphics and image production, expert systems, networking, integration, memory, speed of response, and accessibility makes it an opportune avenue to personal and organizational diagnosis. It was only a matter of time before computer technology would combine with the concepts of performance technology in what we now have come to accept as performance support systems (in PSSs, the term electronic is understood unless otherwise noted).

Using a Performance Support System to Evaluate Employee Development

The examples used in this training plan are based on a simplified performance support system in the area of employee development. The examples here are chosen to support the notion that people, especially adults, learn well by "doing," an old concept in educational psychology that spawned whole fields of educational practice such as progressive education, apprenticeship, and vocational-technical education. Many argue that even learning concepts, procedures, and terminology is enhanced when that learning happens at the point of requirement for use. Supporters of performance support systems talk about competency developing *during* training, not having to wait for "transfer" to the job at a later time. When optimal job performance is supported by a training methodology either through simulation or actual job requirements, companies save time and money on the input part of the productivity equation, productivity = output/input.

It's the *support* part of performance support systems that stretches the imaginations of most trainers. For example, in sales training you might supplement traditional interactive CBT (featuring drill, practice, and corrective feedback or situation analysis videodisc training) with:

- up-to-the-minute information bulletins about price quotes or materials costs
- directories and reference documents that can be instantly accessible during a branching routine in the training module
- competitors' operational financials, latest stock information, and credit ratings that can be called up from external data bases
- a video tour of the customers' places of business and product displays that could be accessed
- product features that could be shown by digitized images or by close up video photography as that information is needed during training

Expert systems leading the trainee salesperson into correct sales strategies could be part of any new salesperson's orientation package.

In the chemical process industry, simulation training for plant operators could be supplemented by:

- up-to-the-minute political and economic analyses from countries rich in petroleum products and other process industry raw materials
- on-line access to numerous journals and worldwide conference proceedings related to the industry
- schematics and animated engineering drawings of examples of process flow
- various video pictures illustrating plant operations or featuring commentary by industry leaders

The possibilities for storing and retrieving information are numerous and the technology is here; what's lacking seems to be a workable human resources development and management organization that can make it all happen.

TIME REQUIRED TO DELIVER THIS TRAINING

Generally in chunks of on-line learning time of less than one hour at the point the trainee needs to know.

LEVEL OF TRAINEE

Performance support systems can accommodate a wide range of levels of trainee, as long as the user is knowledgeable enough to know what information to skip. For this example, the target trainee is any manager or supervisor who is charged with the responsibility to do employee development.

TRAINING OBJECTIVES

- To engage the trainee in hands-on performance support in the area of employee development
- To model for the trainee the performance support system so that the trainee (manager or supervisor) can see the possibilities for employee use of such a system for self-managed development

LEARNING OBJECTIVES FOR THE TRAINEE

- To implement an employee development program through on-line performance support
- To use the performance support system as trainer

METHODS TO EVALUATE THE TRAINEE'S PROGRESS

Success of the trainee in accomplishing these objectives will be indicated by completed employee development forms and by the timely accomplishment of employee development tasks. Both of these success indicators will be tracked by the system in real time and reported at any time to the trainee by simply calling for evaluation data. The formative evaluation program is written into the software.

TRAINING TIPS	*EXERCISES*
1. Major areas of content are contained in modules. In an employee development program, such modules could be: —Performance planning —Performance reviews —Performance evaluation —Skills evaluation —Development planning	1. Each module is independent of the other, yet accessible to each other. Modules are probably constructed in a windows environment and accessed through icons, although accessibility through a DOS menu is also possible. In either case, the first exercise would have to be an on-line tutorial in how to move around the system. Trainers must be sure to provide clear documentation and good on-line help commands to get trainees into the tutorial easily.
2. Other content modules are monitoring modules such as timeline monitoring and trainee evaluation modules.	2. These modules, too, are accessible at all times to the trainee from any module. On-line tutorials in how to get in and out of these system-governing modules must be mastered by the trainee at the beginning of training. If you, the corporate trainer, are working with a manager as he or she learns to use a PSS, you might intervene at this point, simply asking the trainee how she's coming along with navigating the system. Often all you need is a phone call or brief visit to the trainee's work station to see if there are any questions.

(Remember the old marketing trick—"dissonance is greatest right after joining"—give support towards changed behavior, or in this case, towards a change in learning mode, early in the trainee's demonstration of willingness to change. Through this kind of early support, you are more likely to encourage the adoption of the changed behavior you are seeking.)

3. A further breakdown of content within modules could be this:

   Performance planning—
   —job descriptions
   —job designs, work flow diagrams
   —salary charts
   —certification requirements
   —lists of criteria at five performance
   —levels
   —skill needs projections per business unit
   —workforce demographics
   —employee demographics, current and at 3-year intervals

   Performance reviews—
   —videotape library of how to conduct a performance review
   —sample filled-out forms
   —current guidelines
   —this employee's past reviews
   —employee's year-to-date documentation
   —audiotape or videotape information from the employee
   —employee written input
   —incentive history

3. If you have a number of managers and supervisors to train in using this PSS, you might want to get them all together to launch the new system, for example, at a luncheon meeting at which the system is demonstrated. If you, the training organization, want to be involved in PSS, you'll have to find ways to provide service to PSS users. If you expect individual managers and supervisors to manage their own learning, you probably should not run classes in how to use the system, but rather, let the tutorials and user documentation guide the trainee through. One role for you is to be the voice at the other end of the hot line, to troubleshoot navigational or content problems. Another is to be available on call with paper backup if trainees are having a difficult time with on-line forms. Another is to provide one-on-one evaluation interpretation.

Performance evaluation—
—this period's blank form
—this period's completed performance evaluation
—the employee's former performance evaluations

Skills evaluation—
—*job analysis, e.g., a people-data-* things analysis, or a cognitive-psychomotor analysis
—a list of survival skills for this job, i.e., work values and attitudes required for successful job performance
—skills hierarchies in various duties of the job
—checklist for skills to be developed

Development planning—
—employee survey forms
—employee survey results, past years, trends
—labor market studies
—individual employee skill deficits and suggested ways to compensate for them
—training opportunities, e.g., in-house catalogs, external vendor seminars, college courses, on-the-job training possibilities, correspondence courses, and so on.
—professional association directories
—professional association conferences and meetings
—development timeline format and instructions for its use
—progress/results of this employee's last year's development program.

As the trainee goes through all of the content areas of employee development via the PSS, the system monitor programs will be keeping track of the trainee's time per activity and per module. The system will also be tracking completion of forms such as the performance evaluation itself and the employee development plan against the timeline for completion of these forms. The system also could keep a frequency count of training courses recommended for employee development and of skills needed by employees; both of these tallies will be helpful to training planners.

Training's success with performance support systems will depend on the vision training has of a truly learning-based workforce and the ability to communicate that vision to people who can work together to turn the vision into reality.

TRAINING PLAN 5.4

How to Present Employment Opportunities By Using Interactive Videodisc

This training plan is an outline of the key elements, methods, and procedures required to teach managers and supervisors *how to use interactive video* to deal with the responsibility of providing employment opportunities to the workforce. This subject is included here as a training issue because of the changing face of the employee pool—demographics are driving the need for a more varied kind of information dissemination linked with needs for help in *knowing,* that is, not simply having information available. A less educated workforce at the bottom and a more static and older workforce at the top will require help (that is, training) in understanding the range of benefits and opportunities of employment in the 1990s. Litigation will continue to be a fact of life in employee-employer relations, especially as the workforce becomes more diverse. Juries, too, will no doubt continue to decide in favor of individuals in most cases, as they have historically done.

The principle of equal opportunity equally for all continues to be a strong foundation of working life in America. As workers understand English less well, either because of a lack of basic reading and communications skills or because English is their second (non-native) language, employers must find ways to help them get all of the information that they are due regarding benefits, training, and working arrangements (van pools, flextime, day care, etc.). As employers try to economize, especially in areas such as health benefits, and offer menu-type benefits programs, it's up to employers to be sure that employees know enough to make wise choices regarding what's best for them. As benefits programs become more complicated, employees can easily become less able to understand them, creating an opportunity deficit for many individual employees. It's up to managers and supervisors to protect the company by ensuring that the people who report to them are making wise choices.

This particular training technique, training through interactive video, is especially suited to content areas in which pictures speak louder than words. People are used to getting information through television, and, together with films and videotapes, the medium of television presents the context for understanding human relations to which most people can relate. Video pictures of people interacting present more understandable information to most people than binders full of words—especially words written in insurance company legalese. In addition, video picture information supplemented by a system capability for review, pausing, and quick random access build in a personal choice feature that helps to ensure appropriate, customized, and fair applications.

OVERVIEW OF TRAINING METHODOLOGY

As in learning the power and possibilities in performance support systems, the best way for managers and supervisors to learn interactive video training technology is to do it themselves, before they use the technology with their employees. Your initial training role is to be sure that the learning environment is "set," that is, that all hardware is in working order, in place where it should be, clean, and that the trainee knows how to use it. Provide instruction in how to use the hardware, taking the time for a one-on-one demonstration and question-and-answer session. (Most managers prefer that a real live human being show them how to get started, even though a navigational tutorial is built into the system on-line.)

In addition, be sure that software documentation, study guides to the employment opportunities training, and any other printed materials are arranged or notated for this particular trainee. A little bit of training planning on behalf of your particular trainee will pay off both in quality of learning and in time saved during training. For example, your knowing a manager's or supervisor's particular training needs could mean that you flag certain training options in the disc library, or that you put a paper clip in the user guide that explains how the training library matrix is configured. Sometimes just knowing that somebody cares how effectively one learns is enough to increase the effectiveness of that learning. Trainers should never shy away from using electronic technologies because they perceive themselves as "non-techies." Trainers always have the responsibility to design in the *learning* components of training, and this applies to when they train managers and supervisors and when those managers and supervisors train their employees.

Components of an Interactive Videodisc Training System

The components of an interactive videodisc training system include:

- a TV monitor (with optional touch screen and light pen), an extra monitor
- a videodisc player and discs
- a microcomputer with disc drives and magnetic discs
- a joy stick or mouse, keyboard and keypad
- connections between all of the above

This is a load of equipment, often too cumbersome for a cubicle or small office. User manuals and reference books add to the space requirements for such a system, pointing to the probable need for a separate training station to be set up for several offices to share. An analogous situation is the manager's conference room that is shared by several people who report to that manager. A manager's interactive video training station is a similar concept.

Advantages of Using Interactive Videodiscs

The Office of Technology Assessment (OTA) of the U.S. Congress reported that large companies are estimating that by the late 1990s, over half of their training will be delivered outside the traditional classroom using training technology.[1] Interactive videodisc is a training technology with appropriate characteristics to meet this future:

- it can be available at numerous worksites including home, office, and workstation,
- it has excellent transfer to work,
- it is adaptable to most subjects,
- it can cover a wide variety in content,
- it can be used at any time,
- and it is highly interactive.[2]

These factors seem to be in tune with what we'd like training to be in the future, in spite of the technology's high development cost and long lead time for development, and the difficulty of modifying existing videodiscs.

---

[1]Office of Technology Assessment, *Report on Worker Training,* 1990, p. 183
[2]Op cit, p. 186.

Wise training designers will be sure to maximize the benefits of the technology and to minimize its shortcomings. In this training, for example:

- don't rush into creating a videodisc unless the benefits package is finalized and not subject to contract negotiations
- don't use the videodisc for transient information about training opportunities that are one-shot deals; instead, put that information out via an electronic bulletin board
- design self-monitoring programs that address individual differences—for example, include several foreign language-to-English dictionaries and company glossaries, acronym lists, and human resources department members' telephone numbers.

Remember that you are in this business to guarantee equal employment opportunity to your workforce—that is, *access* to opportunities of employment.

Implementing Interactive Videodisc Training

Remember, too, that information never equals behavior; just because you've provided all sorts of information accessible at the touch of a spot on a screen or key, that information will not turn into action just because it's there. Behavior change requires a planned sequence of steps that build upon each other.

Trainers are generally the only ones who understand this and who can do something about the way in which information is presented to turn it from simply strings of words to ideas that result in action.

Interactive videodisc training can take several training modes:

- *Question and answer,* in which a "talking head" on the video asks questions or poses problems to the trainee
- *Simulation,* in which video actors portray numerous actions and solutions to problems based on the trainee's choice of action allowing the trainee to see the effects of poor as well as wise decisions
- *Practice,* in which the video actors, animations, or CBT programs guide the trainee in practice sessions (especially good in training involving learning new procedures)
- *Diagnosis,* in which video actors demonstrate troubleshooting techniques aided by close-up video camera work (especially good in hands-on and technical training), and in which numerous comparisons, examples, and explanations can be provided within a second or two

Each of these training modes reinforces a trainee's ability at problem solving, including the ability to isolate and analyze problems and to identify and qualify solutions to them. In the area of equal opportunity, these are important beneficial characteristics of a training delivery system. Employees need more than just information about benefits, training, and working arrangements—they need to know how to use this information to their own best advantage, to act upon information for their own and the company's success.

The sections that follow give a brief outline of what interactive videodisc training in the area of employment opportunities might be.

TIME TO DELIVER THIS TRAINING

Training time is limited to the playing time of the videodisc plus any pauses for interactive responses, CBT programs, and the trainee's choice of balance between still images and full motion video. Most trainees stick with interactive training between one and two hours at most.

LEVEL OF TRAINEE

Any manager or supervisor who must ensure that all employees have equal access to employment opportunities such as benefits, training, and working arrangements; and ultimately, all employees will become trainees.

TRAINING OBJECTIVES

- To facilitate employees' best choices regarding employment opportunities
- To enable trainees to learn to choose what's right for them through learning how to use interactive videodisc training

LEARNING OBJECTIVES FOR THE TRAINEE

- To understand the range of opportunities available to me as an employee of this company
- To choose the best options for me

(*Note:* an incidental objective for many trainees will be to learn to use the training technology to my own best advantage)

METHODS TO EVALUATE THE TRAINEE'S PROGRESS

Most good training videodiscs have numerous branching programs looking to the trainee like many video vignettes. When the actors interact with the trainee at the keyboard or touch screen, the resulting actions or problems solved are in essence the evaluations of those trainee decisions.

This, of course, is formative evaluation in video format combining pictures, words, perhaps music, and environmental sounds with decision making. All of this context for action works together in a powerful and integrated way to indicate to the trainee through several senses and a holistic bombardment of information just what the consequences of decisions are. It's been said that interactive videodisc training allows one to see both the "forest and the trees."

In addition, a computer monitoring and administrative program can provide tallies, statistical analyses, and reports of all sorts should the trainee want learning management information.

TRAINING TIPS	***EXERCISES***

Note: The following are only a few examples from among a wide range of possibilities.

TRAINING TIPS	EXERCISES
1. Build a personal profile of your own needs for health benefits, e.g., self, family, lifestyle issues, preventive programs, weight management, AA, mental health support, cancer support, and so on.	1. Do this through structured question and answer, either in one-on-one Socratic fashion or by a video discussion group that draws you into participation with them in exploring benefits options and their implications for health. View detailed text regarding selected options. View video portrayals of or actual photos of support groups in action to see if that's for you. View "what if" financial scenarios, given various benefits choices.
2. Get a personal benefits needs profile, on the screen at first, and change any information to alter the profile before concluding.	2. Print out your own benefits needs profile at any point you feel that you've explored as many options as you want to and are ready to make a decision.
3. Call up video clips from courses that sound interesting; search by subject, instructor, duration of course, location, time of year, or any other index to find the best ones for you.	3. Find out what prerequisites there are in terms of experience, months with company, lower-level courses, and so on. Find out costs and scheduling for the training you want.
4. Provide the system with data, i.e., your self-assessment of your own skill needs and career goals; ask the system to match your needs with courses to attend.	4. Use questionnaires and guided practice routines to pinpoint skill deficiencies. Use a question-and-answer structured dialogue to correctly identify skill needs and training opportunities. Review all training modes—classroom, CBT, other self-study, off-site seminars, and so on.

5. Find out how to apply or register for the training you want.	5. Use the system tutorial or example cards as models. Get an optimal training timeline printout, considering your skill needs, career goals, and training available.
6. Run through all options and criteria regarding working arrangements (day care, van pools, work at home, and the like).	6. Assess advantages and disadvantages of each via simulations. Specify choices of interest to you, noting your own constraints.

Chapter 6

Training Managers and Supervisors to Plan

Planning is still the key to effective management, and is still the job most employers expect managers to do. However, in today's world, the pace of change and the proliferation of information are pushing managers into a new mold regarding time and resources, and this affects the kind of planning they do. In previous decades, managers were somehow expected to be lofty and reflective thinkers with time to ponder and test planning ideas, detached at this higher systems level from the people in their organizations, dealing with resources as dollars and as numbers that needed to make sense.

Today's managers, by contrast, are literally closer to the people in their organizations—there are fewer of them, they tend to be involved shoulder to shoulder with those they supervise, their spans of control tend to be across wider varieties of operations, their organizations are flatter with fewer layers of employees, and their time for reflective thought simply isn't there. The structure of today's business requires managers to be fast and flexible when it comes to managing work and workers, and that includes planning for such management.

The proliferation and accessibility of information, too, in recent years has created a resource that is different from the capital and material resources so easily translated into dollars and numbers. Information essentially feeds human resources, and as such is harder to quantify, harder to harness, and harder to measure—largely, again, because of the way in which time affects it. Information comes in discontinuous pieces, often out of sequence for easy understanding, rapidly, in enormous volume, and through a variety of print, electronic, graphic, audio, and visual media.

Managerial planning today still has the goals of creating a smooth-running business that makes a profit from satisfied customers, but teaching today's managers to plan must recognize the realities of the time crunch and the wide spectrum of information-based human resources challenges. Both the instructional techniques and the planning content must build in the time and information factors.

FINE-TUNING INSTRUCTIONAL METHODS FOR TRAINING GROUPS OF MANAGERS

This chapter makes two assumptions about managers: one, that management at your company has undergone some major change recently—probably a reduction in force or a merger, either resulting in broadening of managerial responsibility; and two, that managers are still responsible through people who report to them for operational results—either products or services. Managers still need to know something about comprehensive business planning, such as:

Financial planning
Strategic planning
Operational planning
Market planning
Project planning
Work planning

Managers need to know something about planning work in a time-crunched, information-rich, human resources-dependent environment. Managers need to know about job design and work flow, and about empowered teams. This chapter addresses these work planning needs of managers and supervisors too, recognizing that time and information have a great effect on an employee's sense of control, power, and ability to do a good job.

The instructional techniques chosen as the vehicle for teaching managers and supervisors to plan are both group-based and one-on-one. Business planning methods are handled through a six-week Planning Institute held one day per week for six consecutive bi-weekly periods (that is, over 12 weeks). In the Institute, a variety of group-based instructional methods are suggested such as case study, formal presentation, and role play. Examples of planning content are chosen from the list of six major planning areas. Back on the job, these group techniques in the Institute are interspersed with one-on-one training such as mentoring, coaching, and peer tutoring. Instructional guidelines are included to help you train your managers to be effective one-on-one instructors.

The Planning Institute and Its Reinforcement

The Planning Institute is essentially six days of classroom training spread out over a 12-week time period. This allows one major planning responsibility to be featured during one of the Institute's classroom days and provides a two-week period in which trainees can practice the new planning skill on the job—with planned one-on-one instruction in applying that new skill as an integral part of the Institute concept.

We assume that a group (6-20) of managers and supervisors enroll in the Institute together and complete the six sessions over the 12-week period together. Such an Institute can be offered four times per year to accommodate all managers. Because the engaging part of the classroom sessions of the Institute is the case study, it is relatively easy to construct new case studies as time goes on in order to keep the training current yet without having to significantly revise the instructional plans.

The basic format of each Institute classroom day is this: mornings, formal group session to learn new information, models, procedures, and to practice new skills; and afternoons, small group sessions for in-depth case study. In the mornings, a variety of group instructional techniques are used; two that work well together, role play and case study, are detailed on worksheets following the training plan for the Institute.

The two-week period following each Institute classroom day is a time for planned one-on-one training in the form of mentoring, coaching, and peer tutoring focused on the topics covered during class. By the end of the 12 weeks, trainees will have had a thorough and customized training experience on the subject of business planning, and in a setting that supports the way in which today's managers work.

Topics to Cover at a Planning Institute Training Session

Unlike the topics in quality management (Chapter 1), which required a paradigm shift in thinking, the topics of planning are familiar territory to most managers. The

Planning Institute is organized basically around familiar cognitive learning objectives; persons attending the Institute essentially want to find out the latest information and best ways of doing things. Then armed with new knowledge, they want support as they try to apply it.

The Institute is set up so that one key planning area is the focus of each classroom day. For illustration here, six kinds of planning are featured in the Institute:

- *Financial planning,* including:
  —preparing a budget
  —providing periodic budget reports
  —accounting essentials
  —operational budgeting versus opportunities budgeting
  —use of spreadsheets and software
  —cost-benefit analysis
  —developing profit and loss statements
  —reports to stockholders
- *Strategic planning,* including:
  —analysis of strengths and weaknesses
  —description and projection of future opportunities
  —current resource deployment
  —needs for resource enhancement and redeployment
  —analysis of causes of change (technology, markets, knowledge, demographics, world events) and our relationships to changes
  — scenario-building
- *Operational planning,* including:
  —prioritizing
  —setting time lines
  —providing support
  —setting standards
  —establishing controls, systems, procedures
  —dealing with suppliers and contractors
  —using various operational planning tools (e.g., Gantt chart, PERT chart)
- *Market planning,* including:
  —consumer identification
  —analysis of customer behavior
  —sources of competitive information
  —projection of new opportunities
  —establishment of overall budget
  —allocation of personnel and other resources
  —use of channels
  —domestic and global considerations
  —governmental regulations and laws
- *Project planning,* including:
  —procedures and forms for managing content
  —cost, controls, and implementation schedule
  —communications with internal/external customers and project staff
- *Work planning,* including:
  —job design
  —staffing and placement
  —the organization chart
  —work flow

—performance support
—motivation and rewards
—working in teams

Two of these planning areas are chosen as examples of the two instructional techniques, *running a 6-day Planning Institute* and *one-on-one management training.* These two complementary techniques work together to ensure that your managers and supervisors master various planning techniques.

TRAINING PLANS

Two training plans detail the considerations and procedures involved in executing these two very different but complementary instructional techniques. These plans are carefully chosen to enhance the learning capacity of today's fragmented managers, and they are presented here as a rather advanced-level instructional design and delivery vehicle for management training. The two content areas of project planning and market planning illustrate the two training plans.

Worksheets appended to each training plan detail the kinds of instructional methods typically employed in each kind of training. Group methods such as role play and case study are described, and guidelines are given for doing effective presentations and managing difficult groups. In one-on-one training, the techniques of mentoring, coaching, and peer tutoring are described, and guidelines are provided for development of mastery lists and effective ways to train the trainer.

Training Plans for Chapter 6 include:

management issues	*training techniques*
6.1 Comprehensive business planning	Six-day Planning Institute
6.2 Interdependence and empowerment	One-on-one training

TRAINING PLAN 6.1

Training Managers and Supervisors in Comprehensive Business Planning Through a 6-day, 12-week, Planning Institute

This training plan is an outline of the key elements, methods, and procedures required to train managers and supervisors through a *6-day planning institute spread over 12 weeks*. This Planning Institute features one major area of planning at each of the six days. For the purposes of detailed illustration, one planning area—Project Planning—is featured in this training plan. Similar training plans could be developed for the other five planning areas: financial planning, strategic planning, operational planning, market planning, and work planning. By following the format of this training plan for Project Planning, management trainers should be able to develop similar training plans in each of the other five planning areas.

The Institute is scheduled so that one day of intensive group instruction, the Institute day, is held in a central location every two weeks. The ideal location is a company-owned corporate training center away from the managers' telephones and other day-to-day business and random intrusions. Or, a rented hotel training room in a central location is also a possible setting for such an institute. The aim is to get trainees out of their offices and into a training setting that is the same for all six sessions of the Institute.

In between the six Institute days, trainees are involved in structured one-on-one training that complements the topic of the Institute for that particular two-week period. Training plan 6.2 details this one-on-one training designed to complement the classroom training of the Institute. The total training in planning should be seen, therefore, as a 12-week effort.

OVERVIEW OF TRAINING METHODOLOGY

This training plan (6.1) is based on advanced-level cognitive skills (see chapter 3) such as analysis, synthesis, and evaluation. The Institute concept is one that uses extensively case studies and role play, both of which are group-based instructional methods that require the trainee to demonstrate the skills of analysis, synthesis, and evaluation. In addition, other traditional methods of group instruction are found in the typical institute format. Such methods might include presentations by specialists or company executives or subject matter experts, narrated slide or video presentations, lectures, and panel discussions.

This particular Institute features the traditional group instructional methods in the mornings to present the descriptions and challenges of the "planning area of the day" to trainees, and then focuses on the use of case study and role play for the afternoon session. Because the case study and role play are the special features of the classroom day, these two instructional methods are woven into this training plan and are described more fully in separate worksheets.

One of the main reasons for choosing case study and role play for this Institute is that these vehicles for learning allow the learner to exercise a great deal of intuition and creativity in analysis and synthesis, generally providing encouragement and time for incubation of ideas, the opportunity to try out new modes of thinking and solving problems, and a chance to receive verification from fellow trainees for approaches that work. Case study and role play are not quite real, but they approximate reality if they are done well; at the very least, the skills involved in learning through these vehicles seem to be in tune with the more subjective aspects of management that today's managers are increasingly called upon to exhibit.

Like other training plans, the training plan for the Planning Institute has objectives, evaluation methods, teaching points, and exercises.

TIME REQUIRED TO DELIVER THIS TRAINING

Six 7-hour days, one day every two weeks over a 12-week period

TRAINEE LEVEL

Peer-level managers and supervisors

TRAINING OBJECTIVES

- To present models and ideas in six key planning areas using various methods of group-based instruction each morning of the Institute
- To lead trainees in case study and in several levels of role play during each afternoon of the Institute
- To encourage trainees to be flexible, intuitive, and creative in their approaches to planning models and methods so that results of planning optimize the company's human resources
- To motivate trainees to practice newly learned planning skills
- To guide trainees' practice as appropriate during class
- To initiate planned follow-up of new skills during the two-week periods between classes

LEARNING OBJECTIVES FOR THE TRAINEE

Note: From this point on, this training plan uses content examples from the Project Planning day of the Institute.

- To review several models for project planning
- To study the case of "Training Manual Production," paying special attention to the process dynamics:
  1) system/people interface
  2) shared responsibilities among internal client leadership and project staff
  3) conflict management
- To analyze project documentation forms, using them as a basis for design and construction of better forms for this case
- To participate as a player in role play based on this case
- To engage in group discussion whose aim is to:
  1) identify work within each participant's area of responsibility that could be redefined as a project
  2) orient individual participants' thinking to consideration of projects as people-based rather than as data-based

- To draft an approach to project planning within my own area of responsibility
  —To seek and to give feedback regarding this project planning

METHODS TO EVALUATE THE TRAINEE'S PROGRESS

Evaluating an Instructor-led Presentation (e.g., a Lecture)

Evaluation of the learning that goes on during a lecture is almost impossible to do. What typically happens during an instructor-led presentation to a group is that trainees passively listen, perhaps take a few notes, and silently absorb whatever they can from the instructor's presentation. Instructor-led presentations always run the risk of being information dumps or dissemination activities at best on the periphery of teaching and learning. When the lecturer has finished, you can be fairly sure that the content was presented as planned, and, if the trainees were attentive, you can be fairly sure that they reviewed the models at some basic awareness level.

You should give a lecture—even a lecture supplemented with slides, transparencies, or a flipchart—only under certain considered circumstances: that is, when you must give a specialized or novel body of information to a group of people, your group is homogeneous and at a similar readiness level to accept the information, and each member of your group has a stake in the information (i.e., the members of the group perceive a need for the information or face a personal risk if they don't get it). *Trainer's Worksheet 6.1-A* provides guidelines on how to give effective lectures.

In this kind of training, you are essentially evaluating the communication of information, not the clear conclusion of a learning event. Formative evaluation of a lecture is hardly possible; and, in most cases, the presenter has a time limit and has been given the task of getting through a certain body of content in that allotted time. If you, as an evaluator, can view the lecture part of the Institute day as the very lowest cognitive level, or the descriptive knowledge-based bottom of the taxonomy of objectives in the cognitive domain, you can evaluate that delivered lecture as part of a learning continuum that eventually results in a trainee's being able to adapt the model or other information that was presented in the lecture to his or her own situation. But you won't know this until sometime later over the course of the 12-week span of the Institute.

What typically happens is that the *design* of the lecture gets evaluated at the end of the morning on a "smiles sheet" (with such questions as "was the instructor friendly?" "did the content get covered in sufficient depth?" etc.). But the *trainee's learning* never gets evaluated, leaving the person who paid the bill for the training and the trainee himself/herself in the dark about whether or not anything was learned. To evaluate the trainee's learning, you would have to ask the trainee to correctly identify parts of the model, or to define for you certain terms that the lecturer presented, or to draw the model for you on a flipchart, or to demonstrate to you somehow that he or she can recall the specifics of the lecture. Readers who have taken management training courses themselves will recognize that evaluation of learning by lecture seldom happens.

The model for this kind of evaluation is the high school "quiz" given at the end of a chapter of history or mathematics—a summative evaluation exercise designed to evaluate learning at the very lowest levels of understanding and generally used to generate normative data—how many A's, B's, C's, D's, and F's in the class. Serious trainers in business do not tolerate this kind of evaluation when they want to evaluate learning. Rather, they design, present, and evaluate instruction from a formative evaluation perspective, continuously relating the process of instruction to the accumulation of skills and knowledge that the business requires trainees to apply.

Management trainers so often make the mistake of believing that high-level learning has occurred because a highly-credentialled expert has delivered the keynote lecture at a management institute. The clue to conducting a successful institute as a vehicle for learning is to clearly understand what it is that you are evaluating, and, of course, to have clear objectives for learning in the first place. When you choose instructor-led passive instructional methods for part of your training, be sure to place them carefully in your total training agenda, knowing that low-level skills are probably being demonstrated. Add other group-based instructional methods to the lecture-type presentation, and pay attention to group management techniques in your role as facilitator of learning. *Trainer's Worksheet 6.1-A* provides guidelines for effective instructor-led presentations, focusing on the communication principles that encourage trainees to pay attention and engage in the ideas of the presentation.

Evaluating the Use of Case Studies and Role Playing

The case study used in this Institute session on Project Planning focuses on the single issue of project controls. It does this by directing the attention of trainees to three elements of process dynamics of the case: systems/people interface, shared responsibilities among internal client leadership and project staff, and conflict management. As you and your training assistants or facilitators guide your learners through the case, you will be able to observe each trainee closely to evaluate whether or not he or she is figuring out the key relationships, distinguishing the vital elements from the trivial ones, and formulating strategies for dealing with positive problem-solving actions. In short, by observation built into the design of the instruction, you will engage in formative evaluation of your trainees' ability to *analyze* the case. By having one correct solution to the case as a standard, you can also evaluate your trainees' capacity to creatively go beyond this particular solution and perhaps solve some of its problems in a better way. When it comes to human relations, there are many solutions to problems.

When you evaluate role play in this case or in any other, try to see beyond the character in the play and don't get trapped into evaluating your trainee's acting ability. What you're looking for when evaluating role play is the extent to which your trainee can do the following:

- learn from the characterization to perhaps develop hypotheses about the universal problem(s) illustrated by the case
- synthesize feelings and information from the case
- come to conclusions about a course of action
- and perhaps even begin to articulate his or her own plan of action regarding a project waiting for attention

Role play can elicit a "eureka" discovery; as an evaluator, you want to be there at your trainee's side if that happens, supporting that discovery and gently prodding the trainee to keep going.

The other aspect of evaluation of an Institute day is the evaluation tied to the objectives having to do with practice of new skills. These objectives can be built into some of the morning instruction if the lecture-type presentation is only a short one, or could wait for the end of the day, after the case study and role play. In this kind of learning, your trainees will demonstrate to you, to themselves, or to each other that they have learned the features or characteristics of the models and perhaps the forms and procedures which they'll need to follow as they begin to practice applying the project planning intelligence they've gotten during this day at the Institute.

As you evaluate this kind of learning, watch for evidence that trainees are using all of the relevant concepts from the case study and the rest of the day's training. If trainees have chosen to use project planning forms, give them cues to completing them and guide trainees over the difficult sections. Ask them to define critical incidents, worst-case and best-case scenarios towards solutions, and help them arrive at conclusions that seem workable for them. Help trainees go deeper and broader as they draft project documents of their own. Give specific feedback that causes action.

TRAINING TIPS	*EXERCISES*
Note: These training tips and exercises pertain to case study and role play since these are the culminating instructional methods of the Institute, and since these methods have not been detailed previously in this book. The assumption is that these methods are used every afternoon of the Institute. As in previous sections of this training plan, the content selected for elaboration is the content of Project Planning.	
1. Write the case, "Training Manual Production." See *Trainer's Worksheet 6.1-B.*	1. Limit it to three pages. Prepare a "case note" detailing all who, what, when, where, why information. Keep this handy as you construct the narrative of the case. Also keep a piece of paper handy that states the issue to be addressed by this case, namely "project controls," and the three major process dynamics you want trainees to focus on, namely, "system/people interface, shared responsibilities among internal client leadership and project staff, and conflict management." Build the case around these points, eliminating unnecessary or irrelevant details.

2. Prepare a study sheet for trainees called "Case Analysis Guidelines."

   Substitute fictitious names for actual persons in the case.

2. Limit this to one page.
   - At the top, put:
     —case title, "Training Manual Production"
     —main issue, "project controls"
     —three items on which to focus:
       1) system/people interface
       2) shared responsibilities
       3) conflict management
   - Name and describe the characters
   - List and date the major events
   - Summarize the case in a paragraph
   - Suggest how this case might relate to your own company
   - Provide study guidelines such as "look at the relationship between...," "uncover motivations for...," "define feelings of..."
   - Include the model for project planning against which this case will be studied. Point out the critical features, for example, in the model which includes the key elements of content, cost, schedule, and control, the fourth element, "control," is the critical feature on which to concentrate in this case study.

3. Give the case write-up and the single page "Case Analysis Guidelines" to trainees at least 3 days before the Institute session.

3. By doing this you accomplish at least two things: you encourage trainees to be prepared, that is, to achieve a "mental set" regarding training, and you allow "incubation" time for those who might be thinking creatively about planning problems.

4. Break the larger group into about three smaller groups for case study.

4. Before trainees enter the classroom, arrange the seats around round or square tables so that trainees are equidistant from and rather close to each other. Let them choose to sit however they please, that is, don't direct or assign the seating.

5. Begin the case study by referring to the "Case Analysis Guidelines" sheet, perhaps reading the summary paragraph and items of focus and concentration.

5. After the openers to get trainees focused, ask several general questions to try to get at least one person from each table to respond. Keep asking general questions until each table comes alive. Questions related to what certain characters did or did not do to contribute to either success or failure are often good engaging ways to start. This character approach is especially useful if you follow your case study with role play.

6. Introduce several project forms during the early large group stages of case study.

6. Because several learning objectives deal with use of project planning forms, use selected forms as "props" during your introductory questioning. Get trainees in the frame of mind to see the forms as helpful tools for problem solving.

7. When you are sure that each table has gotten involved, turn over leadership of the case study to each small group.

   Remind them that they have about two hours in which to redesign the project so that it works.

7. Direct them to each focus on the issue of better project controls, based on the problems the project had in the three process areas of system/people interface, shared responsibilities, and conflict management.

   Tell the groups that they can solve the problem of project controls any way they want to—e.g., generating new schedules, reassigning staff, different communication patterns, better forms, re-worked design for the project deliverables, and so on.

8. Have groups role play their solutions. See *Trainer's Worksheet 6.1-C.*

8. At the end of the project rework time, probably 1–1½ hours into the small group work, retake your leadership role and address trainees as a large group.

   Have members of each small group assume the roles of various characters in the case, acting out their solutions to the other groups. Give the groups about 15 minutes to prepare for role play.

   Lead role players into thinking about their roles as "task" roles driving their solutions forward, or as "process" roles enabling the human resources aspects of the solutions to work. After each group's role play, ask them to identify the task contributions and the process contributions of the new roles, contrasting these with the apparent former task and process misbehavior of the character they played.

9. Try for consensus regarding the best solution. Record the agreed-upon best solution (or solutions) on a flipchart.

   Consensus is difficult, even in very structured training as this. *Trainer's Worksheet 6.1-D* provides techniques for dealing with troublesome groups.

9. Move a flipchart to a central place where all groups can see it. Conclude the afternoon with this consensus-building exercise:

   After the role plays, instruct the groups to each contribute their best ideas, one at a time. The small group as a whole must agree on each point contributed. Call on one group, then another, then another, for one point at a time. Record that point on your flipchart and keep it there only if all groups agree that that is a good idea. Keep the ideas coming, point by point and in the same group order until all ideas have been exhausted. Cross out any points on which you do not get consensus. By the end of this exercise, you should have a solution to the case study that does in fact reflect the people in your company—and hopefully, that will set the stage for these people to use project planning as a workable tool in their areas of responsibility.

10. Send trainees home with a packet of project planning forms and the challenge to rethink their areas of responsibility and perhaps reshape some of it into projects, especially if "control" of the process is a problem.	10. See *Trainee Handouts 6.1-E, F,* and *G,* as examples of forms.
11. Remind trainees that a one-on-one training program during the next two weeks will focus on adapting project planning models and forms to work in your company, and that they can be expecting you to contact them within a day or two.	11. (Training Plan 6.2 details this one-on-one training.)
12. Hand them an Institute schedule highlighting the remaining sessions as they exit the training room.	

Trainer's Worksheet 6.1-A

LECTURE PRESENTATION TECHNIQUES

These are guidelines to follow when presenting a training lecture to a group of trainees whom you do not expect to interrupt you. Be aware that lecture is considered the least effective training technique. It should be used rarely and in combination with other group-based interactive instructional methods. It is appropriate for a keynote address or luncheon speech at a training institute or conference.

1. Come prepared, having checked the sequence of your visuals and pages of lecture notes. Be sure equipment works and sight lines are adequate from all trainee seats. Be sure that a table is available on which you can organize your materials as you proceed. Time your presentation to be sure it fits within your allotted place on the agenda.
2. Be enthusiastic, credible, patient, and natural.
3. Memorize and rehearse your first two sentences and your last two sentences—distractions like late comers and end of lesson relaxation sometimes interfere with your trainees' attention at both ends of your presentation. Memorizing your start and finish will help you not to yield to these distractions too.
4. Select visuals (slides, overhead transparencies, videotapes) to supplement and illustrate what you say, not duplicate it word for word. Visuals support, not supplant, instruction. Learners can be expected to retain about 50 percent of what they hear and see, contrasted to about 20 percent of what they hear only.
5. Know your transition points and key transition words; highlight these in your lecture notes. You need to help listeners conclude one thought before going on with the next one.
6. Give trainees a copy of your outline, key points, visuals, and a list of reference materials before you do your presentation so that they don't need to take notes while you are speaking.
7. When writing your lecture, keep in mind that:
   a. Learners need to make associations with what they already know—give several examples of how the topic of your presentation has implications for their jobs.
   b. Learners like learning goals—tell them what you hope they'll get out of your presentation.
   c. Learners need organization and consistency—develop your lecture around several key points; define, describe, and explain in that order. Use examples and analogies from your trainees' experience base.
   d. Learners will send you non-verbal cues as you speak regarding their comprehension—be alert for signals that you're going too fast or too slowly, or that you misjudged their experience levels. Adjust your presentation accordingly.
8. Structure the end of the lecture.
   a. Synthesize important information.
   b. Rephrase and reemphasize key points.
   c. Send them away challenged and smiling.

Trainer's Worksheet 6.1-B

CASE STUDY INSTRUCTIONAL GUIDELINES

A. Prepare or choose a case to fit your need, your trainee audience, and the time allotted for training

1. Be sure it is not overly complex
2. Be sure it illustrates precisely the problems you face
3. Be sure to allow enough time for problem analysis: the current situation, the desired situation, and the actions necessary to reach resolution
4. Tell trainees why you chose this case; state learner objectives

B. Provide each trainee with the narrative of the case

1. Lead trainees into the case with a brief description of your own
2. Give them time to read and analyze the narrative—overnight, if necessary

C. Provide each trainee with case analysis guidelines

1. Be sure all trainees know what problem has to be discussed; if there is more than one obvious problem, be sure each one is differentiated from the others
2. Provide character descriptions
3. List major events in the case
4. Point out how this case relates to their work
5. Provide study guidelines such as "look at relationships; uncover motivations; define feelings...."

D. Lead the discussion of the case in a "brainstorming" fashion, setting an informal, non-judgmental, accepting, and creative tone

1. Accept all comments as valid
2. Involve all trainees in discussion
3. Steer discussion toward conclusions only after all trainees have contributed ideas several times—new ideas grow from old ideas
4. Close the training session by asking trainers to relate what they learned from case analysis to their own jobs

Source: Carolyn Nilson, *Training Program Workbook & Kit*, Englewood Cliffs, NJ: Prentice Hall, a division of Simon & Schuster, 1989, p. 209.

Trainer's Worksheet 6.1-C

ROLE PLAY INSTRUCTIONAL GUIDELINES

Following are general guidelines for role play.

A. Present the role with great clarity
   1. Present facts
   2. Present descriptors of the fictitious person in the role
   3. State the problem simply: Challenge the role player to solve it
   4. Prepare a written briefing sheet containing these first three items for each trainee who is performing the role
   5. Choose a role player who identifies with some part of the character

B. Structure the observation
   1. Give each trainee a chance to be both role player and observer
   2. Instruct observers to look and listen for specific things during the role play, and to write down their observations. These are the basics:
      - body language
      - attitudes; tone of voice
      - bad behavior
      - assertiveness
      - turning point in problem solving

C. Have fun
   1. Make the situation believable and the problem real, but interject the exercise with humor
   2. Do several "warm up" exercises to set trainees' minds for role play. Choose exercises that will make trainees smile or put them at ease. This can be done through simple questions and statements like these:
      "Did you ever notice that Lynn always looks in the left corner of the room when she's doing a presentation?"
      "I'll bet you didn't know that I always have to remove my loose change from my pockets before work so I don't rattle it at meetings!"
      "Do you remember that TV commercial about the guy who makes the donuts—does he remind you of anyone around here?!"
      "Can you think of a time when your teenage daughter willingly cleaned her room?"

When role play is used with case study, as in training plan 6.1, the general guidelines are adapted to allow for the deeper information base about the characters that trainees already have because of having done the case study. That is, the role clarity (point A) will probably already be rather good; it probably will not be necessary for you to provide a written briefing sheet for the role play itself. Tying role play to case study and the consensus exercise are adaptations of point B; you might still want to suggest some kind of structured observation if you think that it will facilitate arriving at the optimum solution to the case.

Source: Carolyn Nilson, *Training Program Workbook & Kit,* Englewood Cliffs, NJ: Prentice Hall, a division of Simon & Schuster, 1989, p. 208.

Trainer's Worksheet 6.1-D

HOW TO DEAL WITH DIFFICULT GROUPS

The perceived quality of training delivery often rests on the trainer's skill in managing the group. In most groups, people will try to avoid conflict, and when a group runs into trouble, group members withdraw and lose focus. An effective trainer will recognize that when conflict occurs, it needs to be skillfully managed, because most people have not learned strategies to deal with conflict. (An effective instructor will support those few group members who take the risk to resolve the conflict.)

The following techniques can be useful in which energy is low, dominance by a clique or individual is obvious, tempers are too hot, and in many other situations where "process" is important to accomplishing "task."

IF:	THEN:
1. The group is bored,	**1. Introduce a new piece of data.** *Example:* "You might be interested to know that at the Iowa Conference they found out that. . . ."
2. The group is dull and passive,	**2. Change places.** *Example:* Move from in front of the lectern to the back or side of the room.
3. Small groups aren't working,	**3. Regroup into smaller or different sets.** *Example:* Break into pairs instead of fours or fives; organize a "fishbowl" in which half the class is active and the other half functions as observers around the perimeter of the active group.
4. The group is argumentative,	**4. Present feedback to the group.** *Example:* "I observe at this very moment that we seem to be. . . ."
5. The group is out of control and noisy,	**5. Make an assignment.** *Example:* "STOP—shift gears, find a pencil and piece of paper. List there things that. . . ."
6. The group "can't see the forest for the trees"—nitpicks, and has lost focus,	**6. Focus on the uses of the report or decision.** *Example:* "Let me remind you that the state of New Mexico has agreed to fund this study as soon as we get the functional specifications finished."
7. A group member behaves badly,	**7. Give immediate behavioral feedback, but refrain from judgmental remarks.** *Example:* "Manny, you are smoking in a 'no smoking' area; please extinguish your cigar."

Source: Carolyn Nilson, *Training Program Workbook & Kit,* Englewood Cliffs, NJ: Prentice-Hall, a division of Simon and Schutser , 1989, p. 201.

Trainee Handout 6.1-E

PROJECT NOTEBOOK FORMAT

An essential project management tool is the project journal or notebook. This journal is kept in a standard 3-ring binder, and is comprised of daily documentation about the project. Information in the project journal is organized behind the four tabs, Content, Cost, Schedule, and Control, which provide space to document and study the four basic elements of the project.

CONTENT	Objectives Scope Staff Tasks List of products/services
COST	Salary, expressed as person-days Materials Computer time Purchased services (accounting, legal, photography, art) Overhead
SCHEDULE	Milestones Person-days to complete each task, and total person-days Lapse-time to complete each task, and total lapse-time
CONTROL	Roles and responsibilities Relationships among project staff, tasks, and time Communications, correspondence, status reports to clients In-process reviews End-of-project evaluation

Source: Carolyn Nilson, *Training Program Workbook & Kit,* Englewood Cliffs, NJ: Prentice Hall, a division of Simon & Schuster, 1989, p. 347.

Trainee Handout 6.1-F

PROJECT STATUS REPORT FORM

________________________________ ________________
Project Name Date of Report

____
Time Period Covered by this Report

Accomplished:

-
-
-
-

To Be Accomplished:

-
-
-

Constraints and Concerns:

-
-
-

____
Project Manager Signature

Source: Carolyn Nilson, *Training Program Workbook & Kit,* Englewood Cliffs, NJ: Prentice Hall, a division of Simon & Schuster, 1989, p. 357.

Trainee Handout 6.1-G

PROJECT MONITORING PROFILE FORM

This form can be used as an interim documentation and monitoring tool before the project is completed, or as an end-of-project evaluation tool. It can be effectively used during personnel discussions regarding performance standards and expectations for project staff, and as one kind of evaluation base for analysis of corporate support that might be required for successful project implementation across the company.

Keep in mind that this is a very brief documentation; complete records and backup information should be available in other project file cabinets or in the Project Journal.

Project Name:________________Date:_______Project Manager:____________

Commendations and Concerns		Not at All	Some-what	To a Large Extent
	MANAGEMENT			
	1. Planned tasks have been completed on schedule.	❑	❑	❑
	2. Changes are consistent with original project objectives	❑	❑	❑
	3. Reports are succinct and nontrivial.	❑	❑	❑
	4. Staffing has been effective.	❑	❑	❑
	FINANCES AND RECORDKEEPING			
	1. Expenditure records are current.	❑	❑	❑
	2. Revenue records are current.	❑	❑	❑
	3. Records indicate that resources have been allocated in support of deliverable products/services.	❑	❑	❑
	4. Costs have been justified.	❑	❑	❑
	PERFORMANCE			
	1. Required information has been assembled.	❑	❑	❑
	2. Data is accessible and easy to use.	❑	❑	❑
	3. Deliverables have been produced according to design.	❑	❑	❑
	4. Deliverables are available for review.	❑	❑	❑
	5. There is evidence that the target audience accepts the project as complete.	❑	❑	❑

Source: Carolyn Nilson, *Training Program Workbook & Kit*, Englewood Cliffs, NJ: Prentice Hall, a division of Simon & Schuster, 1989, p. 361.

TRAINING PLAN 6.2

How to Use One-on-One Training with Managers and Supervisors as a Complement to Planning Institute Group Instruction

This training plan is an outline of the key elements, methods, and procedures required to train managers and supervisors through various *one-on-one, on-the-job training techniques.* Among these are mentoring, coaching, and peer tutoring. These three major kinds of one-on-one techniques are considered together in this training plan because together they work towards similar business goals, are driven by the same kinds of work pressures, and are generally successful vehicles for similar kinds of learning objectives.

From a corporate training perspective, they can be seen as a "program" of management training that requires a systematic analysis, design, development, implementation, and evaluation approach as disciplined and careful as any course, seminar, workshop, conference, or institute. This training plan presents the components of one-on-one training with this systems framework in mind.

This kind of management training is included here in the chapter on planning because so much of what a manager does in terms of planning is done in short clips, is based on an intuitive sense of operations, and involves the manager's roles as resource allocator, conflict manager, "fire fighter," coordinator, and spokesperson. Training managers and supervisors to be better planners requires not only good planning models, workable goals, and the latest information but also some reinforcement, support, and clarification at critical moments on the job precisely when that new planning skill is practiced.

Today's managers and supervisors, in response to broader spans of control, compressed time, and exploding information, seem less and less willing to do self training by spending time away from their jobs at multiday seminars and training events. Training is being seen more as a mixture of self-directed and experience-based learning with instructor-led and trainer-facilitated instruction. Video, computer, and telecommunications technologies have given trainers wonderful new tools to serve today's business leaders with instructional aids appropriate to one-on-one and self-directed learning. The trick is for trainers to choose the one-on-one training delivery method with its learning aids to lead the manager or supervisor trainee towards effective self-directed learning of skills the business needs. Management training must recognize that managers on the job do a lot of learning by themselves; they "bathe" in information, sometimes processing it, sometimes disseminating it, and sometimes not; and they perform hundreds of different people-intensive and data-intensive tasks every week.

Managers, too, are being prodded by the quality movement and by the "bandwagon effect" of other companies' publicized successes to become team players with other managers and to also organize their own work groups as empowered teams. Managers are being asked to behave like followers and leaders at the same time, to *want* to contribute to the greater good of the team as it works out its grander corporate mission. Managers and supervisors are being expected to generously pitch in shoulder to shoulder with other employees who share a common purpose. They're expected to know how to organize a team's work through all of its internal and external relationships. Managers and supervisors are being expected to know how to allow and encourage team efforts—to give employees and themselves "permission" to share control of work in its fullest and best sense.

Managers and supervisors need a training methodology, especially in the planning area, that recognizes the realities of today's time and human resources challenges of their jobs. Effective one-on-one training holds promise for being one such learning vehicle. Together with the Planning Institute, it can serve well.

OVERVIEW OF TRAINING METHODOLOGY

One-on-one training methods can provide these person-to-person supports if this kind of training is designed and delivered well. Too often, on-the-job training is a haphazard, non-accountable, ill-planned venture. To prevent falling into the trap of paying no attention to what happens on a person-to-person basis (corporate trainers love to count person-days of attendance in class and multiply that sum by numbers of courses), treat this kind of management training as a carefully planned program of instruction that is particularly in tune with the nature of management today.

Tying the structure of one-on-one training to the structure of an institute such as the Planning Institute outlined in the previous training plan is one way to approach it. Building the one-on-one training around the twelve weeks of the Institute, giving a two-week emphasis to each kind of planning is the plan suggested here. For illustration, training plan 6.2 uses topics in Market Planning as it is developed. Each other Institute planning topic (financial, strategic, operational, project, and work planning) can be developed as a focus for one-on-one training using similar techniques.

Like other training plans, it begins with objectives for the training as a whole and then includes objectives for the learner. Evaluation methods are tied to the learning objectives. Teaching points and exercises related to the various kinds of one-on-one training complete the training plan. Helpful worksheets follow it.

Advantages to One-on-One Training

In addition to being practical and in harmony with today's management challenges, one-on-one training has some particular strengths as an instructional technique. These are:

- The individual learner is obviously the focus.
- Instruction is designed for one learner's needs.
- In the give and take of instructional delivery, the learner's learning styles are specifically addressed.
- The learner's speed of learning can drive the pace of instruction to the learner's benefit.
- Learning errors, misinformation, false starts, wrong approaches can all be corrected right away.
- Formative evaluation is constantly occurring, facilitating and enhancing the quality of instructional design and delivery.
- One-on-one instruction tends to quickly build confidence in the learner, leading learners into a self-directed learning mode more easily.
- One-on-one instruction is empowering for both the instructor and the learner.
- One-on-one instruction gets to learners at the point when they need it most, and therefore has the potential for being highly successful in facilitating transfer of new knowledge and skills to the job.
- One-on-one instructors have an excellent chance of being credible in the eyes of the learner, enhancing motivation to learn.

- One-on-one instruction can also efficiently and effectively teach corporate survival skills as mentors, coaches, and peers interact as corporate spokespersons with fellow employees in a learning context.
- One-on-one instruction at the learner's job site is inexpensive to deliver and easy to cost out.

Guidelines for Setting Up a One-on-One Training Program

Here are some guidelines for "how to do it." As a corporate trainer, you'll probably be responsible for setting up the one-on-one training program. Use these following ideas as train-the-trainer techniques for those who will be doing one-on-one teaching:

1. **Present the big picture**. Relate the topic (from the Planning Institute) to what you know about the company's mission, key business goals, special strategies or plans. Let the trainee see that his or her job has meaning in terms of the big corporate picture.
2. **Review the requirements**. As a company spokesperson, you have a good idea of what rules, procedures, standards, and specifications have to be followed. Be sure that your trainee knows these things too at the very beginning of training.
3. **Fill in the gaps.** Your trainee will have some information from having attended the Institute. However, this information most probably is in some disarray and needs an applications focus before your trainee can use it to full advantage. It's your job as an expert, by virtue of your experience, to help the trainee get it all together. Fill in the gaps for the trainee so that he or she can truly use the information.
4. **Walk in your trainee's moccasins.** Appreciate your trainee's situation—your trainee's sense of urgency, personal and career goals, responses to job pressures, and his or her past job successes. Let your trainee know that you appreciate his or her competencies and already-made contributions to the company. Make the one-on-one trainee feel personally adequate, not inadequate.
5. **Use a problem-solving approach to instruction.** Set up your lessons to encourage the trainee to see the possibilities for success by using the information or skills. Encourage the trainee to figure out procedures; use analogies to strategies the trainee has probably used in past situations; give cues, but let the trainee figure out the solution.
6. **Talk about the good results of using the planning tool.** Focus on the expected outcome of good learning in terms of favorable business results.
7. **Provide frequent feedback** to the trainee during instruction, giving praise when it's warranted, and take the time to correct errors as soon as they occur.
8. **Give the trainee a crutch.** Take the heat off yourself by providing a chart, model, manual, illustrative videotape, or some other tangible training aid that helps the trainee remember what to do on his or her own after training has ended.
9. **Have a plan for follow-up.** Show the trainee that you have a stake in his or her ability to use this planning tool. Plan to contact your trainee again periodically, put your trainee in touch with your own network of helpful people on the subject, set up regular breakfast or luncheon meetings just to keep in touch. Demonstrate to the trainee that you are available to answer the trainee's questions.
10. **Separate training from other aspects of work.** Work from a training check sheet of items to be mastered by your trainee. (*Trainer's Worksheet 6.2-A* contains some helpful hints regarding mastery.)

Make it clear that training is different from performance review; referring to training as mastery of learning points or objectives clearly identifies the encounter as training, not as supervision or salary review. Set aside a training time and space without interruptions. Have a clearly recognized end to training so that training can be accountable.

Some Differences Among the Types of One-on-One Instruction: Mentoring, Coaching, and Peer Tutoring

As you design a one-on-one training program, try to sort out the characteristics of the trainees and the business environment to arrive at the best conclusion about which one-on-one technique to use. Of course, consider using all three in the appropriate situations.

Mentoring. Mentoring is either a formal or informal mentor-protégé relationship generally for the purpose of career development of the protégé. Mentoring is based on a combination of expert modeling and career counseling. The protégé is most often a new manager or supervisor, or a new employee; the mentor is most often an older or obviously more experienced "company person."

Critics point out that in hierarchical, top-down style companies, formal mentoring seldom works because there are not enough mentors to go around; fewer people are left at the top, and those who are don't want to feel imposed upon to put their own performance on hold while they support a newcomer. Proponents of mentoring say that it's the best way for novice managers and supervisors to learn company norms and get the most effective initial training. Companies who've tried mentoring with success often pair up persons from different organizations, thereby eliminating the "inside track to promotion" syndrome. If long-term career development is your goal, consider a mentor program.

As in other kinds of training, a mentoring assignment means that one becomes a teacher with responsibilities for assessing the trainee's needs, designing instruction with learning objectives in mind for the protégé, deciding how best to deliver that instruction, and evaluating those instructional times together. Like other kinds of training, mentoring should have a beginning and an end with monitoring, feedback, and accountability.

Coaching. Coaching, too, is instruction based on a counseling model. Unlike mentoring which generally is based on a long-term relationship and long-term goals, coaching generally is a shorter-term relationship with more immediate performance objectives. Companies moving towards empowered teams very often try to set the stage for breaking down a hierarchical chain of command through coaching.

Coaching is essentially a communication process between coach and "player" that emboldens the player to peak performance. The first prerequisite to good coaching is a coachable player, that is, one who shares the coach's commitment to excellence. Like all good communicators, coaches spend a good deal of time listening to the perceived shortcomings of the player, giving feedback that results in redirected efforts (formative evaluation that informs instruction), and focusing on the critical few changes that the player must make in order to achieve that goal of excellence. If empowered and possibly unpredictable high performance is your goal, consider coaching.

Peer Tutoring. Peer tutoring is a form of one-on-one training that looks more like traditional instruction. It generally is skill or knowledge based, and is not counseling. It has the advantage of a level field, that is, peers or persons of equal status are paired for the learning experiences. The approach in peer tutoring is "we're in this together." A structured peer tutoring program can work well among managers and supervisors, especially in the situation such as a Planning Institute, where, indeed, they all are in it together. In this case, peer tutors can come from among Institute attendees or from among the other management staff who have been with the company a bit longer. In peer tutoring, it's the skill level that determines who could be a tutor.

A peer tutoring program is easier to design and implement than mentoring and coaching because it is tied to skills that have standards and can be codified into competency lists. There are fewer potential psychological traps in peer tutoring than in mentoring or coaching. Peer tutoring can help to create a sense of camaraderie and an effective network of expertise. Choose peer tutoring when specific skill deficiencies are the issue. *Trainer's Worksheet 6.2-B* contains guidelines for peer tutors. These can be used in a train-the-trainer program for peer tutors.

TIME REQUIRED TO DELIVER THIS TRAINING

Six weeks of short, specific one-on-one training interspersed with the six Planning Institute days of group instruction.

LEVEL OF TRAINEE

Peer-level managers and supervisors

TRAINING OBJECTIVES

- To guide trainees in the practice of planning skills and implementation of planning models through one-on-one instruction
- To run an organized program of one-on-one instruction for 12 weeks as part of the Planning Institute, focusing on each Institute topic for a two-week intensive one-on-one training period following each Institute day
- To facilitate interdependence and empowerment among managers and supervisors

LEARNING OBJECTIVES FOR THE TRAINEE (FOR ONE TRAINEE)

Note: From this point on, this training plan uses content examples from the Market Planning day of the Institute and focuses on the 2-week period of learning based on one-on-one instruction. Similar learning objectives can be developed for the other five 2-week periods following Institute days.

- To refine my ability to project new market opportunities.
- To establish a self-improvement program in conversational German to be completed in eight months prior to my assignment in Berlin.
- To learn more about this company's use of market channels from both historical and future perspectives.

METHODS TO EVALUATE THE TRAINEE'S PROGRESS

In one-on-one training, the trainer and trainee together are the best judges of the trainee's learning progress because it is these two persons who together have agreed on what must be learned.

Setting realistic training and learning objectives for individual trainees is the first step in getting good evaluations. Writing these objectives down for both trainer and trainee to work towards is one of the first tasks that persons involved in one-on-one training should do.

Remember, in this case, you are dealing with a two-week period of instruction. The assumptions are that the training department maintained a list of potential one-on-one instructors, with their fields of expertise described, and used this list to confer with Institute attendees regarding individuals' needs for guided practice during the two weeks following the presentation of the planning model on the Institute day. Evaluation of progress is a simple matter of using a checklist of tasks and their mastery criteria related to objectives for this one trainee only. Evaluation is usually a matter of trainer and trainee agreement regarding progress. Some kind of evaluation record should be maintained for the two-week period, preferably with some notation at the end of each one-on-one training session.

In this case, instruction uses all three types of one-on-one instruction: a peer tutor for the first objective, a coach for the second objective, and a mentor for the third objective.

Peer tutoring was chosen for this trainee because a number of excellent peer experts are available who can show the trainee how to use models for projecting market opportunities, how to fill out the bi-monthly report forms, and some tricks for using existing documents and personal information sources to do projections. The needs to be addressed by this objective are skill-based; the first objective is a classic cognitive objective. Formative evaluation should occur as the trainee uses these various documents during the peer tutoring sessions.

For the trainee's "just-in-time" German study, *coaching* was chosen as an effective training technique. Several people in the company have recently had to quickly learn a language for a similar business reason, and could be particularly helpful in telling the trainee on what to concentrate as he or she gets started. Such a coach could also help with connections for the trainee among the bilingual employees in the company, and could possibly facilitate ongoing German conversation practice sessions over the next several months. Evaluation of this objective focuses on the quality and workability of the plan for language study.

Mentoring was chosen for the third objective for this trainee because of the past and future dimensions of the trainee's concern, and because the concept of channels is fundamental to understanding the nature of our business. A mentor-protégé relationship around the issue of channels should pay off in the long run for this particular trainee. Getting started now with this long-term relationship capitalizes on the enthusiasm and interest of the trainee following the Institute presentation of the challenges of channels.

After the one-on-one training instructor (mentor, coach, peer tutor) has been identified, both trainer and trainee are then on their own to schedule the training at their mutual convenience. The thing that will make the Institute and the one-on-one support phases a success is the shared commitment to excellence of all one-on-one instructor participants and Institute attendees—excellence in training, and excellence in business practice.

TRAINING TIPS *Peer Tutoring*	***EXERCISES*** *Peer Tutoring*
1. Identify gaps in trainee's knowledge of the two acceptable projection models presented at the Institute.	1. Check correctness of terms, acronyms, understanding of all variables. Then check trainee's knowledge of the new organization chart and regional responsibilities. Be sure trainee knows key players in European Community, Taiwan, Singapore, and Russia.
2. Assemble all relevant forms and instruction sheets.	2. Make working copies of all forms for use during training. Take the trainee step by step through each form, working in red ink so trainee can use these working copies as samples later.
3. Focus on the issues of qualification of clients and scope of project opportunity.	3. Get copies of marketing plans and weekly sales reports. Show trainee how clients are coded for profit potential. Show trainee how to read the trends regarding scope in these reports (i.e., focus on line of business breakdowns and percentage of high-end products and services). Show trainee how to quickly estimate project value.
Coaching	*Coaching*
4. Agree on the "product" of the coaching sessions, i.e., how detailed should the plan for German study be?	4. Get the trainee to be realistic about his or her available time and preferred learning style. Find out who else needs to see this plan.
5. Assess the trainee's weaknesses regarding learning a language.	5. As agreement is reached regarding weaknesses, list each on the vertical axis of a Gantt-type timeline. List many items, possibly combining several at a later date.
6. Divide the weaknesses between coach and trainee, assigning solution investigation equally.	6. Build confidence and competence in the trainee. Demonstrate the coach's interest and stake in the trainee's success.
7. Agree on a reporting-back schedule and stick to it.	7. Assemble a pile of reference materials including names of persons who can be helpful to give to the trainee.

8. Read through the materials together to allow the trainee to see the possibilities.	8. Make notes on the materials so the trainee can refer to them later.
9. Develop the timeline and complete the plan.	9. Assign a timeline and instructional method or contact person to each item of weakness. Combine items if this makes sense.
Mentoring	*Mentoring*
10. Get the trainee to clarify his or her career goals for the short term as well as the long term.	10. Listen and withhold comment until several sessions later. Give the trainee the chance to test the reality of the goal statements as well as to establish some credibility.
11. Find out what the trainee knows about our historical selection of channels.	11. Meet in the corporate library with a reference librarian to review the company's historical dependence on channels. Point out key market changes, namely those which were technology-driven and those which were constrained by Latin American political stability.
12. Discuss worldwide trends in business organization that influence our current and future selection of channels.	12. Suggest a few current articles for the trainee to read prior to our next training session. Use these as jumping off points for discussion of why we see channels differently today than we did 30 years ago. Meet in mentor's office.
13. Set up a regular luncheon engagement with the trainee to continue discussions after the Institute is over. Make tentative plans to include the trainee in several marketing strategy meetings over the next six months.	13. Schedule luncheons in executive dining room, not in public restaurants.

Trainer's Worksheet 6.2-A

DEVELOPING AND USING MASTERY LISTS

Time and achievement seem to be dichotomous variables. If we choose to allow learning time to vary, as in one-on-one instruction, we can continue training until optimum achievement has been reached. (If we hold learning time constant, as in a lecture to a group, we see achievement varying.) Being committed to one-on-one instruction carries with it a commitment to specifying the achievement levels we're aiming for and a commitment to a flexible, ever-improving training process that recognizes both the individuality of the learner and the difficulty and importance of the learning task.

Developing and using mastery lists follows four basic steps:

1. Analysis of the job
2. Coding or weighting the tasks of the job to be learned
3. Setting a standard or criterion for each task
4. Evaluating the trainee regarding competency

Simplified examples of each step follow:

1. Analysis of the job of operations manager:

People Duties	Data Duties	Things Duties *
conducts operational reviews	tracks sales and service results	manages van fleet
implements corrective programs	evaluates methods and procedures	maintains automated tracking system
sponsors promotional programs	monitors quality assurance efforts	maintains product introduction center
coordinates product introductions	prepares budget and balance sheet	
conducts service audits		
supervises staffs		
attends headquarters staff meetings		

2. Coding the tasks of the job, Receptionist:

Category: Greeting tasks	*Index 1*	*Index 2*	*Index 3* **
Index 1 difficult level (hard, medium, easy) Index 2 value to client (high, medium, low) Index 3 value to superior (high, medium, low)	**Difficulty h, m, e**	**Client Value h, m, l**	**Supervisor Value h, m, l**
1. Say "Good Morning" to employees	easy	low	high
2. Greet clients who phone in	medium	high	high
3. Take employee sick calls	medium	low	medium
4. Get business cards of walk-ins	easy	high	high

*Source: Carolyn Nilson, *Training Program Workbook & Kit*, Englewood Cliffs, NJ: Prentice Hall, a division of Simon & Schuster, 1989, p. 28.

**op. cit., p. 70.

Trainer's Worksheet 6.2-A (continued)

3. Setting the standard for each task of the job, Receptionist:

   For the items above:

   1. to each employee (100%)
   2. use name of client and own name on at least 80% of calls
   3. get five items of information: time, illness, employee's location during illness, contact person, likely return date
   4. or substitute name, address, phone number (100% of walk-ins)

4. Evaluating the trainee, e.g., a group instructor, regarding competency:

	low competence				high competence
1. Check operations of training equipment	1	2	3	4	5
2. Verify class list	1	2	3	4	5
3. Establish a comfortable atmosphere	1	2	3	4	5
4. Establish learning objectives	1	2	3	4	5
5. Introduce lessons	1	2	3	4	5

Trainer's Worksheet 6.2-B

GUIDELINES FOR PEER TUTORING

CONTENT GUIDELINES:

1. *Remember to tell the trainee what the objectives are for each lesson.* Plan a lesson for 15 minutes' worth of time.
2. *Be sure that you define all terms and acronyms that the trainee might not be familiar with.* Don't make assumptions that the trainee knows what seems obvious to you.
3. *Use a variety of mental structures to explain things — stories, analogies, examples, case studies, equations, diagrams, maps, graphs.* Remember that your trainee needs to have intellectual ways of connecting what's new with what's already part of his experience.
4. *Be logical.* Present information so that the trainee can use what he has just learned as a basis for learning the next lesson. Don't skip around. Make logical transitions.
5. *Give the trainee cues.* Point out the critical steps in a new procedure; differentiate the very important from the not so important. Tell the trainee which features of a model are the significant ones and which ones are generic or common to other models. Help your trainee discriminate and differentiate.
6. *Teach by nonexample too.* Tell or show the trainee what something is as well as what it is not. Help your trainee to fix in his mind the information on which you are focusing by showing him the ways in which alternatives are not acceptable.
7. *Ask the trainee to relate new concepts and procedures to his job.* Help the trainee understand how to apply new learning by asking the trainee to tell you.
8. *When the trainee talks, listen.* You might have to reorganize some content or modify some objectives "on the fly" depending on how your trainee is synthesizing and integrating the information you are teaching. Remember that this person is our peer, and has some good ideas too.

PROCESS GUIDELINES

1. *Give the trainee a chance to tell you what he expects to get out of the training.* Get the trainee to write it down on an index card and tape it to the wall during training. Refer to this statement later during your teaching when the trainee begins to accomplish what he expected to accomplish. Do this early in your peer training to let your trainee know that you will be instrumental in this accomplishment and that you care about the trainee and his learning successes.
2. *Give the trainee a chance to establish his own credibility.* Do this by asking how he got to be where he is now, and discussing how his former positions or schooling will probably play a part in the new position. Generate some enthusiasm for the current training by relating it to the trainee's previous successes.

Trainer's Worksheet 6.2-B (continued)

3. *Be aware of your pace of presentation.* Be ready to adjust it if it seems too fast or too slow, too dull or too animated.
4. *Answer the trainee's questions.*
5. *Give and receive feedback.* Be gracious; remember you're in this together.
6. *Maintain smiling eye contact.*
7. *Use the "mirror" technique if a trainee gives you a wrong response.* Say back to the trainee exactly what he or she has said, giving the trainee a chance to hear and analyze that response. Preface your mirroring with the statement, "I believe I heard you say ...." Follow it up with, "Is this what you meant to say? Have you thought of this other approach?" or "What do you imagine would be the end results if you acted upon this?" Try to let the trainee figure out what was wrong with the response, then identify and list the errors as a review for the trainee. Use errors as an opportunity for good teaching. Never ignore them or make light of them.
8. Give the trainee time to practice new mental or physical skills under your supervision.

Chapter 7

Techniques for Training Managers and Supervisors in Personal Competence

Many people in corporate America believe that competence cannot be taught, that is, that managerial and supervisory competence is born, not made. This point of view has had some adherents, perhaps, in the days of the last decade or two when companies had a full complement of managers at many levels—the "good old days" of middle management and many managerial slots into which to transfer and promote a company's many rising stars. The fuller managerial ranks of the recent past decades could generally find places for managers to easily fit and demonstrate the skills and personal abilities that they had already acquired. It was easy, in those days, to spot and place a person who seemed ready-made for the position—a manager seemingly born to succeed with just a little bit of grooming. There were simply more people and more managerial and supervisory openings then.

Today things are different. Businesses throughout the country are downsizing, combining departments, and pushing managerial responsibility lower and lower. At the one end of the employee pool, ordinary workers and worker teams are assuming many tasks formerly reserved for management; and, at the other end, managers and supervisors are being called upon to perform many tasks that formerly were done by their superiors. Management is shrinking, both in terms of the numbers of management and supervisory jobs and the numbers of people ready to perform those jobs. It is less realistic today to expect to find a person at either end who can just walk into a job demonstrating all of the competencies that job requires. Management jobs are more complicated these days, and employees are less prepared to handle them.

Along with this flatter management organization, companies are being challenged by ethnic and gender diversity of the incoming workforce and by domestic and international competition regarding quality of product and service. Managers and supervisors are being called upon to have a personal vision regarding how to make the corporation work within these new staffing, production, and marketing challenges. Managers and supervisors are required to be both bottom-line focused regarding financials and operations and introspective regarding managerial style and one's ability to relate to styles that are different from one's own. Businesses are demanding that managers and supervisors be sensitive to their own personas as well as able to mold the workplace to accommodate enormous individual differences among the workforce.

Three essential skills regarding personal competence can be taught within the framework of this more complex management and supervisory workplace profile. These are the skills of managing time, solving problems, and providing leadership.

TRAINING TO HONE THE PERSONAL SKILLS OF INDIVIDUAL MANAGERS AND SUPERVISORS

Competency training for managers and supervisors is seen here as a set of skills grounded in the learning domains of both psychomotor skills and cognitive skills. Thus, skill-building exercises are cast within the framework of subsets of these skills, providing trainers with the structures they need to facilitate learning.

Presenting competency training as a set of differentiated skills maximizes the occurrence of transfer from classroom to the job and provides the trainer with an interesting, solid, theoretical as well as practical base upon which to design and deliver training in this sometimes controversial area of management training. Companies that encourage their managers and supervisors to develop and implement management practices that work best for individuals are more likely to achieve good bottom-line "people management" results in the company as a whole. The secret to training personal competence is to treat the trainees as individuals and, in turn, enable them to deal with their management responsibilities through the individuals who report to them. This kind of training for today's workforce is a one-by-one-by-one approach, not the model or method or dictum from on high that says "this is how we do it here."

The managers in your class on time management, problem solving, or leadership are far more different than they are alike. They are each expert in a certain functional area or line of business, have different jobs to do, different internal and external pressures to deal with, and different personal priorities and beliefs. They are required to be very flexible in how they manage their human and material resources. They will typically learn best themselves and contribute the most to the learning situation for their classmates by being able to fit their own jobs, expertise, and personalities into the skills they need to learn.

In each of these three major skill areas, the classroom situation is the preferred setting because each manager can contribute to the learning by the other managers, thereby creating a cross-fertilization of ideas and better appreciation of the special expertise of many different people. Conducting effective "individualized" classrooms, however, requires a training approach that combines large group work to get ideas out in the open, small group work to flesh out details, and guided time for individual reflection and self-analysis. The trainer must be able to move among instructional techniques smoothly and effectively.

Your own preparation for these kinds of individualized lessons should include updating your own knowledge of the major responsibility area of each manager in your class. Start by memorizing the managers' names and responsibility areas ahead of class. Be sure that the registration form has a space for the manager to state his or her primary responsibility area, and that it in fact asks the manager to do so at registration time. You will make the class feel very personalized if you have done your homework and go out of your way to show them that you know and care about what they do. Through this simple preparation, you can set the personalized tone that you want to carry throughout the class.

Make the time to prepare yourself adequately. Don't depend on a "cheat sheet" or your superior memory during student introductions. Test yourself ahead of class to be sure you, in fact, have the critical information memorized. Only when you have committed the critical personalized information to memory will you be free enough to use it appropriately during class. Feel that you know the individuals who are your students. Keep the class size to no more than twelve persons to ensure that each gets individualized attention.

The scope of these lessons has to be both broad and narrow—broad because you have to appeal to many different areas of expertise and responsibility and narrow because you want to keep it focused on introspection and very personalized expression. Be confident about your teaching agenda. Be very sure about what you want to do first, second, third, and so on. Managers will probably be eager to talk about themselves and their special ways of doing things. It's easy to get lost in such a class—that is, to find yourself having to jump around in your instructor's manual in order to cover all the material. Don't let this happen. Pay attention to the sequence of instructional events. Know what needs to come first, second, third in order for your trainees' insights and skills to build. Above all, stick to your sequence. Know when to cut off a freewheeling discussion and how long to let an exercise continue in order to make the point. Don't be intimidated by the assemblage of managers in front of you—remember, you're in charge right now.

In lessons like these that use a variety of group sizes and depends on various kinds of interactions, it is important to be sure that there is space for each kind of learning situation. Check out your classroom or training space (even if it's a hotel halfway across the country) to be sure that comfortable, well-lighted spaces with comfortable chairs and tables for taking notes are available for large group instruction, breaking into smaller groups, and for individual reflection and self-analysis. If you expect each small group to each use a flipchart, be sure enough flipcharts have been ordered and in fact get delivered to your classroom.

Be sure all supplies are available—this often means bringing them yourself in your own briefcase. Plan carefully. For example, if you expect your trainees to make their own overhead transparencies, be sure you have "write-on" acetates and nonpermanent markers. Be sure all your equipment works. If you are delivering your class in a field or remote location, get there a day early to set things up exactly as you want them to be, to assemble your supplies, and to test all equipment.

You are the person responsible for the quality of this course, and in these kinds of personal competence courses especially, you will not want to waste your trainees' time by having to do last-minute housekeeping chores. Managers in your audience will see that wasted housekeeping time as the time when they can disappear to make just one more phone call back to the office. Remember that you're dealing with a collection of individual experts who will expect to be greeted and paid attention to as individuals. Treat them as individual clients. Make each one feel that you are devoted particularly to him or her. It's their business that you are interested in; they are not there to be interested in yours. Try to make the business of running the course as invisible as possible. Do this by meticulous attention to the setting of each part of the lesson.

TRAINING PLANS

Four different training plans provide a comprehensive sample of training techniques for teaching managers and supervisors skills of personal competence: to manage their time, be efficient problem solvers, and to provide leadership for today's diverse workforce, new organizational patterns, and widespread competitive challenges.

Where appropriate, worksheets are appended to each training plan. Each training plan with its appendices is intended to give you, the trainer, the instructional design and presentation guidelines that you need. In these training plans, we do the conceptual work for you—you need only to flesh out the plans with your own company jargon, names, and specific data.

Training plans in Chapter 7 for training managers and supervisors in personal competence include:

management issues	*training techniques*
7-1 Managing Time	Team teaching
7-2 Delegating	Organization analysis workshop
7-3 Solving Problems	Sports psychology weekend
7-4 Leadership	Self-analysis through peer group analysis using video vignettes

TRAINING PLAN 7.1

Training Managers to Set Very Personal Goals Regarding Time

This training plan is an outline of the key elements, methods, and procedures required to train supervisors and managers using a *team teaching approach to classroom training*. Often in a company there are several professionals outside of the training department who can be effectively teamed with a seasoned instructor to present information and facilitate learning of a personal nature. One such professional is the company doctor, nurse, or psychologist. In this training plan, we choose the psychologist; however, any health professional can be substituted according to your company's staffing in the medical organization. This training plan for time management teams the management trainer with the staff psychologist.

This training plan is structured to enable the trainer to create an instructor's guide or course outline from it. It begins with objectives for training and for the learner, and with evaluation methods tied to the learning objectives. Teaching points related to the content of a manager's or supervisor's area of responsibility provide the foundation for topics covered during training. Sample exercises suggest ways to deliver instruction. Helpful worksheets follow the training plan.

OVERVIEW OF TRAINING METHODOLOGY

The subject of personal goals regarding time management is a highly individual matter, requiring a training methodology that encourages individual expression. The following plan provides the basics for this kind of methodology, suggesting ways in which to deliver training in goal setting to individual supervisors or managers. The methodology is structured to deliver maximum impact on individuals, yet is set within a group where the instructional design leads to helping individuals feel understood through being supported by the group.

It is presented in a classroom setting to save time and costs. In addition, team teaching is used to provide a dual thrust of management skills that are good for business and of personal growth skills that are good for the individual. The addition of a member of the company's medical staff in the role of instructor/facilitator will help individual trainees to focus inward towards managing their own productivity regarding management of their own critical resource of time. Managers typically find it easier to focus outwardly on work flow and operational time management; they frequently need help learning to focus inwardly.

Discussion will probably occur on the personal competence expectations of the company regarding the manager's work-related social time (golf with clients, Friday nights at the pub, early morning breakfast meetings). You can also expect the discussions on time management to digress somewhat into the related subject of stress management, and for this, too, it's a good idea to have a medical staff member on hand as a trainer. A competent industrial psychologist or other medical professional will be able to both help individuals focus on themselves and also enable others in the group to give encouragement and support.

Limit the class size to 12 persons. Minimum class size is four. If you don't have four people who need the course, wait until you do. This training plan assumes a class size of 12.

TIME REQUIRED TO DELIVER THIS TRAINING

2 hours
The secret to the success of these two hours is detailed planning ahead regarding personal information about each trainee and careful coordination between you (the instructor) and the psychologist regarding learning objectives, content, and timing.

TRAINEE LEVEL

Any level manager can benefit from this course, and a wide variety of managers can be trained together. Expect great individual differences in the trainees' abilities to be introspective—looking inward is not part of a manager's standard experience base or academic preparation for the job.

TRAINING OBJECTIVES

- To use a variety of instructional techniques in order to encourage focused and in-depth contributions from each trainee
- To conduct a very personalized class through use of each manager's proven track record, and through facilitation techniques such as eye contact, swift and plentiful feedback, and creating opportunities for trainee participation at many points in the class
- To collaborate with the company psychologist in delivery of this course

LEARNING OBJECTIVES FOR THE TRAINEE

- To create a personal goal statement regarding time management
- To share points of view and information about time management with other manager/trainees in the group
- To encourage and support other trainees during learning

METHODS TO EVALUATE TRAINEE'S PROGRESS

Evaluating trainees' progress is best done at many times during the delivery of training, and in a friendly and somewhat informal way. This is called *formative* evaluation, because it is evaluation that helps to form or shape instruction. It is also known as *in-process* evaluation, contrasted to *end-of-process* evaluation. Formative evaluation is developed in relationship to a specific learning objective, thus contributing to the effective accumulation of understanding and skill during a lesson.

In this kind of *goal-setting training* that tends to get down to the bare facts—the personal values, attitudes, errors in judgment, essential beliefs, biases of individual trainees—you ask trainees to take risks by asking them to expose their personal preferences and ways of managing. Be aware of when you do this, and cue your psychologist facilitator at those moments to give some overt positive feedback to the risk-taker.

What you're interested in here is to reward the process of introspection, thereby using the formative evaluation action to propel the introspection forward. Remember that the learner's goal is to create a personal goal statement regarding time management. The job of the team of instructor facilitators is to help the learners work through the process of introspection in order to be able to draft such a goal statement. Trainees will reach their learning objectives successfully only to the extent that they probe deeply enough into their own values and individual management styles on their way to creating their own goal statements. Supportive and frequent formative evaluation helps them get there faster.

Here are some specific things you and your partner instructor can do:

- Look at each manager's attempts at a goal statement. Don't wait for a finished product. Check for unique points; provide positive feedback on each unique point to encourage honest self assessment and creative expression.
- Assign a buddy manager (fellow classmate) to any manager having trouble. Check with the buddy and the manager to be sure work on the statement is progressing correctly.
- Spread leadership around—give each trainee some visibility in a leadership role during small group sessions. Don't be afraid to give up some of your position of authority as an instructor. Remember that this is a group of corporate leaders who are accustomed to functioning in a leadership role. They will enjoy doing this in a classroom situation, and will generally add a great deal to the positive atmosphere in the classroom when they are asked to become instructional leaders.

Putting a trainee in a leadership position also gives you an excellent opportunity to provide in-depth formative evaluation as that person performs a specific leadership role. Encouragement tends to be contagious, and acts as a motivator for others to model the positive behaviors of the leader.

By using this technique in small groups, you positively compound the effect of instructional leadership, and you structure and contain the natural tendency of this particular trainee audience to fall into leadership roles. By using this as an evaluation exercise, you retain and enhance your overall position of authority and you send your trainees the signal that you trust and respect their leadership abilities.

The following roles are typical roles that you might want to assign to your manager trainees: brainstorm session recorder, leader of a triad small group, recorder at small group discussions, or presenter of his or her work on overhead transparencies before the small group or the larger group as a whole.

Carry out the evaluations of small group work by getting around the room to do a mental check of who is contributing and who is more hesitant; readjust assignments to balance the participation level.

The secret to successful evaluation is to use the unique responses of the individuals in your class to foster creative thinking among other trainees. This ensures that you will reach the many interest and experience levels represented by your trainees. Take the time to really listen to your trainees' points of view, and to make truly appropriate comments about the good points and not-so-good points in each person's response.

TRAINING TIPS	***EXERCISES***
1. Focus on the task at hand, that is, to help each trainee create a personal *goal* statement regarding time management. (Refer to *Trainee Handout 7.1-A.*) Share the instructor role with your company psychologist. See *Trainer's Worksheet 7.1-B* for tips on team teaching.	1. Brainstorm the notion of "reality about time in this company." See *Trainer's Worksheet 7.1-C.* Seek input from each trainee. Record it on whiteboard (so you can spread out and easily change a contribution—a flipchart will do in a pinch, but tends to limit brainstorming discussion because of its narrow dimension).
2. Choose three items from the brainstormed ideas that are especially important to you. Prioritize the items. Sample responses might be: time on the telephone, processing paperwork, follow-up on expense reports, meetings, social obligations, generating letters oneself on the computer, electronic mail rather than hard copy, travel time, the time dimensions of stress, interruptions, procrastination.	2. Break into triads (groups of three people) to talk about why each of these three items on each person's list is a problem. Instruct triad leaders/recorders to stay focused on the individual's unique situation and possibility for problem solving. Don't try for agreement; try for quality of individual expression. It sometimes helps to use the mistakes a person knows he or she makes as a means to discuss corrective action and zero in on goals. See *Trainer's Worksheet 7.1-D.*
3. Upon reflection, recast or reprioritize your three items. State them as goals, not as problems. (Encourage trainees to set more than three if they are finding the exercise easy.)	3. Go back to original seats. Take five minutes of silent reflection time to assess your own special situation and personal capacities. Be realistic.
4. Read all goals to the group.	4. Hand-pick several managers to present their goals on a self-made transparency to assure a good variety among early responders. Encourage the rest of trainees to volunteer in random order to present their goals to the group. Compliment honesty, creativity, and attainable goals. Send them back to their jobs with a renewed sense of purpose, with reachable goals. Save the development of plans and timelines for another training session.

Trainee Handout 7.1-A

HOW TO WRITE GOALS

Goals have to do with output—results. They can be measured and verified. They provide targets for action, give structure to the context of work, provide closure for efforts, and enable employees working toward them to attain a sense of achievement.

These are the three essential characteristics of goals:

1. Driven by a valid business purpose.
2. Attainable and perceived to be attainable.
3. Have a direct payoff to the individual—tied to the company's reward systems and values.

Keys to characteristic 1, *Driven by a valid business purpose:*

Typical business drivers include:

- increased production
- quantity of new ideas
- increased sales
- lower inventory
- faster turnaround
- days worked
- cost savings from innovation
- reduction in customer complaints
- lower litigation costs
- improved course evaluation reports
- number of publications

Keys to characteristic 2, *Attainable and perceived to be attainable:*

People want to know that their work is meaningful, that is, that their efforts will contribute in a direct way to the good of the business. Managers and supervisors especially have a personal stake in how the company fares in its marketplace.

When you construct a goal, think about and talk about the resources related to the goal that are currently available, consider the constraints to reaching the goal, and consider the means or the systems that need to work in order to accomplish the goal. Goals must be reachable and be perceived to be reachable. Consider your own personality and your own physical and mental resources and constraints regarding work toward attaining the goal.

Keys to characteristic 3, *Have a direct payoff to the individual:*

Answer yes to these questions:

are you able to measure your own progress regarding this goal?

do you value the output implied by this goal?

are your resources, constraints, and systems in balance so that the effort you expend toward this goal is appropriate and not overwhelming?

is the payoff clear?

do you have the ability to do the work?

do you want the reward?

Trainee Handout 7.1-A (continued)

Working Form for Goal Setting

Date ____________________

Manager's name ______________________________________

Statement of the goal ______________________________________

____

____

____

Measures ______________________________________

____

____

____

Resources available or needed ______________________________________

____

____

____

Constraints______________________________________

____

____

____

Systems, methods, plans ______________________________________

____

____

____

Completion target date ______________________________________

Trainer's Worksheet 7.1-B

TEAM TEACHING GUIDELINES

Before two or more instructors work together in front of a class, get together to review these guidelines:

1. Clarify each instructor's role—that is, will one be the "task master" and prod the group onward through the content, and will the other one be the "process facilitator" and cajole, console, give cues, and pay attention to individuals' emotional responses? Or, will one be a "presenter" and the other be a "recorder"? Or, will some other roles be taken?
2. Make notes in your instructor's manual or outline as to who does what and when. Instruction is part drama, and you want to be sure that you have the stage directions down pat.
3. Go over what you think might be the rough spots, especially the content transition points in your lessons. Map out a "plan A" and a "plan B" in case the trainees have a hard time. Role play these spots as part of your instructor training several days before your class is due to begin. As a team of instructors, be sure that you know what the instructional goals are for those transition points. Be sure that each team member is comfortable with flexibility of method at these points, and that each is clear about the goals for these transitions.
4. Be aware that a group will typically go through phases of orientation, conflict, and cohesion before the class is finished. If you've never seen this in a group, take the time as a team to observe another instructor's class. Learn to recognize these three phases of group dynamics. After class, review your own class outline and identify where you think these three phases will come. Discuss what you believe to be appropriate responses to your trainees in these various phases. Decide who will lead through conflict, and how long you'll let the conflict go before you mold the group into cohesion. Talk about these things ahead of time so you're not surprised when your group changes dynamics.
5. Make sure each team member can do all of the following typical functions of an instructional leader:
   - Guide learning through your own analysis and interpretive feedback to trainees
   - Suggest methods and procedures for accomplishing different objectives
   - Ask questions that encourage individual growth
   - Give emotional support to individuals as they learn (learning can be risky and lonely)
   - Encourage the group to embrace individuals
   - Control the pace of learning
   - Evaluate the quality of learning, both of individuals and of the group

If you are a little shaky on your ability to do any of these instructional functions, practice ahead of time—on your family, your friends, or a "pilot" group of trainees, and talk with other more seasoned instructors about items you need to know more about.

Trainer's Worksheet 7.1-C

BRAINSTORMING GUIDELINES

Brainstorming is an exercise that helps individuals share ideas without being interrupted or evaluated as they speak. It works well in peer groups who struggle with similar problems.

In a brainstorming session, the leader is responsible for raising the energy level of the group, for keeping the pace lively, for encouraging participation from each member of the group, and for preventing evaluative or derogatory comments from being made . A smooth-functioning group should be able to produce at least twenty responses ("brainstorms") per minute. When responses come quickly and with enthusiasm it's helpful to have two instructors on hand, one of whom records exactly what the trainee says and the other of whom keeps the responses coming.

Trainees' responses are best recorded on a blackboard or whiteboard in front of the class. If only a flipchart is available, tear off three sheets and mount them side by side on a classroom wall. You'll need horizontal space in which to work.

Many people believe that quality of ideas depends on quantity of ideas. The aim of brainstorming is to get a sufficient quantity of ideas from a group that quality will result from refinement of the strongest ideas during later exercises.

You might want to turn the following list of *Brainstorming Rules* into a handout for each trainee or into an overhead transparency. Begin the session with a review of these rules:

1. Single ideas are important. Each person is limited to one idea at a time.
2. Each idea has value and potential. Criticism and evaluation of ideas are not permitted.
3. The session should be free spirited. Wild and unconventional approaches are just fine.
4. Quantity of ideas is the goal. Play a word association game if you can in order to generate more ideas.

This is an example of how a 30-second brainstorming session on the time management problem of "too many constant interruptions" might progress. In this exercise, the group was asked to brainstorm all of the *causes* of interruptions, see Figure 7.1-C.1.

Another brainstorm session might be held to consider the solutions to interruptions. In the training plan on setting personal goals regarding time management, you might want to brainstorm both the causes and the solutions to some typical time management problems before you break the group into triads to work on their own goal statements.

Trainer's Worksheet 7.1-C (continued)

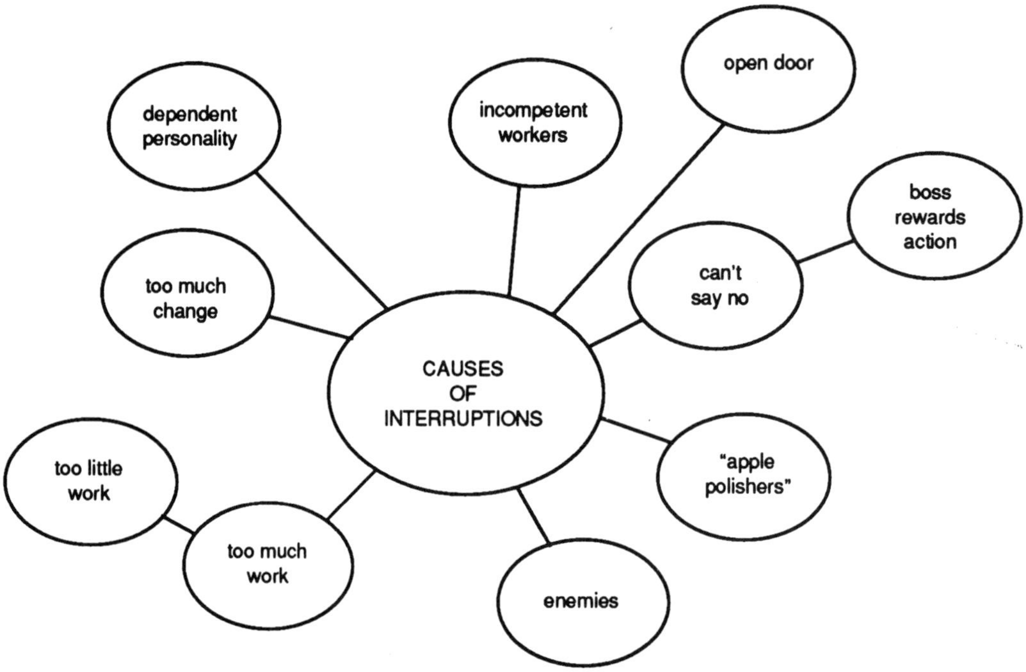

Figure 7.1-C.1 Sample Brainstorming Diagram

Trainer's Worksheet 7.1-D

HOW TO FACILITATE TRIADS

The most obvious question a trainer asks is, "Why triads?" What is there about groups of three, as opposed to groups of four, five, or six that makes it ideal for continuing a discussion that began as some other exercise, for example, as brainstorming?

The answer is that triads offer an opportunity for maximum contribution of all three members in a constricted time frame, for example, 15 or 20 minutes. Triads permit flexibility in relationships among the points of view—the probability of two points of view against one, or of three different points of view provide a dynamic that thrusts the group forward. This is in contrast to the two- or four-person small group which can too easily become stalemated and weak. In triads, because the group is small, there is a high involvement level and a resulting opportunity for each member to adopt part of each other group member's point of view. Triads encourage the most complete use of ideas and often lead to collaboration of various sorts after training is done.

The secret to successful facilitation of triads is simple: prod each triad member to seek a higher quality of ideas through these suggestions:

- modify
- substitute
- combine
- elaborate
- enhance
- rearrange
- reverse
- translate
- magnify

TRAINING PLAN 7.2

Training Managers and Supervisors to Manage Their Time Through Delegation

This training plan is an outline of the key elements, methods, and procedures required to train managers and supervisors through the medium of *a half-day workshop*. The workshop is planned as an in-depth analysis and problem-identification session for no more than eight trainees.

This workshop outline is structured to enable the trainer to create lesson plans, an instructor's guide, or a course outline from it. It begins with objectives for the presentation of the workshop itself, objectives for the learner, and with evaluation methods tied to the learning objectives. Teaching points related to the content of a manager's or supervisor's area of responsibility provide the foundation for topics covered during training. Sample exercises suggest ways to deliver this kind of instruction. Helpful worksheets follow the training plan.

OVERVIEW OF TRAINING METHODOLOGY

Developing your managers' skills in delegation through the medium of a half-day workshop will be hard work for you because the three hours of training time will be intense and fast-moving. The best format for the workshop is two square tables, each of which accommodates four people, one at each side of the table (square is better than round because there's more space to spread papers out to the sides). Leave at least four feet between the tables so that you can move between the tables easily.

The ideal number of trainees is eight, although you can also run the workshop with four trainees. In a class of only four persons, it's always a judgment call whether or not it's worth the time; eight trainees makes the class more cost-effective.

This format of a short workshop is chosen to fit the topic of delegation because of the workshop's "roll up the sleeves and get to work" thrust and the topic's analysis and problem-identification requirement. That is, the medium for training is selected to fit the nature of the content.

Trainers sometimes make the mistake of going for only the immediate "bottom line" regarding delivery of training in a topic such as delegation and choose a videotape to show to a large group—no doubt an inexpensive per head training cost, but also probably a delivery mode that is inappropriate for the nature of the subject and therefore ultimately a waste of time for the trainees and an unjustified cost to the company in the long run.

Choice of methodology is a critical issue in training because of many business reasons:

- cost, pricing, accounting, and budgeting
- cost-benefit questions
- relationships among what gets measured and what is valued by the company
- the time it takes to transfer what was learned in class to the manager's job
- equal employment opportunities

The medium by which you deliver training affects the resources you spend in planning for that delivery, the personnel time, the materials you purchase, the space you use or rent. It also affects what happens after training is done, how much follow up is needed and whose time-sheet gets charged for doing it, how expensive is the time lag between the end of training and the implementation of new, better, resource-saving skills. The choice of methodology also affects employment opportunity—in general, the more diverse trainees you have together in a class, the greater the risk of bias in the methodology and the greater the chance of diminished opportunity for some.

In a subject such as delegation, with its personal competence overtones, you want to be sure that the methodology supports individual problem identification and analysis so that there's no chance of a structural bias inadvertently built into the presentation itself. Keeping the class small and well controlled is your best guarantee of providing equal opportunity to learn.

TIME REQUIRED TO DELIVER THIS TRAINING

3 hours, with approximately 30 minutes preparation time by each trainee several days before the workshop

TRAINEE LEVEL

Any manager or supervisor who must delegate work to subordinates

TRAINING OBJECTIVES

- To lead trainees into identification of delegation problems.
- To guide trainees in a preparation assignment regarding organizational analysis (use *Trainee Handout 7.2A*).
- To help trainees analyze the risks and rewards of delegation according to their own and their subordinates' personality needs (*Trainee Handout 7.2-B* and *Trainee Handout 7.2-C*).

LEARNING OBJECTIVES FOR THE TRAINEE

- To identify delegation problems.
- Prior to the workshop, to complete a self-analysis of organizational structures or practices that impede one's own ability to delegate (use *Trainee Handout 7.2-A*).
- To define the personality factors and skills of subordinates and of oneself that represent problem areas that work against effective delegation (use *Trainee Handout 7.2-C*).
- To integrate the organizational challenges and personality characteristics to arrive at the beginnings of a plan for more effective delegation.

METHODS TO EVALUATE TRAINEE'S PROGRESS

Evaluating trainees' progress is best done at many times during the delivery of training, and in a friendly and somewhat informal way. This is called *formative evaluation* because it is evaluation that helps to form or shape instruction. It is also known as "in-process" evaluation, contrasted to "end-of-process" evaluation. Formative evaluation is developed in relationship to a specific learning objective, thus contributing to the effective accumulation of understanding and skill during a lesson.

This particular *half-day workshop on delegation* focuses on the two similar and rather low-level skills of identifying and defining. In this case, trainees are asked to identify and define problems so that they can later go about figuring out how to solve them—but the skills you'll be evaluating are the "up front" skills of problem finding. It's critical for you, in your role as evaluator of the trainee's progress, to be very clear in your own mind just exactly what it is that you are evaluating. It's very tempting to get carried away with the solutions aspect of class discussion and to lose sight of the learning objectives, which are "to identify..., to define..., and then to integrate...." Evaluation tasks are made so much simpler if you remember to relate them directly to the learning objectives for the trainee.

There are many ways you can evaluate trainees' learning. You can:

- check each trainee's *Trainee Handout 7.2-A* as they enter the training room
- walk around the room as trainees are assembling and ask to see their completed *Trainee Handout 7.2-A*
- ask each trainee to read aloud and talk about his or her responses on *Trainee Handout 7.2-A*
- ask for a volunteer to write a list of problems on the whiteboard or flipchart and initiate discussion with the group about areas of agreement or disagreement
- spend time at each table of trainees to verify that each person has completed *Trainee Handout 7.2-C*
- engage trainees in elaboration of items in the various checklists on *Trainee Handout 7.2-C* in an attempt to elicit better and more responses
- set up "what if" scenarios and ask various trainees what they believe would be the ideal delegation solution

In all of these evaluative situations, interact verbally and nonverbally with your trainees, giving feedback to each on the quality of decision-making—on each's ability in "identifying, defining, and integrating."

TRAINING TIPS	***EXERCISES***
1. Make the point early in the workshop that this is *their* workshop, that is, that the focus of effort is the trainee's own organizational analysis and self-study. Make it clear that you are there to facilitate their best efforts—they are the source of the wisdom, not you.	1. Focus early on the pre-workshop assignment on organizational analysis. Collect the completed *Trainee Handouts 7.2-A,* or have one in your hand as trainees are assembling. Make it obvious by your action that you intend to get right to the heart of *their* contributions.

2. Encourage trainees to be comfortable and spread out their books and papers.

2. Walk around each table, greeting each trainee as he or she is getting settled. Take a position near the center of the room where all can see you and distribute *Trainee Handout 7.2-B* on Minimizing Delegation Risks. This kind of instructional control action sends the signal that you're still in charge, even though the focus will be on their ideas. This kind of control action complements the "get comfortable" invitation and brings the context into balance.

3. Begin interaction with trainees and encourage interaction among trainees by hearing their responses on *Trainee Handout 7.2-A.* Suggest that anyone who didn't get a chance to do this ahead of time might like to get caught up now.

3. The small group set-up of only four trainees per table and plenty of elbow room should help foster interactions and motivate a working atmosphere.

4. After trainees get freer with each other and have been interacting equally, suggest that they tackle *Trainee Handout 7.2-C* on personality factors and skills.

4. This can be done in several ways. Choose a presentation method that fits the mood of the workshop at that moment. If discussion has been lively and you want to cool it off, do this as an individual quiet exercise. On the other hand, if you want to liven up the discussion, ask several trainees to each read a checklist or two aloud and lead the class in discussion. If you need to regain control of an unruly class, read aloud all of the checklists yourself as trainees silently check off the appropriate items.

5. Lead some kind of "integrating" or synthesizing exercise about half an hour before the workshop is due to finish. Send trainees back to the job with plenty of ideas for planning to delegate more effectively.

5. At this point, help the class bring together their insights about the organization and the personality factors they identified as problems. Start their thinking about priorities of attack, systems and procedures that need to be realigned or created, and human and material supports that need to be engaged in order for problems to be solved. Try to prevent the workshop from being too future-focused; its purpose is to stay at that *identification* and *definition* level.

The best and quickest way to keep the focus where you want it is to use the worksheets themselves, building directly upon the trainees' work during class. Ask general questions that generate responses from many trainees, having the effect of magnifying the right direction. Above all, in a class like this, listen to your students!—and be ready to get them back on track according to the stated objectives for learning.

Trainee Handout 7.2-A

PRE-WORKSHOP PREPARATION: ORGANIZATION ANALYSIS

Instructions to the trainee: Anytime during the week immediately preceding the workshop on delegation, take about 30 minutes to analyze your organization according to this model. During training, you will share these responses with other trainees.

Write your responses on this worksheet.

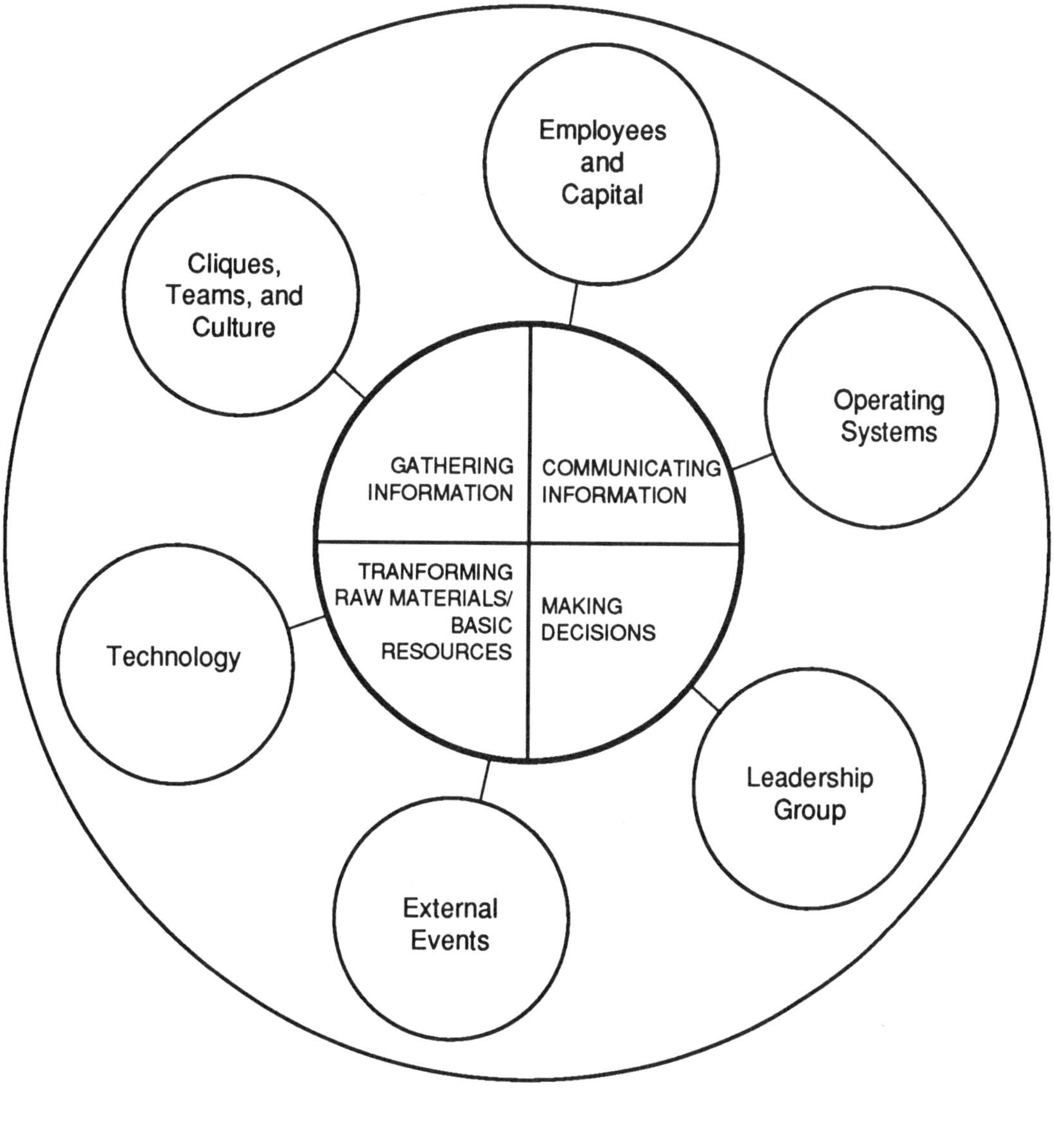

Based on a model of organizational dynamics developed by John P. Kotter, professor at Harvard Business School. From J.P Kotter, *Organizational Dynamics.* © 1978, 1981, by Addison-Wesley Publishing Company, Inc. Reprinted with permission of the publisher.

Trainee Handout 7.2-A (continued)

1. Try to identify where in the organization you have the most difficulty with delegation for any reason at all. This is a basic step in simple identification and definition. Focus first on the inner circle of four key organizational processes and then expand your thinking to include the factors in the outer band that affect the central basic business processes. Feel free to add to or modify this model; it is included here simply to spark your imagination. Your response can include any number of citations.

   Response: ______________________________

   ____

   ____

   ____

2. Explain briefly any citation that you feel might not be clear to other trainees or that you feel has especially broad implications for other managers.

   Response: ______________________________

   ____

   ____

   ____

3. Give your responses a "weight" in terms of how difficult that area is for you to delegate (1 = low, 5 = high). Place a number next to each of your responses in item #1.

4. Draft a brief statement of what you think are the organizational problems that prevent you from being totally effective as a delegater. (In the model, the six factors in the outer circle typically affect one or more of the key processes in the center.)

   Response: ______________________________

   ____

   ____

   ____

Trainee Handout 7.2-B

MINIMIZING DELEGATION RISKS

Managers are hesitant to delegate for two basic reasons:

(1) they fear loss of control, and

(2) they believe their subordinates lack the ability to handle the delegated task.

The following list will help managers who operate under the second reason. Here's how to minimize your risks regarding your subordinate's getting the delegated task done:

1. Assign the authority gradually, one major piece at a time. Be clear in your own mind what pieces you'll give up and what you'll retain. Have a timetable for finally delegating the whole task.
2. Retain the right to final approval. Allow your subordinate to evaluate options and to make major decisions during early stages. Give your subordinate real power and real control, but limit it to the first stages of the decision or project.
3. Set a plan for checkpoints and reports. Stick to it.
4. Delegate the "what" but not the "how." Establish performance and procedural standards and methods. Keep the process elements intact with little flexibility—slowly is okay, but eliminating or greatly modifying methods is not.
5. Give deserved recognition and thanks.
6. Step in to correct errors early before they multiply.

Trainee Handout 7.2-C

MANAGER/SUBORDINATE PERSONALITY INVENTORY

This assessment inventory will help you focus on what can be changed so that delegation becomes easier and more effective. These various checklists will help you isolate the problems and the constraints that work against delegation. Remember, the purpose of this analysis is to *identify* the problem areas.

Check all the items in which a person has difficulty. Complete a separate form for each person in the delegation situation—that is, one for yourself and for each subordinate to whom you intend to delegate work. After this analysis, focus your effort on solving the problem—or at least recognizing it—before attempting to delegate.

One of the major difficulties in delegation is that solutions are often proposed for the wrong problems; it's easy to get confused about what's the problem and what's the solution. This is an exercise in problem finding, not solution finding. It's the first and most important step in successful delegation.

PERSONALITY INVENTORY FOR ________________________
(person's name)

Instructions: Check each specific problem area.

A. Personal Skills
___ 1. Being cooperative
___ 2. Sharing
___ 3. Being persistent
___ 4. Being loyal
___ 5. Being on time
___ 6. Taking initiative
___ 7. Being a follower
___ 8. Being a leader
___ 9. Working for quality
___10. Minding one's own business
___11. Being friendly
___12. Being accessible

B. Intellectual Skills
___1. Curiosity efforts
___2. Mental flexibility
___3. Originality
___4. Depth of knowledge
___5. Breadth of knowledge
___6. Fluency of verbal/oral expression
___7. Fluency of written expression
___8. Thinking on one's feet
___9. Common sense

C. Communication Skills
___1. Listening
___2. Speaking
___3. Writing
___4. Giving feedback
___5. Using feedback

D. Learning Skills
___1. Finding information
___2. Recognizing patterns
___3. Evaluating one's own ability
___4. Monitoring one's own efforts
___5. Working independently
___6. Working collaboratively
___7. Seeking help
___8. Planning
___9. Implementing plans

Trainee Handout 7.2-C (continued)

E. Proble- Solving Skills
- ___1. Finding facts
- ___2. Making inferences
- ___3. Classifying
- ___4. Defining options
- ___5. Modification
- ___6. Analysis
- ___7. Synthesis
- ___8. Evaluation
- ___9. Adoption

F. Manipulative Skills
- ___1. Visual, auditory, tactile acuity
- ___2. Ability to focus and attend to cues
- ___3. Eye-hand coordination
- ___4. Finger dexterity
- ___5. Ability to accurately repeat motions

G. Mathematical Skills
- ___1. Accounting
- ___2. Computing
- ___3. Estimating
- ___4. Projecting
- ___5. Solving equations
- ___6. Using statistics
- ___7. Creating graphs
- ___8. Interpreting graphs

H. Attitude (Affective) Skills
- ___1. Interest
- ___2. Motivation
- ___3. Integrity
- ___4. Consonant value system with company values

TRAINING PLAN 7.3

How to Teach Managers and Supervisors to Solve Problems

This training plan is an outline of the key elements, methods, and procedures required to teach managers and supervisors one specific part of problem solving, that is, the search for and generation of alternative solutions. Most management trainers agree that managers learn to solve problems by solving problems, and that the best kind of class to run on problem solving is a class in which a real business problem is solved during class according to some systematic problem-solving methodology.

There are some trainers, however, who believe that *simulated business problems* can provide the same opportunity to learn problem-solving skills—that problem-solving methodology is generic, and that as long as a trainee's work group is learning the methodology together at the same time and in the same context, the problem-solving skills will be able to be practiced back on the job. Advocates of this approach believe that the shared experience forms the foundation for ongoing willingness and ability to work together to solve actual problems back in the workplace, and that the key to learning problem-solving skills is the intensity and reality of the problem-solving experience while in the learning situation.

In recent years, a network of training companies has sprung up across the country to teach problem solving, teamwork, and other leadership skills through "outward bound" -type programs, survival training, and sports psychology weekends. Proponents of this kind of simulated problem training believe that the elements of taking educated risks, overcoming fear, stretching one's capability, and depending on one's peers for physical and emotional support can and do transfer readily to the essential management and supervisory task of problem solving in the real workplace.

This training plan uses one small example from a sports psychology weekend to illustrate how to teach the essential problem-solving skill of generating alternative solutions. Because this subject is one in which there is still considerable debate about the pros and cons, I will suggest points of disagreement and highlight the issues you'll need to consider as you think about possibly teaching problem solving through this kind of delivery method.

As in other training plans, this plan begins with objectives for training as well as objectives for the learner, and with evaluation methods tied to the learning objectives. Because this training plan is only a small part of a larger curriculum on problem solving, the objectives are for only this lesson's focus on "generation of alternative solutions." In this training plan, you'll see the wedding of a traditional problem-solving model and the nontraditional instructional delivery mode of a sports psychology weekend in the mountains with the management team. The intent of this training plan is to show you the possibilities for effective management training using this unconventional approach by alerting you to the training challenges in the design of this one small part of the program.

OVERVIEW OF TRAINING METHODOLOGY

The critical issue in choosing this training methodology over conventional classroom teaching is the issue of what you believe the manager's job actually is. If you believe that the manager's job is characterized by reflective and systematic planning, you would probably not choose sports psychology as a training medium. If, on the other hand, you believe that the manager's job is characterized by discontinuity, quick decisions, dealing with weak links, and an action orientation, you might consider it as a medium of choice to deliver instruction in problem-solving skills.

Coupled with your belief about the nature of managerial work is your perspective on learning. If you believe that the skills of problem solving are best learned through cognitive studies emphasizing logical and rational approaches, you would not choose sports psychology as a delivery context. On the other hand, if you believe that problem-solving skills are best learned through an experiential medium, you might consider it. As in any other kind of training, you must make the key decision early in the design of instruction about the match of the message to the medium.

In choosing sports psychology, you run the additional risk of having the medium become the message. Unless this kind of training delivery is approached with the same care in instructional design as more conventional training, the real situation (i.e., business situation) which the training simulates fades into the background. Trainees can easily get carried away with the immediacy of the physical challenges and camaraderie that accompany the sports-like tasks confronting them. The obvious immediate goals of crossing the rapids, making the leap off the rock, or scaling the wall tend to become ends in themselves unless there's careful instruction related to the business goals driving the course in the first place.

Proponents of this kind of training tell you that the experience of literally leaping together into unknown territory or being led blindfolded down a rocky ravine by a fellow manager will help you to make leaps into risky business territory or to innately trust your peers. Opponents will tell you that you're asking for separated rotator cuffs, disability payments, costly lawsuits, invasion of privacy, and going against one's religious beliefs. The skeptics will tell you that simulated exercises bring simulated trust.

The crux of the matter regarding methodology is to choose appropriately and design it for learning. To help you see the value in choosing sports psychology and a weekend in the mountains as a methodology for teaching and learning problem-solving skills, this training plan focuses on just one small segment of instruction in problem solving.

It uses the exercise of getting the team over a 13-foot wall as a way to learn the part of problem solving that illustrates the skill of generating alternative solutions. Almost any problem-solving methodology you can find in training books everywhere breaks the skill of problem-solving down into parts generally called "problem finding" and "solution finding." In most problem-solving schemes, "generating alternative solutions" comes at the beginning of the solution-finding phase. In this exercise on "the wall," we make this assumption: that other problem-finding skills have been taught earlier in the weekend, using other trust exercises and sharing tasks typically built into such weekends. This lesson uses the wall exercise as a simulation in solution finding, specifically in generating alternative solutions.

TIME REQUIRED TO DELIVER THIS TRAINING

40 minutes plus 10 minutes debriefing several hours later, including 5 minutes orientation, 10 minutes planning time, 20 minutes of "the wall," and 5 minutes wrap-up upon completion of the exercise.

TRAINEE LEVEL

Any level manager or supervisor. This kind of exercise is best done with a small (6-10) group of peers or persons from the same business organization. No particular fitness level or sports acumen are required. General good health is required, although persons with minor problems such as trick knees, weak ankles, or bursitis often participate. (In fact, part of the challenge of this exercise is to deal effectively with the "weak links" in order to accomplish the task.)

TRAINING OBJECTIVES

- To present a model of solution-generating through challenges posed by "the wall." (Use the "Keys to Generating Options" in the model on *Trainee Handout 7.3*).
- To challenge trainees to all get over the wall in only 30 minutes.
- To lead trainees safely over the wall (it's your responsibility as the trainer to guarantee the safety of the equipment and the task).
- To keep time.
- To lead trainees in articulating what the challenges were.
- To lead trainees in specifying the possible solutions.
- To lead trainees in identifying correlations between wall challenges and business challenges.

LEARNING OBJECTIVES FOR THE TRAINEE

- To get everyone over the 13-foot wall, including the last person, within 30 minutes.
- To identify a variety of ways to meet the challenge.
- To articulate pros and cons of the options.
- To specify plans, systems, and supports that worked or didn't work and why.
- To identify the universal truths inherent in this exercise and state how the results of meeting the challenges of the wall translate into job-related actions.

METHODS TO EVALUATE TRAINEE'S PROGRESS

Evaluating trainees' progress in this kind of fast-moving, active, physically challenging task seems to come naturally. As trainees are working feverishly to get all persons over the wall, those already over yell assurances and encouragement to those helping others along, great hurrahs explode when the next trainee makes it over, and loud and frequent feedback comes from many quarters as the exercise progresses. You will undoubtedly add your own enthusiastic words of encouragement and congratulations.

Your task as instructor is to keep the process moving along safely. During your five-minute introduction to the exercise, urge trainees to pay special attention to correct knee-bending, lifting, stretching, and pulling. Suggest that during their ten-minute planning time, they take into account the weight of various people and any physical weakness (tennis elbows, back problems, and so on) that might require special planning or techniques.

It is also your job to be sure that trainees understand that they are to be looking for alternatives and paying attention to the mental processes they're going through as they pursue their goal of getting over the top. Be sure that they understand they'll be called upon later at the debriefing session to talk about "process" issues.

As a way to make your evaluation job easier, you might want to note the number of different solutions or solution approaches that you observe. During the debriefing session later (e.g., after dinner), these notes will come in handy as you help trainees see the problem-solving model that underlies the physical exercise. Immediately after the wall exercise, let trainees "cool off" physically and mentally without pressure to think a great deal about the nature of problem solving; tell them that you expect their analysis and feedback at the debriefing session later. (On a typical sports psychology weekend, the wall would be one of many exercises. The evening debriefing session might include analysis of several different exercises.)

Sports psychology is often seen to be at its best here—the psychological and physical support of team members, the roar of the approving crowd, the exhilaration of winning, the motivation to do more and exert more completely. This is also formative evaluation at its best—feedback informing instruction, motivating more and better learning.

TRAINING TIPS	***EXERCISES***
1. Challenge the group to plan for and get over the 13-foot wall in the specified time (30 minutes for 6-8 people). Suggest that the group from now on think as a team.	1. Point out that there is a platform for standing on directly on the other side of the wall near the top. Point out that there are no handles to grab to. Invite trainees to inspect the wall.
2. Review the objectives of this lesson, that is, to generate options for solving the problem of getting over the wall. Take about five minutes to do this, being sure that each trainee understands that there's an intended correlation between the wall and the workplace. Read the "Keys to Generating Options" (*Trainee Handout 7.3*) to the trainees before trainees begin to work on the problem.	2. Post an enlarged copy of *Trainee Handout 7.3* on a nearby tree or out-of-the way section of the wall to remind trainees that there's more to this exercise than just getting over the wall. Allow trainees the chance to express doubts, anxieties, frustration, or misunderstanding before they get started. Suggest that there will be obstacles both in the planning and the execution of the task, and that those who encounter obstacles should make mental note of them and be prepared to discuss them after the exercise.
3. Encourage group cohesion by suggesting that they focus intently on the planning phase (10 minutes) so that each person will get over the wall. Part of the challenge of the exercise is for the group to maximize its own resources.	3. If the group leaders haven't noticed, point out that some people have stronger backs/legs/arms/shoulders than others. All bodies do not work equally well as human ladders. Challenge them to remember how they dealt with the weak links. Suggest that they be ready to find solutions in unexpected places—that talent for a new task can be uncovered in a variety of ways. Awareness of differences is important.
4. Keep track of the time; tell the group when it's half-time (i.e., 15 minutes remaining to completion)	4. Be firm about the end of the 10 minutes of planning time. Get them off planning and onto execution as fast as you can. Don't let them get "analysis paralysis"—get them into action quickly.

5. Conduct a five-minute wrap-up session after the time is up and the task is accomplished.

5. At this time, your task is to go with the flow of their enthusiasm but gently remind them that you'll see them all later at the debriefing session. Don't let them lose sight of the objectives regarding problem solving and solution finding as they go off to the rest of their day's activities. Refer briefly —even just by gesturing in the direction of the posted "Keys to Generating Options"—to the learning objectives for this exercise.

This exercise isn't finished until the debriefing is done. Before they leave the site of the wall, it's your job to "set" their thought direction so that each person can think through the exercise and be prepared to contribute her or his own interpretations at the debriefing session.

6. Later in the day, conduct a 10-minute debriefing session. Ask the trainees how many different options they tried, even briefly. Ask trainees to talk about the pros and cons of each option and to say why some options failed. Ask trainees if they can see any similarities to work problems and the approach to solving problems.

6. To maximize the time spent in debriefing, get right to the point of the exercise. Let the trainees relive some of the exciting moments of the wall exercise as they are congregating before the session begins. Smile with them, but don't get too involved in the diversion.

It's up to you to bring the discussion back to the objectives for the lesson. The best way to do this is to simply ask trainees a series of questions about problem solving and team effort, eventually focusing on their generating solution options. Use *Trainee Handout 7.3* (posted on a tree or the wall) as a "cue card" for yourself if you need it to be sure that you cover the content of generating solution options. All of this takes a very short time, so your best defense is thorough preparation of the questions you intend to ask them. Use the worksheet as a handout if you want to send the trainees away with a reminder of the exercise. (If you work with the handout during the debriefing, it will take you more than 10 minutes. The best way to meet your time requirements for cost-effective training delivery is for you to be thoroughly prepared so that you can quickly and systematically lead trainees through an analysis of solutions.)

Trainee Handout 7.3

KEYS TO GENERATING OPTIONS

A problem can be seen as separated roughly into two parts, the "WHAT IS" part and the "WHAT SHOULD BE" part. In developing your skills in problem solving, you should concentrate considerable effort first in an analysis of the WHAT IS part, and secondly in a somewhat imaginative speculation about the WHAT SHOULD BE part.

This worksheet suggests several keys to generating options for solutions. It is part of the WHAT SHOULD BE part. These are the key operations for each specific solution. First, briefly describe or give a name to each possible solution. Then, for each option, follow these steps:

1. Specify what has to be changed to get to WHAT SHOULD BE. Consider systems, resources, products, services, standards, performance, job design, workflow, and relationships.
2. Find out if some employee has special expertise in this area.
3. Find out if some employee has had similar experiences.
4. Specify the personnel gaps you have regarding successful problem solving. Consider personal limitations and weak links.
5. Specify where to go to find information you need.
6. For each option, specify:
   - costs
   - business risks
   - political acceptability
   - technical feasibility
   - probability of success

TRAINING PLAN 7.4

Training Managers and Supervisors How to Be Leaders

This training plan is an outline of the key elements, methods, and procedures required to teach managers and supervisors how to be leaders through one kind of leadership training, *self-analysis through peer group analysis using video vignettes.* This outline is structured to enable the trainer to create lesson plans, an instructor guide, or a course outline from it.

Leadership, by all accounts, is demonstrated most often by a capacity to be intuitive and communicative, by an experience-based ability to ask the right questions, figure things out and get things done. Many would say that leadership training is a waste of time, that leaders burst forth when conditions are right for a particular kind of talent, and that leadership is more of an art than a skill to be learned. Many students of leadership believe that it is so dependent on context or situation that a single body of knowledge or skill development simply cannot possibly exist. Many believe that an individual's highly personal psychological need and desire to lead are what drives a leader to leadership position, and that these things cannot be taught.

So the questions become, "What do we teach people about leadership?" and "How do we teach people to become leaders?" Most organizations are interested in cultivating leaders, and are wrestling with the list of characteristics that their own leaders should possess. As companies become flatter with fewer management levels and more project teams, the characteristics and competencies of leadership change. What used to be a solid value regarding the probable accumulation of corporate wisdom in a few individuals who were clearly seen as *the* leaders has been steadily changing in recent years so that this value now seems to more and more place the accumulation of corporate wisdom within organizations and peer groups. The concept of leadership is indeed hard to define and even harder to develop a training methodology for teaching it.

So we return to the questions, What do we teach? How do we do it? and Is it worth the effort? This training plan makes the assumption that because leadership is such an individual thing, the best approach to teaching managers how to become leaders is a self-analysis approach. In this kind of training, honest and accurate self-analysis is the goal, using video vignettes and character and style studies to provide the trainees with a focused opportunity to take a look at recognized leaders in action, thereby becoming better at self analysis.

This training plan makes the assumption that it is worth the effort because leaders are both essential and inevitable, and they are especially important in meeting today's changing organizational and human resource challenges. The ability to be a leader comes from both an accumulation of integrated experiences, a strong sense of self, and a drive to lead. In each of these elements of leadership the ability to analyze oneself is of great importance, and this is what this training plan attempts to facilitate.

A training plan begins with objectives for training itself as well as objectives for the learner, and with evaluation methods tied to the learning objectives. Training points related to the content of a manager's or supervisor's area of responsibility provide the foundation for topics covered during training. Sample exercises suggest ways to deliver this kind of instruction. Helpful worksheets follow the training plan.

OVERVIEW OF TRAINING METHODOLOGY

There are several assumptions we make before embarking on leadership training. They are that:

1. Managers and supervisors want to be leaders
2. The company wants managers and supervisors to be leaders
3. Leadership is largely a matter of individual style, and leadership is enhanced when a person acts in accordance with the strengths of his or her particular style
4. There are some generic leadership skills that can be taught, such as communication skills, team-building skills, and quality management skills.

Before designing leadership training, it's important to think about the difference between management and leadership. For example, it's fairly easy to make a list of what a manager does at work and of what skills and behaviors the job description states. It's very difficult, on the other hand, to make a list of what a leader does. And it's this difference that makes leadership training so tricky.

This training plan will not outline generic management skills, but will rather focus on the *skills of self-analysis* in an attempt to improve a would-be leader's integrity and sense of self. If, in fact, a leader's job is to figure things out and get things done in the broadest sense and at the highest level and in the most risky environments, then a clear sense of self—one's style, limitations, and strengths—is an appropriate goal. The kind of training presented here can lead toward that end.

TIME REQUIRED TO DELIVER THIS TRAINING

3 hours
Probably delivered as a block of time either morning, afternoon, or evening during a two- or three-day leadership training course. Time requirements could expand considerably if the members of the class do their own videotaping or have themselves videotaped to use in class. In this case, taping time should be added to the three hours of class time.

TRAINEE LEVEL

Any level manager or supervisor who wants to be a leader.
This methodology works best with people in the same organization, i.e., who work together frequently.

TRAINING OBJECTIVES

- To show four to six 10-15-minute video clips ("video vignettes") of well-known leaders who clearly illustrate style differences, for example, facilitator, dictator, visionary, power broker, judge, analyzer, big talker, negotiator, organizer, problem solver, and so forth.
- To lead general discussion of leadership types represented by the video vignettes, suggesting that trainees try to identify their own leadership type or style, either related to the videos or some other entirely different type or style.
  Note: Commerical videotapes are available from many training companies that feature well-known national figures (presidents, prime ministers, generals, senators, CEOs) as leadership types. Use some of these tapes if you can find ones that illustrate your own ideas of leadership. Check into several sources before doing

your own taping. Adjust your training time accordingly, or stick to the 15-minute limit by editing any longer commercial tape. Do your own taping only if you have an in-house video studio and good equipment and time in which to capture clear examples of different leadership styles among your own managers at work.

- To lead trainees in self-analysis through questionnaire/lists as individual exercises. (See *Trainee Handouts 7.4-A, 7.4-B, 7.4-C* as options.)
- To lead trainees in self-analysis and feedback through questionnaire/lists through peer pairs. (Use *Trainer's Worksheet 7.4-D*, and *Trainee Handouts 7.4-E* and *7.4-F.*)

LEARNING OBJECTIVES FOR THE TRAINEE

- To differentiate various leadership styles after viewing 4-6 video vignettes of famous leaders.
- To identify characteristic behaviors of leaders associated with each various type of leader.
- To engage in a self-analysis of one's own leadership style and behaviors using several worksheets that represent different approaches to the self-analysis task.
- To pair off with another trainee to give feedback on that person's leadership style by using *Trainee Handout 7.4-E.*
- To pair off with another trainee to receive feedback on your own leadership style by using *Trainee Handout 7.4-F.*
- To discover your own leadership profile, incorporating the results of your self-analysis and the feedback from your trainee peer.

METHODS TO EVALUATE TRAINEE'S PROGRESS

Your role as evaluator in this kind of self-analysis, somewhat psychologically risky exercise is to give trainees constant feedback on the quality of their analysis efforts. Be careful not to comment on the nature of their self-revelations—for example, don't say things like, "Aha! We all thought you were too organized all along" or "That proves you're not very trusting." It's very easy to get caught up in the characteristics that are being talked about and to give evaluative feedback on these characteristics instead of on the *process* of analysis. Remember, you're trying to teach the skill of self-analysis, not to change the basic personalities of your trainees.

Here are some pointers regarding the analysis process.

Understand just what analysis is: it is the breaking down of material into its constituent parts, the determination of the way the material is organized, and the identification of relationships among the parts within the overall organization. Analysis is a cognitive skill; it can be taught, learned, and measured. For a more thorough discussion of analysis, see section 4.00 of Part II, *Taxonomy of Educational Objectives, Book 1: Cognitive Domain*, by B.S. Bloom, 1956, and the general discussion in Chapter 2 of this book, especially pages 71 and 72.

Thus, when you attempt to evaluate the process you see going on before you during this training, you'll want to pay attention to the *parts*, the *organization*, and the *relationships*. Evaluating the analysis process is akin to being able to spot the differences between structure and function, "anatomy" and "physiology," and to determine how it all works together.

Interject your own objective point of view often during training because in this kind of introspective exercise, it is very difficult for trainees to remain objective—especially as they begin to get feedback from their peers. Suggest to a trainee that he or she might have missed a certain part of the scenario (e.g., an important characteristic of an altruistic leader on the video); for example, has misinterpreted the place of talent for consensus-building in the larger organization of team-building, or that the trainees as a group passed right over the relationship between vision and measurement in a certain video vignette. Throughout the video portion of the training, try to establish the elements of analysis through active feedback to individual trainees and to the group. This kind of evaluative feedback builds capacity and competence (formative evaluation).

As you progress through the lessons on analysis of the trainees' own styles of leadership and the individual exercise, again keep your analysis model in mind as you give feedback. At this point, be sure to give plenty of positive feedback to reinforce the good analysis that your trainees are doing. They'll need a solid foundation of confidence as they go on to the paired exercise.

Here are some typical kinds of analysis errors:

- *Gross errors*—totally "missing the boat," not being able to figure out primary and secondary characteristics or relationships, misidentification
- *Errors of inadequacy*—overlooking some parts or relationships, "sins of omission," narrow interpretation, shallow perception
- *Errors of excess*—seeing too many "trees" and therefore missing "the forest," a tendency to concentrate on form at the expense of substance, crowding one's analysis approach with too many biases and too much "excess baggage," losing focus and time by making the task more complicated than it is

As an evaluator, always keep your training objectives and the trainees' learning objectives in mind. In this case, that means to pay attention to how those trainees are learning the skill of self-analysis. The foregoing discussion gave you suggestions about the analysis part; the ensuing discussion gives you some ideas about the "self" dimension of evaluating self-analysis skill-building.

Again, you need to remember that you are not evaluating the quality of "self" ; you're evaluating the quality of self-analysis. In this training plan, trainees' self-analysis skills are most acutely tested and demonstrated in the paired exercise. Your role as evaluator in this exercise should focus on the giving and receiving of feedback.

Use *Trainee Handouts 7.4-E* and *7.4-F* as checklists against which to evaluate trainees as they give and receive feedback. Pay special attention to how they receive feedback from a peer; this is often an area of weakness in managers who would be leaders—they can usually give it more easily than they can receive it! Intervene often with praise ("good," "keep going," "good comment," "right on target") and with suggestions for correction. And when a trainee obviously tries to correct a response, notice it and compliment the trainee on a good try.

Structuring this self-analysis feedback exercise in pairs means more work for you as you get around the room to all of the pairs, but it also means that each trainee has the opportunity for maximum practice of both giving and receiving feedback and of getting constructive evaluation during the exercise.

It's the guided, evaluative, peer-supported skill-building environment that will yield the best results in leadership training—if you believe that leadership essentially requires a strong sense of self, the ability to integrate experiences, and the drive to lead. Knowing oneself is a fundamental prerequisite for leadership.

TRAINING TIPS	***EXERCISES***
1. Choose video vignettes that clearly demonstrate distinct leadership styles. Ask trainees to write down style characteristics of each featured leader, being as analytical as possible, noting how the exhibited characteristics in each person are integrated. Tell trainees to make notes as they view the video.	1. View each 10-15-minute video vignette, pausing for a minute or two after each to allow trainees to write and refine their lists of characteristics. Wait until all video leaders have been viewed before starting the analysis discussion.
2. Give them cues to get their minds "set" for this task. Suggest these typical leadership roles: coach, mentor, monitor, teacher, prophet, cheerleader, visionary, company commander, mother, priest, attorney, or choreographer. Suggest to trainees that leader characteristics are found in persons in many roles.	2. Suggest that they try to look beyond the obvious characteristics and try to also find the more subtle and therefore more distinguishing traits each leader shows. Challenge trainees to see the differences between "determined" and "persevering"; between "forceful" and "influential"; between "motivating" and "demanding." Get them started by stretching their range of perception regarding analysis.
3. Guide a general discussion about leadership style, encouraging an ever-increasing focus on individual characteristics. Get trainees to the point of introspection, in preparation for the next exercise. Do this by having them isolate and evaluate unique characteristics.	3. Start with the "big picture" of each leader on the video. Do them one by one, that is, finish one before going on to the next. Let the discussion continue freely for a few minutes, then bring the group around to thinking about what very specific traits this particular leader has, and about the unique way in which all these traits work together in an integrated way to form his or her special style of leadership.
4. Lead trainees in an individual self-analysis exercise using a structured style list such as *Trainee Handouts 7.4-A, 7.4-B, 7.4-C.* Many such lists are readily available commercially, or develop your own worksheets as examples. Ask trainees to hold onto their responses until the peer pair exercise when they might choose to share their analyses with their partners.	4. Ask trainees to mark the descriptors that most nearly match their own personal style. Suggest that there are no rights and wrongs; that the important thing is for leaders to know what makes them tick.

5. Facilitate the pairing of trainees for the purpose of sharing information. The trick here is to keep the exercise non-defensive, analytical, and supportive. Lead the group in pairs through the exercise of first recording their own self-analysis to the items on *Trainee Handouts 7.4-D* and *7.4-E*; and second, recording how each trainee views his or her pair partner.	5. Ask trainees to pair off, in any way—with the person seated next to you, behind you, born in same Zodiac sign, with whom you seldom have any professional contact, and so on. Tell them that the goal of this exercise is to share information about themselves, in order to understand themselves better as leaders. Review with them the guidelines for giving and receiving feedback, *Trainee Handouts 7.4-F* and *7.4-G*. Use these as handouts to each trainee before they break into pairs.
6. Facilitate the pairs' giving and receiving feedback on each trainee's individual leadership style.	6. Remind trainees to follow the feedback guidelines, keeping in mind that the point of this exercise is to share information that will help individual managers understand themselves and their leadership styles better. Visit each pair to be sure that each is receiving feedback in a productive way. (It's always easier to give than to receive.) Interject your own comments only when you feel that the feedback session is not specific enough—stay focused on the quality of analysis, encouraging trainees to work toward getting an accurate sense of their "integrated selves" from this training session.
7. If necessary, bring the trainees back into a single group to give them a sense of unity of purpose at the end of class. This is not necessary if the session seems finished at the end of pair feedback.	7. A good wrap-up technique is to review the guidelines for receiving feedback and the model for analysis (parts, organization, relationships). If you still need finality to the training, call on one or two especially good trainees to share their own newly self-discovered leadership profile with the group.

Trainee Handout 7.4-A

A SELF-ANALYSIS CHECKLIST FOR PREFERRED LEADERSHIP BEHAVIOR

This handout is organized into three columns of typical preferred behaviors associated with three leadership styles. Use this as an individual exercise by checking each descriptor that applies to your own leadership style. Add more descriptors to each column, or add more columns of descriptors according to your own unique organization.

There are 10 descriptors in each column. When you've finished the exercise, total your checkmarks for each column and make a bar graph indicating the profile of what you believe your leadership style to be.

	✓	FACILITATOR	✓	DICTATOR	✓	DIAGNOSTICIAN
1		trusting		directive		analytical
2		supportive		decisive		detailed
3		patient		controlling		cautious
4		organized		powerful		systematic
5		encouraging		noisy		factual
6		motivating		up-front		explicit
7		developmental		competitive		perfectionist
8		caring		demanding		close-to-the-vest
9		stimulating		active		rational
10		problem solver		achiever		inquisitive
		TOTAL (FACILITATOR)		TOTAL (DICTATOR)		TOTAL (DIAGNOSTICIAN)

SELF-ANALYSIS PROFILE OF PREFERRED LEADERSHIP BEHAVIOR

Note: Construct your own leadership behavior profile using totals from each column above.

10						
9						
8						
7						
6						
5						
4						
3						
2						
1						
	FACILITATOR		DICTATOR		DIAGNOSTICIAN	

Trainee Handout 7.4-B

SELF-ANALYSIS ACCORDING TO MYERS-BRIGGS TYPE INDICATOR

The Myers-Briggs Type Indicator and MBTI are registered trademarks of Consulting Psychologists Press, Inc. These products are sold widely to educational institutions and businesses for a variety of uses in counseling, career guidance, and organizational improvement efforts.

The MBTI is the most widely-used measure of personality preferences. It is used often in management development work both in the personnel department and by trainers to identify leadership style, improve teamwork, resolve conflict, support career development, and improve communication.It is self-administered and requires about twenty minutes to take.

Scoring sheets and interpretive information are also available from the publisher. The MBTI provides four bipolar scales that can be reported as continuous scores or reduced to a coded response type. The four scales are:

Extroversion ———— Introversion
Sensing ———— Intuition
Thinking ———— Feeling
Judging ———— Perceiving

According to the catalog description of the MBTI scales, the scales indicate relative preferences for:

Extroversion—Introversion index reflects whether a person is oriented primarily toward the outer world or toward the inner world of ideas;

Sensing—Intuition index describes an interest in perceiving the objects, events, and details of the present moment or the possibilities, abstractions, and insights imagined in the future;

Thinking—Feeling index describes a preference for making rational judgments by using objective and logical analysis or by weighing the relative person-centered values;

Judging—Perceiving index describes a preference for organizing and controlling events or the outside world or for observing and understanding such events.

According to Myers and Briggs, the various combinations of these preferences result in 16 personality types.

Trainee Handout 7.4-C

THREE WAYS TO THINK ABOUT LEADER BEHAVIOR

In addition to the more familiar kinds of leadership style assessment devices, these three representative approaches described here indicate the range of possible ways to think about leader behavior. These three references are included to spark your imagination about how to train employees to provide leadership.

M. Sashkin, **LEADER BEHAVIOR QUESTIONNAIRE (LBQ)**
Available from Organization Design and Development, Inc., 2002 Renaissance Blvd., Suite 100, King of Prussia, PA 19406

The LBQ has 50 items measuring ten different leadership scales. In general, it measures the extent to which the respondent uses visionary leadership behaviors and possesses the personal characteristics required of visionary leaders. LBQ identifies six general patterns of leadership behavior characteristic of the visionary leader:

- the charismatic individual
- the visionary thinker
- the organizational thinker
- the visionary charismatic
- the organizational architect
- the organizational planner

The ten different scales include:

- focus
- trust
- risk
- empowerment
- organizational leadership
- communication
- respect for self and others
- bottom-line orientation
- length of vision span
- cultural leadership

The LBQ comes in a set that includes one self-assessment and two feedback instruments.

E.H. Porter, **STRENGTH DEPLOYMENT INVENTORY (SDI)** *Group & Organization Studies,* March 1976 (1) (1), 121-123, published by University Associates, LaJolla, CA.

The SDI is a self-administered instrument based on the notion that a person's motivation for seeking interactions with others is the gratification offered by interpersonal relationships. Strengths are defined as appropriate behaviors.

The SDI yields three scores on how an individual uses his or her strengths when things are going well and three scores on behavior when faced with conflict. The instrument requires respondents to choose from three sentence-completion statements, with resulting various point values.

Trainee Handout 7.4-C (continued)

Three scales include these interpersonal dimensions:

altruistic—nurturing
assertive—directing
analytic—autonomizing

A sample sentence completion exercise is:
"It is most like me to...

1. develop the ability of others to make decisions
2. take the lead to influence decisions
3. study thoroughly fact, opinion, and rumor before making a decision"

S.P. Springer and G. Deutsch, **BRAIN LATERALIZATION** *Left Brain, Right Brain.* W.H. Freeman & Co., San Francisco, 1981.

Neurological and physiological studies in the 1970s resulted in a proliferation of works that attempted to apply the remarkable results of research on the human brain to a variety of practical purposes, including training.

Since those early days we have come to refer to people as "left brained" or "right brained," or at least have described people's behaviors as left-brained or right-brained behavior. In a nutshell, this is what brain lateralization means: certain kinds of thought seem to be controlled by or dominated by one hemisphere of the brain or the other. Here are some of the most common descriptors:

Left Hemisphere	Right Hemisphere
verbal	nonverbal
sequential	simultaneous
analytical	synthesizing
rational	intuitive
Western thought	Eastern thought
convergent	divergent
digital	analogic
deductive	imaginative
discrete	continuous
concrete	abstract
realistic	impulsive
directed	free
explicit	tacit
objective	subjective

Trainer's Worksheet 7.4-D

PEER PAIRS FEEDBACK AND DISCUSSION WORKSHEET

Use this worksheet and *Trainee Handout 7.4-E* as an assessment instrument for analysis work in pairs, as in the final exercise of the leadership style training session. Give each trainee one of these Peer Pairs Feedback Rating Forms. Tell them to fold it lengthwise on the dotted line. First, ask trainees to give themselves a rating on each item, then give the folded paper to their peer partner. Next, the peer partner rates the trainee on each item also, but without looking at the self-assessment ratings. Use this five-point scale:

to a very small extent	to a small extent	to some extent	to a great extent	to a very great extent
1	2	3	4	5

Conclude this exercise by giving and receiving feedback within the peer pair, comparing responses item by item. Approximately 20 items are suggested.

Trainee Handout 7.4-E

PEER PAIRS FEEDBACK—Evaluation Criteria

Create your own items or use these leadership-related ones:

1. Accurately assesses work situations
2. Communicates a clear vision
3. Works with others to set work directions
4. Inspires others to make commitments
5. Mobilizes others to work towards goals
6. Develops workable teams
7. Demonstrates support for quality implementation
8. Manages conflict
9. Manages change
10. Recognizes contributions of others
11. Shows integrity
12. Operates from an adequate information base
13. Promotes the development of individual talent
14. Cares about employees as persons
15. Has courage
16. Is flexible regarding plans
17. Deals effectively with diversity in the workplace
18. Exercises mature judgment
19. Communicates standards
20. Builds followers

Peer Pairs Feedback—Rating Form

to a very small extent	to a small extent	to some extent	to a great extent	to a very great extent
1	2	3	4	5

Instructions: Rate yourself, and have your partner rate you on 20 leadership items according to this five-point scale. Fold this rating form so that your partner cannot see your responses. Use this completed form for discussion and feedback, comparing item by item.

Trainee Handout 7.4-E (continued)

	1 2 3 4 5		1 2 3 4 5
1.	______________	1.	______________
2.	______________	2.	______________
3.	______________	3.	______________
4.	______________	4.	______________
5.	______________	5.	______________
6.	______________	6.	______________
7.	______________	7.	______________
8.	______________	8.	______________
9.	______________	9.	______________
10.	______________	10.	______________
11.	______________	11.	______________
12.	______________	12.	______________
13.	______________	13.	______________
14.	______________	14.	______________
15.	______________	15.	______________
16.	______________	16.	______________
17.	______________	17.	______________
18.	______________	18.	______________
19.	______________	19.	______________
20.	______________	20.	______________

Trainee Handout 7.4-F

GUIDELINES FOR GIVING FEEDBACK

Feedback is the attempt to reduce distortions between the message a person intends to convey and the message another person actually receives. It is given and received in a spirit of personal learning and improvement.

These are guidelines for *giving* feedback:

1. Get agreement from both partners that they are willing to both give and receive feedback.
2. Make your comments descriptive, not evaluative.
3. Describe behaviors and actions, not total impressions.
4. Make specific suggestions, not general ones.
5. Include both positive and negative observations.
6. Begin your comments with yourself, that is, "I believe that you..." rather than with "You did...." Don't accuse; simply report what you have noticed.
7. Maintain smiling eye contact with your partner.
8. Maintain an open, somewhat informal posture; pay attention to your body language and send a nonverbal message of acceptance.
9. Beware of your own biases, attitudes, and hidden agendas, and don't get trapped in your own frailties.
10. Be considerate of the receiver's feelings, readiness, trust level, tolerance limits, and self-esteem. Don't press on if the emotional climate needs fixing.

Trainee Handout 7.4-G

GUIDELINES FOR RECEIVING FEEDBACK

Feedback is the attempt to reduce distortions between the message a person intends to convey and the message another person actually receives. It is given and received in a spirit of personal learning and improvement.

These are guidelines for *receiving* feedback:

1. Pay attention; listen actively; remain open-minded.
2. Ask for clarification and elaboration of specific points if you want them.
3. Request descriptive information on specific points. (If your actions need changing, it will be much easier to make change if you have an accurate description of very specific points.)
4. Be willing to hear both positive and negative reports.
5. Acknowledge feedback. (It's hard for some people to give feedback.)
6. Ask for your partner's ideas on specific improvement tactics if you believe that you could benefit from them.
7. If you've had enough, tell your partner by saying, "Thanks, that's enough feedback on this item," and continue to the next item. Keep it item-specific.
8. Avoid being defensive. (This is feedback, not salary review.)
9. Be aware of your body language and attitudes so that your partner doesn't become defensive about giving feedback.
10. Sort out and select which elements of the feedback you will act upon. Do this soon after the training session and in private.

Chapter 8

Training Managers and Supervisors to Manage Information

It used to be that those at the head of operations saw their locus of power, control, leadership, and ultimate worth to the company in their responsibility to plan and direct the work of others. Authority and competency meant being at the top of an organization chart with more numbers of people and dollars of resource control than other managers and supervisors. Managers had privilege and proximity which regular employees didn't have. Climbing the ladder of success usually meant getting to be a manager and rising on the organization chart.

Today, managers and supervisors are looking at things from a different perspective. Organizations have less people in them, levels are fewer, functions are integrated, electronics have brought people into each other's planning and operations spaces, information access is broad, and empowered employees are working smarter and harder to stay that way. Ladders are shorter: old metaphors have changed. Perhaps the linked chain is a better metaphor for the avenue of organizational success today.

Availability of information has challenged those at the head of organizations to be quick, flexible, and correct in ways never dreamed of a generation ago. According to Ken Olsen, CEO, Digital Equipment Corporation, "Power no longer comes from telling people what to do; it comes from knowing what goes on." Members of work groups and teams often each take turns doing each other's work, being leaders, subject matter experts, negotiators and process experts as they cooperate to meet their goals; each has access to and responsibility for a greater range and quantity of information in order to perform good work. There is joint ownership of broad kinds of information.

Networks of information bind employees within and between groups in lateral, not hierarchical, kinds of ways as empowered teams see work through from start to finish. To function at the most basic level in a team environment people at work need skills of communication, personal self-management, and strategies for learning to learn.

WHY MANAGERS NEED INFORMATION AT THE MACRO LEVEL

According to the Bureau of Labor Statistics, employment growth from 1990 to 2005 projects that executive, administrative, and managerial jobs will grow by 27.4 percent; and the likely job categories of employees to manage can be expected to be in the information-dependent jobs of technicians and related support (growth by 36.9 percent), marketing and sales (growth by 24.1 percent), and administrative and clerical support (growth by 13.1 percent).[1] It seems clear that managers and supervisors will have to know how to facilitate and maximize productivity of those who report to them, and this means, especially in these growth jobs, how to manage information. Managers and supervisors need to make it easier for people to work together through information; their roles as sources or filters of information are no longer valid as employees themselves become able to access information at the touch of a button on a keyboard, mouse, or through an icon on a screen.

Changing Economic Factors

Also, economic factors create information challenges. Many companies in a search for cheaper or higher quality labor locate their factories or assembly operations in places geographically widely separated from headquarters. Firms searching for tax breaks or lower property prices move workers and engage in building projects in many parts of the country. Companies who want to compete internationally place people and resources anywhere in the world. An AT&T manager, for example, tells of running the production process control system for a chip packaging plant in Bangkok, Thailand in real time from a computer in Allentown, Pennsylvania. Asea, Brown, Boveri, an engineering and equipment conglomerate, has a conscious strategy of having many small factories throughout the world to optimize the human resources and communication functions of the localities where they operate. In retailing, bar codes, scanners, caller IDs, and other front-end technologies produce and send data to corporate data bases to be searched for highly qualified meaningful information for uses anywhere and everywhere that people have access to it. Information management ties all of this together, and challenges managers and supervisors in many new ways.

Information-Sharing Requirements

The presence of external service workers also can be expected to grow, from around 6 million jobs in 1990 to around 8 million in 2000 (A. Carnevale, *America and the New Economy,* Jossey-Bass, 1991, p. 139).[2] Consultants, independent technical professionals, and temporary workers of all sorts will have to be integrated into projects with a company's regular employees. The information-sharing requirements and communications needs of such a situation are obvious—and another challenge for managers and supervisors. Data security and integrity become increasing concerns in such situations.

Information Obsolescence

A downside of the information challenge is that information-based skills become obsolete quickly and must be updated and replaced continually. Hardware and software change so fast that employees' current skill levels are often inadequate to keep up with the new tools. *Information Week* (October 28, 1991, p. 16) reported that only 28 percent of the current crop of programmers have skills "in synch" with corporate needs, and that companies could be expected to compensate by trying to hire new development staff to integrate with present staff or to outsource programming work—or they'd simply fall behind.[3] The November 25, 1991 issue of the same magazine ran a cover story of two giants, Chicago-based Continental Bank and the high-technology corporation General Dynamics, who both recently outsourced billions of dollars worth of applications development, long-considered too strategic a function to hand over to others. The same article included a chart indicating that other areas of information services would be outsourced by companies across the U.S.: systems integration, network management, data communications, and data center operations, in that order, all could be expected to find their ways out from under company management and into the professional services arena. Such moves will create new ways of pricing information services and of managing the work. This kind of outsourcing organizational arrangement responds to economic downturns, overstaffing capacity, and skill obsolescence—and illustrates just one of the dichotomies between information abundance and trouble with harnessing it.

Accessing Critical Data

Deciding what information you need to do your job today is the critical issue for managers and others whose jobs are surrounded by it. Just being interested enough in data to know its range and to imagine its uses is often difficult for managers more accustomed to dealing with a narrow scope of responsibility and with a top-down sort of organization. How to access the information you need while avoiding the irrelevant information, how to find quick answers when you need them, and how to be sure that the information you find is the latest available are important questions for managers and supervisors. The element of time has changed in our information-rich business environment; jobs change quickly, even from day to day, and managers need to know *when* they need what kind of information.

Barry Raybould of Ariel PSS Corporation, Mountain View, CA, in his article "A Case Study in Performance Support" in the October 1990 edition of *CBT Directions,* p. 26, talks about how the user of large information systems depends upon the quality of the designer, and that in the most common query-based retrieval techniques even the most experienced user often finds less than 80 percent of the information he or she needs. Full text searching can suggest a cumbersome design and access situation; inexperienced users, according to Raybould, can experience "hit" rates as low as 20 percent. Concept hierarchies, hypertext, and natural language processing are all ways in which designers are experimenting with information representation—and, of course, influencing the ways in which managers and supervisors need to think in order to maximize their use of that information.

Data and Information Quality

Confirming the quality of data—knowing intuitively as well as objectively that the data is good for the work that needs to be done and for the people who need to do it—is a key requirement for managerial effectiveness. Peter Senge, director of the Center for Organizational Learning at MIT's Sloan School of Management, in his book, *The Fifth Discipline: The Art and Practice of the Learning Organization,* Doubleday/Currency, 1990, says it's the discipline of "personal mastery" that allows us to develop our capacity to clarify what is most important to us as we work in groups, in organizations (Chapter 9). Senge talks about Royal Dutch/Shell's management change in perspective as group planners there changed the way they did their jobs—from delivering information to the decision makers to helping managers rethink their worldview.[4] Information management has that personal mastery quality about the management task—that requirement to be in touch with ourselves, to be intuitive about what we need to know. To many out there on the front lines of corporate responsibility, this carries with it the burden of an uneasy need for a change in fundamental thinking about data, information, and learning.

Data Security and Integrity

Managers and supervisors also are called upon to make decisions about who has access to what information. Data security and integrity are major responsibilities of managers from the simple reading, writing, sending, and receiving electronic mail to accessing and acting upon customer, competitor, and strategic corporate information. Who owns information assets, who protects them, how risks are managed, and how data is secured are no small tasks for managers and supervisors in businesses ranging in size from an office with six PCs and spreadsheet and database software to corporate giants communicating via satellite and fiber optics with their far-flung installations on seven continents. Designers of databases, too, have an interrelated role with managers as they, at the front end of the information process, must decide how to organize information, how to design navigational and retrieval strategies, how to build in capacity for rapid updates, and how best to distribute information.

WHY MANAGERS NEED INFORMATION AT THE MICRO LEVEL

Managers and supervisors are also being called upon to be more sensitive to the personal needs of their employees as the "do it because I'm the boss" mentality gives way to "we're in this together." Information-based workplace stress seems to be a fact of life in the contemporary workplace. From the new PC user who gets no training to the assembly worker who now has to set up the day's schedule on a computer instead of doing the work to the salesperson who documents the morning's transactions on a laptop computer in his or her car on the way to the afternoon's appointments, information challenges employees to more complex ways of thinking and pressures the psyche to cope with new work stresses. Managers and supervisors must be wise in the ways of guiding and facilitating workers in dealing with information-related learning stresses.

Employees who work at a terminal or PC often experience both physical and psychological isolation from other employees. Essential oral communication skills such as listening, negotiating, engaging in dialogue, explaining, persuading, challenging assumptions, and offering suggestions can easily atrophy if they're not used—skills that seem more and more in demand as decision making is conducted at lower and lower levels in organizations. Also, when one has access to enormous amounts of information, one's expectations for communication about it can far exceed one's ability to communicate, leading to cognitive dissonance and a sense of dis-empowerment. Managers and supervisors must be sure that employees continuously refine their person-to-person communication skills to keep up with their increased mental manipulation of data.

Information overload can be a problem, too, tending to make a person withdraw from that which seems tangential, to narrow one's focus, or to play out in a "I don't even want to know" sort of approach. Managers and supervisors must ensure that employees have access to enough information to stretch their imaginations and capacities, but not so much that they turn off or spend their days "going shopping" through files as if they were computer games. Consonance in information-processing skills should be the goal: managers and supervisors must be aware of potential problems and know where to go to get help in solving them.

Much has been written about the effect of television on children's reading and language abilities. Not as much is known about the effect of video learning on adults. At a very basic level, managers and supervisors who choose videotapes or video-based classes for training their employees have to wrestle with the passive nature of most tapes—that is, training by videotape seldom engages the learner in anything except watching moving images and temporarily thinking about what was said on the tape. Watching information requires very little direct involvement with it, and requires no practice or feedback—activities usually associated with solidification of concepts, retention, and transfer. For example, "learning to" cook by watching television or "learning to" fix your house through a TV program probably do not result in a cooked meal or fixed house; at best, they probably result in enthusiasm or motivation for cooking or home repair, or in *information about* cooking or home repair. Only practice—the experience of doing it—results in accomplishment. The point in video learning is for managers and supervisors to be clear about what the medium is all about and to not expect certain kinds of results that can never happen.

Today's pool of young workers is the television generation. This generation of workers is used to vicarious experience in areas of learning that used to be characterized by more direct involvement of mind and body. Managers and supervisors must know how to make learning at work meaningful to new workers who generally know only passive ways of approaching new information.

Information management at the micro level is no less a challenge than at the macro level. There have been attempts in recent years to help managers and supervisors. Accelerated learning, speed reading, mind mapping, courses in critical thinking, brain dominance, learning styles, and problem solving have been included in many management training programs. Writing and literacy courses abound in nearly every mid- to large-size company. Information processing is an important concept in the psychology of learning.

MANAGERS' SKILL REQUIREMENTS FOR MANAGING INFORMATION

The following discussion suggests some information-gathering, accessing, processing, and communicating skill requirements for managers and supervisors—and ultimately for all people at work. First, managers and supervisors must know something about equipment—cameras, recorders, and projectors of all sorts, modems and fax machines, and computer hardware and software. They'll need to know enough not to "get snowed" by advertising or sales pitches, and enough to know the range of uses for which they'll need the equipment. They'll need to know realistic estimates of capacity, and how much and what kind of equipment their priority projects will require. These things can be learned in planning workshops, and by working closely with manufacturers during product orientation.

In addition, information managers need to know:

- Where to find up-to-date information
- How to assure the quality of information
- The difference between relevant and irrelevant information
- When to stop collecting and to start analyzing
- The difference between "the forest" and "the trees"—concepts and details
- Ranges and limits to information sources
- How to interact with information—evaluate, challenge, defend, choose, discard, discredit, accept, integrate
- How to share and disseminate information

Managers and supervisors need to be clear about the types of information they use or that they require their employees to use. Procedures are different from facts, the function of information is different from its structure; if/then rules, brainstorm networks, linear logic, and hierarchical trees are all options in representing information. Managers and supervisors need to know enough to differentiate the types of information so that they can make cost-effective decisions about information's accessibility and usefulness. Being aware of categories and options is the starting point. Defining and selecting what you need is the first step forward.

13 Steps to More Skillful Thinking

Michael J. McCarthy, an expert in accelerated learning, suggests thirteen steps to more skillful thinking. These are useful in building information management skills. They are:

1. Get all the information you need—necessary and sufficient is the guideline. As you gather information, stop and assess whether or not you are getting all that you need.
2. Check the source of information—be sure it's credible, complete, and not biased.
3. Be flexible and open-minded—cultivate your curiosity and reach out to people and ideas outside your own belief system.
4. Be sure you understand—be quick to admit your ignorance and take steps to correct it.
5. Make connections—consciously relate new information to what you already know.
6. Consider alternatives—look for alternatives; expand your thinking first and then focus it on the best solution.
7. Think ahead—visualize the future, imagine what will happen, and plan.
8. Organize your thoughts—think about things systematically, one step at a time; see how the parts relate to the whole.
9. Use writing and mind mapping to help clarify your thoughts—write down what you need to do and as many ways of doing it as you can think of; write down your feelings, pros and cons, about each of the alternatives.
10. Read to stimulate your thinking—when you're running out of ideas, read, not for information, but to generate new ideas.
11. Analyze and learn from setbacks—view every crisis as an opportunity; learn from experience by analyzing the inappropriate actions that got you in trouble.
12. Tune in to your intuition and inner knowing—be open to the inner level of your being and trust your innate intelligence.
13. Be patient—take the time to sit and think; analyze new information, synthesize ideas into a new whole, and evaluate what you have learned. Higher-level thinking takes time.[5]

Management trainers need to recognize the challenges that information management presents to managers and supervisors and to meet those challenges with a variety of paradigm-expanding training and product-specific know-how. Courses, seminars, institutes, workshops, field trips, guided discussions, self-study, cross-training, mentoring, computer-based training—all of the older and newer delivery methodologies need to be used to help managers and supervisors change the way they deal with information. As Anthony Carnevale, ASTD's chief economist, notes in *America and the New Economy,* "The unity of design, execution, and control is returning" to jobs as the past years of segmented and non-integrated business organizations give way to an information-based workplace—as Carnevale says, a "hands-off" workplace.[6] Managing more unified work demands a greater involvement with both the scope and depth of information and a holistic rather than a piecemeal approach to it—from specific to general, concrete to abstract. Above all, managers and supervisors must know how to learn.

Endnotes

[1]Sylvia Nasar, "Employment in Service Industry, Engine for Boom of 80s Falters, *The New York Times,* January 2, 1992, p. D4.

[2]Reprinted with permission, Jossey-Bass, Inc. Publishers

[3]Reprinted with permission, Information Week.

[4]Reprinted with permission, Doubleday/Currency, a division of Bantam, Doubleday, Dell Publishing Group, Inc.

[5]Michael J. McCarthy, *Mastering the Information Age,* © Copyright Jeremy P. Tarcher, Inc. Los Angeles, CA, 1991. Reprinted with permission, St. Martin's Press, Inc.

[6]Anthony P. Carnevale, *America and the New Economy,* Jossey-Bass, Inc., Publishers, 1991. Reprinted with permission.

TRAINING PLANS

Two training plans are included here as training delivery vehicles that mirror the holistic nature of information. Obviously, the task of managing information must be taught through a variety of training techniques and within a systematic and planned curriculum. These two training techniques address the management issues of finding the information you need, and choosing to outsource information services.

The first issue is one of personal competency regarding information, and the second is a business issue. The issues require different approaches to learning success, different questions to be asked, and different relationships to information during training. These issues are chosen to illustrate differences in training design and purpose.

Training Plans for Chapter 8 include:

management issues	*training techniques*
8.1 Finding the Information you Need	College course
8.2 Choosing to Outsource information Services	Field trip

TRAINING PLAN 8.1

Sending Managers and Supervisors Off to College to Expand Their Thinking

This training plan is an outline of the key considerations, procedures, and responsibilities of the training department when you send your managers and supervisors to a *college course*. In this case, the general goal of the training is to expand their thinking about information management, and specifically to learn to find the information they need.

A training plan begins with objectives for training itself as well as objectives for the learner, and with evaluation methods tied to the learning objectives. Teaching points related to the content of the course provide the foundation for topics covered, and sample exercises suggest ways to deliver this kind of instruction.

This particular training plan shows you some of the differences between instruction delivered this way and the more traditional training that goes on in corporate training rooms.

OVERVIEW OF TRAINING METHODOLOGY

Sending people away to college is expensive, even with government tax credits. If they go on company time and are still on the company payroll, the costs seem at least double, especially if college costs include living accommodations. The company, of course, is gambling that their expected increase in productivity and quality work upon their return will more than make up for the expense of a semester away from work. Trainers must be reasonably sure that chosen campus programs are exceptionally good and that persons chosen to attend them are committed to returning to work—a clause in the training agreement to "encourage" that commitment is not a bad idea.

There are many kinds of college programs from which to choose. A popular option is the semester-long think-tank management development program offered by major universities such as the Sloan School of Management at Stanford University and MIT. Business colleges such as the Wharton School at University of Pennsylvania and the University of Michigan Business School have programs of shorter duration, too, with many of the live-in collegial features of full-semester programs. And, at the most familiar level, the single course at a college within commuting distance is an attractive option for many managers or supervisors and their companies who prefer not to disrupt the regular work schedule by sending them away from the job for several months.

The option chosen for this training plan is the course at a college within commuting distance. The assumption is that this course meets two evenings per week, and the employee attends class on his or her own time. The company allows the manager or supervisor four hours per week of time away from work during the day to do library work or homework. The company pays all expenses of the course—tuition, fees, books, supplies, travel—on a "refund basis," obligating the trainee to earn a grade of B or better before expense vouchers are honored.

These are some of the reasons why you might choose a college course for your managers or supervisors:

- The subject is broad and is best handled over an extended period of time to allow instruction to unfold hierarchically

- The learner can benefit from having time to synthesize information
- Learning is enhanced by individual investigation, library work, extra reading assignments, written papers, presentations, or computer analysis work
- Diverse learners, possibly a mix of graduate students and managers or supervisors from other companies, will stimulate each other to see differing points of view
- Being in a campus environment is different from work, possibly encouraging broader or more creative thinking
- Thinking about the problems of other companies in a learning context helps clarify thinking about your own problems
- The course is what you want
- Your company needs an infusion of new ideas, and you don't want to hire new people
- Your own management staff is interested in attending the course
- Those chosen to attend have an attitude of "what can I learn in order to make a new contribution to company growth?"
- You are assured that the people you send will make a return on the investment through improved work

There are also some reasons why the particular managerial problem of *finding needed information* is one whose solution can benefit from managers' having been through a college course on the subject. First of all, if managers and supervisors are not making use of the information available to them—and it's not a problem with knowing how to make the machines go—you might suspect that their horizons aren't broad enough in terms of types of information, where it can be found, how to judge its quality, and knowing when what one has is enough. It's easy to get in the same old rut of leafing through printouts based on old or no longer relevant numbers generated by persons far removed from one's own organization. Managers and supervisors sometimes need mind stretching to be able to know enough to pursue hitherto untried avenues, to question the obvious, and to explore options.

College courses are good at refreshing one's memory about important definitions that might have become fuzzy and undefined under the labor of doing one's job day after day. In a course on information, one might be reminded of distinctions among the terms order, structure, function, relationship, level, scope—all terms that could help a person look in the right places for information. Being challenged to simply organize information resources better is often an early spinoff of such a course; and, feedback from quizzes, papers, and classroom dialogue helps steer a student in a direction to meet such a challenge.

College courses are also often very good at stimulating creative thinking and action. Managers and supervisors are generally practical people who can be very inventive when they take the time to play with options; learning set outside the workplace often provides that time to play. Trainers can encourage the transfer of classroom inventiveness into innovation on the job by checking with the course attendee from time to time during the semester, asking about application of the new ideas in the course to the person's job. Don't make the mistake of paying the bills and forgetting about the training and the trainee.

TIME REQUIRED TO DELIVER THIS TRAINING

One semester, two evenings per week, at the college
Time off work during the day (4 hours per week) for homework

TRAINEE LEVEL

Manager or supervisor

TRAINING OBJECTIVES

By taking the college course:

- To broaden trainees' thinking in these areas: identifying sources, investigating tools, formulating strategies, constructing systems
- To develop trainees' skills in inquiry, dialogue, and collaboration regarding information
- To teach new procedural, data interpretation, and data evaluation skills
- To create models for finding useful information

LEARNING OBJECTIVES FOR THE TRAINEE

- To identify, define, and explain new sources, functions, and structures of information
- To construct models and systems for information
- To follow new procedures for using and evaluating data
- To practice new skills in inquiry, dialogue, and collaboration regarding information

METHODS TO EVALUATE THE TRAINEE'S PROGRESS

Evaluating trainees' progress is best done at many times during the delivery of training, and in a friendly and somewhat informal way. This is called formative evaluation because it is evaluation that helps to form or shape instruction.

Instructors in the best college courses will engage in formative evaluation, although this unfortunately has not been the model of evaluation in most college classrooms. College teaching, especially in tough times when student populations are low and institutions are in economic hard times, has developed into the model of impersonal lecture by a big-name professor before a group of 200 students, of recommended reading lists, and of tutoring groups. Don't waste your corporate money sending managers and supervisors to this kind of course.

A recent study funded by the Andrew W. Mellon Foundation at Harvard University sought to find out what kinds of classes students found most valuable. An overwhelming number of present students—corroborated by alumni—told researchers that language classes were at the top of the list. These are the reasons the students gave for their high regard of language classes[1]:

- Instructors insist each student must contribute regularly
- Frequent quizzes give students constant feedback, so each student can make repeated midcourse corrections
- Classes demand regular written assignments each week
- Students are encouraged to work in small groups outside of class

[1]Light, R.J. *The Harvard Assessment Seminars, Second Report,* 1992, p. 76. Reprinted with permission, Professor Richard J. Light.

Students said that these features were most valuable for "enhancing their engagement with" the content of the course (a foreign language), and with helping them learn.

The first three features, above, are all associated with formative, or in-process, evaluation, and at Harvard, and elsewhere, have been valued *by learners* as strong contributers to the success of the learning experience. When you're looking for a place to which to entrust the intellectual expansion of your managers and supervisors, look for a course that has characteristics similar to those language courses. The midterm or final exam might be good for determining a norm-referenced grade for the course, and your company might require this to see how your managers and supervisors stack up against other course attendees, but the test-takers probably won't learn much more than how to cram for an exam as a result of the experience—a skill that probably will be rather useless back on the job.

In this hypothetical college course in finding information, formative evaluation should occur by various investigation and feedback processes over the duration of the semester. Student presentations, writing research papers or doing laboratory or library work, developing models with other students, receiving guided practice on new information-locating skills and on hands-on experimentation with new information-accessing equipment are just some of the kinds of exercises requiring formative evaluation that could be built into such a course. Don't assume that the course will be structured for learning just because the college or the professor has a big name; check it out first before you commit your hard-earned corporate resources to this kind of training.

TRAINING TIPS	***EXERCISES***
These are some of the kinds of things that could be included in a one-semester college course in "Finding the Information You Need."	
1. Discover sources of information. Suggest defining a topic such as global marketing, outsourcing contracts, psychological effects of replacing your assembly line with robots, and so on, looking for information about it in the following places: —periodicals —newspapers —books —reference sources —surveys —market research —annual reports —government documents —media documentaries and news —audio and video tapes	1. Send trainees on a hunt for basic types of information using many different tools: college library, public library, corporation library, on-line searching, CD-ROM, and private for-profit research services, government documents, and so forth.
2. Guide class discussions about how information is organized and classified.	2. Build upon the students' experiences (exercise 1) to have them select the categories for classification. Suggest procedures, concepts, facts, opinions, systems, rules, and so on.

3. Evaluate information.	3. Through dialogue, writing papers, doing presentations in class, and structured feedback, guide students in questioning information by asking and answering: —Is it believable? —Is it fact or opinion? —Is it important to me? —What is its function? —What is its structure? —Is it timely? —How does it relate to what I already know? —Where can I find more of it?
4. Help students synthesize and integrate new information into their experience base.	4. Guide students in comparing and contrasting, in aggregating like cases and in discarding that which does not fit. Teach by example and by nonexample. Devise exercises to allow students to practice procedural reasoning skills, interpretation skills, "what if" scenarios, and information management skills. Help them to accrete new information, restructure their memories as they adopt new information, and to fine-tune and elevate their expectations as a result of new learning. Suggest projects of importance to their jobs in which to apply what they learned.

TRAINING PLAN 8.2

Organizing a Corporate Field Trip to Train Managers and Supervisors How to Outsource Information Services

This training plan is an outline of the key elements, methods, and procedures suggested when you use *a field trip* as a training technique.

Like other training plans, this one begins with objectives for training itself as well as objectives for the learner, and with evaluation methods tied to the learning objectives. Training points related to the manager's or supervisor's area of responsibility provide the foundation for topics covered during the field trip. Sample exercises suggest ways to deliver instruction this way.

OVERVIEW OF TRAINING METHODOLOGY

Taking managers and supervisors on a field trip is an excellent alternative to more traditional ways of training that tend to be directive and formal. Learning from being surrounded by something new, by getting out and seeing for yourself, is a kind of learning environment that many people respond to very favorably.

There are many reasons why this is so. People like information presented in chunks, large clusters of related information as well as small groups of elements that make sense together. This kind of whole presentation of information appeals to the part of us that likes to "get a feel for" the subject under investigation all at once. It's a kind of informal approach, in that there are no explicit rules for entering the learning situation; learning happens sort of all at once. Some might say that learning this way is more "right brained" in approach, depending on spatial interpretation, simultaneous stimuli, intuition, and imaginative observation as organizers of learning.

On a field trip, people get a chance to exercise personal preferences about learning. They get to be interested in a variety of things to which they're exposed and to try out learning approaches that might not exist for their own jobs or in traditional classroom training. For example, a manager whose job is primarily a job dealing with people might focus on the data-intensive jobs that he or she observes on the field trip; a warehouse supervisor who deals mostly with things on the job might devote most of the field trip time to questioning the host manager of communications to get a better feel for that kind of job.

People perceive and conceptualize things differently, and the overall learning environment of a field trip presents the opportunity for learners to experience a variety of ways to learn. For example, on a field trip you'll readily hear people give clues about the way in which they're learning—"I *see* what you mean," "I *believe* that's a good idea," "I *hear* things to support that every day," "I *figure* that's the right approach," "I *needed* someone to reinforce this," and "You obviously can *prove* that," are all different ways of talking about a similar observation. The continuousness and richness of the variety of stimuli during a field trip generally bring out a corresponding richness of response from the trainees. People are often encouraged to learn in a multitude of ways during a field trip.

A field trip allows an individual to both exercise a preferred learning style and to experiment with learning in new ways. A learner saying mostly "I figure" probably learns most easily by manipulating logical relationships, and that person might find it a totally new learning experience to learn by responding to "needs." One who needs to "see" things probably would find it difficult to learn simply by listening. As a trainer, it's great fun to go along on a field trip to see and hear the differences your trainees exhibit, and of course to make note of these to guide the design of future training.

Field trips are also good settings for people to get answers to their concerns about making the innovation they're observing on the field trip work for them back on the job. Individual managers and supervisors can be expected to exhibit different levels of concern and varying degrees of anxiety about possibly replicating the things they see on the field trip. Some trainees will be interested only in information at the lowest level—they'll ask a lot of "what" questions—What is that called? What did it cost? What is included? Some trainees will already be at the implementation level in which they recognize the need for help—they'll ask "who" questions—Who makes decisions? Who should be on your team? Who needs to know about that? Some trainees will be anxious about the consequences of adopting the new practices—they'll focus on "if...then" relationships and show concern about the effects of certain decisions on their own jobs—they'll ask questions like "If we do that, will I end up with the responsibility?" or "How many headcount will I lose if I choose that solution?" Field trips are good for letting trainees get their feelings out in the open and get their questions answered at their own individual comfort levels.

Good field trips begin several weeks ahead of the scheduled visit. Aside from the obvious announcements of the essentials—who, what, when, where, why—about the proposed trip, you'll want to have some kind of orientation for those who sign up to go. This is when you finalize the objectives for the field trip and talk about it as an opportunity to learn something. Tell your potential trainee group when and where the orientation session will be at the time you announce the other particulars about the field trip.

The following details use the example of a field trip to a company who has accomplished outsourcing of information services. The field trip could be followed by another trip to the company who provided the outsourcing services. This training plan, however, includes only the visit to the company making the decision to outsource.

TIME REQUIRED TO DELIVER THIS TRAINING

Two hours of time on-site in the host company plus travel time

TRAINEE LEVEL

Manager or supervisor

TRAINING OBJECTIVES

- To take trainees on a field trip to a host company which has accomplished outsourcing, an innovation that our company is considering
- To prepare trainees for learning while they are on the field trip
- To facilitate trainees' learning while they are on the field trip

LEARNING OBJECTIVES FOR THE TRAINEE

- To investigate outsourcing by seeing how another company has done it, talking with successful decision-makers and seeing how things are done at the host company

- To synthesize the variety of information gathered on the field trip in order to facilitate our own company's decision making

METHODS TO EVALUATE THE TRAINEE'S LEARNING

A field trip can be a very active encounter, especially if trainees choose contact persons to talk with or observe at work while they are there—like taking a family shopping in a supermarket—one heads for the cereal, another for the produce, another for the dairy shelves, and another for the frozen food. If a host manager gives a presentation to your entire group, the question-and-answer period associated with it can be quite animated. Examination of documents can engender all sorts of involving questions, and engage your trainee at various levels of concern.

It is difficult to follow all of these kinds of individual involvement activities and to give appropriate feedback to your trainees. Often the best you can do is to keep track of who is where, and to keep everyone on schedule.

For the trainees you have direct contact with you can observe the ways in which they are interacting with your hosts, and can tell whether or not they're at a low level of awareness information or at a higher level of concern about cause and effect of their decisions. In a question-and-answer period following a presentation, you can judge the quality of the interaction and the significance of the questions that your managers ask of their host counterparts. You can prompt your trainees to ask deeper questions and give them evaluative feedback if you are standing right beside them, but on a field trip, it's rather unlikely that you can give each trainee the same kind of attention.

So, evaluation of a field trip occurs mostly after the trip is done and the synthesizing work begins to be felt back in your company. Field trips always require follow-up to help trainees integrate what they experienced; trainees on a field trip don't always realize what they learned. Trainers can help.

One way to get started in follow-up is to visit or telephone each trainee during the week after the field trip to get a quick assessment of what they considered strong points of the trip. Listen carefully, and then ask each trainee in a personal way what he or she expects to be able to use on the job—in essence, get trainees to try to tell you what they learned. Ask them just one question about application, and tell them that you'll be back in about one month to talk with them again.

About four weeks after the field trip, use a mailed or electronic questionnaire to trainees or interview each using a prepared interview schedule that focuses on their assessment of and adoption of any practices they observed during the field trip. Use open questions, that is, ones to which trainees cannot answer just yes or no. Ask questions such as :

1. How soon did you/do you intend to use information you got on the field trip?
2. What have you found most helpful about the field trip?
3. What have you found least helpful about the field trip?
4. How would you modify the field trip for better learning?
5. What constraints have you encountered here that have prevented/will prevent you from implementing ideas you got on the field trip? (money, time, support, equipment, systems, personnel, training, etc.)
6. How would you change organizational structures, systems, and communications here to accommodate the changes you think will work?

The role of beliefs and expectations is very important in setting the stage for change. If you use the delivery method of a field trip for training, work hard on the expectations aspects of the experience—before it happens, while it is happening, and after it has happened. The field trip can be a powerful training technique, especially for managers and supervisors who by nature mostly have a bent for action.

Note: The following section contains guidelines for you, the trainer, as you handle the field trip from an instructional perspective.

TRAINING TIPS	***EXERCISES***
1. Hold a briefing session for all who want to go on the field trip about one week in advance of the scheduled trip. Suggest that each trainee prepare three questions to ask when they get there. Consider questions like speed, timing, flexibility, precedents, pricing, costs, obsolescence, effects on existing staff, the role of the CIO, effects on customers.	1. Discuss the objectives for the trip, namely, to investigate outsourcing and to synthesize what they learned—two rather high-level cognitive skills. Tell them to go with all antennas up, with a questioning and open perspective. See if there are any other objectives specific trainees have, and add them to the list. Then give trainees information about the place to be visited and the preliminary agenda. Tell them to be expecting the final agenda as they board the bus to depart for the host company.
2. Give trainees an information packet of several pages to read on the bus during the travel time.	2. Include data about the host company, especially data about that company's use of information sources. Include key names and titles of host company personnel.
3. Greet your host and remain visibly in charge of the people from your company. Get around to as many of your trainees as you can for observation and feedback.	3. Be sure that each knows where to go first and help them get there. Be sure that each host company spokesperson sees you; thank each individually.
4. Plan and implement follow-up to the field trip.	4. Do a brief "smiles test" assessment by phone or in person several days after the trip, and a formal evaluation about four weeks later, as outlined in the evaluation section on page 271.

Bibliography

Adams, C. and Huff, L. "Videotape Instruction Is the Alternate Method to Classroom Training" in *Personal Computing,* November 1988, pp. 151-152.

America's Choice: High Skills or Low Wages! Report of the Commission on the Skills of the American Workforce, National Center on Education and the Economy, Rochester, NY: June 1990.

"Best of Baldrige" in *Training & Development Journal,* April 1991, p.12.

Bloom, B. S., ed. *Taxonomy of Educational Objectives, Book 1, Cognitive Domain.* NY: Longman, 1954/1980.

Brown, M. G. *Baldrige Award Winning Quality.* White Plains, NY: Quality Resources, 1991.

Carnevale, A. P. *America and the New Economy.* San Francisco, CA: Jossey-Bass, 1991.

Consulting Psychologists Press, P.O. Box 10096, Palo Alto, CA 94303-0979.

Cook, M. F. *Human Resource Director's Handbook.* Englewood Cliffs, NJ: Prentice Hall, 1984.

Crosby, P. B. *Let's Talk Quality.* NY: McGraw-Hill, 1989.

Crosby, P. B. *Quality Is Free.* NY: Mentor, 1979.

Dorio, M. A. *Personnel Manager's Desk Book.* Englewood Cliffs, NJ: Prentice Hall, 1989.

Drucker, P. F. *Managing in Turbulent Times.* NY: Harper & Row, 1980.

"Ergonomic Concerns Stiffen Rules Regarding VDT Use," in *Personnel,* vol. 68, no. 4, American Management Association, April 1991.

Freudenheim, M. "More Aid for Addicts on the Job," *The New York Times,* November 13, 1989, pp. D 1, D4.

Gagne, R. M. *Conditions of Learning.* NY: Holt, Rinehart & Winston, 1977.

Galagan, P. A. "Tapping the Power of a Diverse Workforce" in *Training & Development Journal,* March 1991.

Geber, B. "Managing Diversity" in *Training,* July 1990.

Gery, G. J. "Closing the Gap" in *Authorware,* vol. 2, no. 2, 1990.

Gery, G. J. "Electronic Performance Support Systems" in *CBT Directions,* June 1989.

Gery, G. J. "The Quest for Electronic Performance Support" in *CBT Directions,* July 1989.

Gilbert, T. F. *Human Competence: Engineering Worthy Performance.* NY: McGraw-Hill, 1978.

Greenhouse, L. "Court Refuses to Hear Occupational Safety Appeal," *The New York Times,* October 3, 1989.

Guilford, J. P. *Intelligence, Creativity, and Their Educational Implications.* San Diego, CA: Robert R. Knapp, 1968.

Hagedorn, A. "Turning Safety Into a Competitive Issue," *The Wall Street Journal,* July 25, 1989, p. B1.

Hannum, W. *The Application of Emerging Training Technology.* Alexandria, VA: American Society for Training and Development, 1990.

Herzberg, F. "One More Time: How Do You Motivate Employees?" in *Harvard Business Review,* vol. 65, no. 5, September-October 1987.

Horton, T. R. "The One Indispensible Relationship" in *Management Review,* American Management Association, April 1991, p. 4.

HRD Quarterly published by Organization Design and Development, 2002 Renaissance Blvd., Ste. 100, King of Prussia, PA 19406.

"Ideas & Trends" in *LOTUS,* March 1990, pp. 15-17.

Institute of Electrical & Electronics Engineers (IEEE). IEEE *Standards for Software Quality Assurance Plans.* NY: 1981.

Introduction to Performance Technology. Washington, D.C.: National Society for Performance and Instruction, 1986.

Juran, J. M. *Juran on Leadership for Quality.* NY: The Free Press, 1989.

Juran on Quality Leadership (videotape). Wilton, CT: The Juran Institute, 1989.

Kackar, R. N. and Shoemaker, A. C. "Robust Design: A Cost-Effective Method for Improving Manufacturing Process" in *AT&T Technical Journal,* March/April 1986, vol. 65, no. 2, pp. 39-67.

Kanter, R. M. *The Change Masters.* NY: Touchstone/ Simon & Schuster, 1983.

Karr, A. P. "OSHA Proposes Stiffer Standards for Protective Gear," *The Wall Street Journal,* August 17, 1989, p. A7.

Kilborn, P. T. "Rise in Worker Injuries Is Laid to the Computer," *The New York Times,* November 16, 1989, p. A 24.

Kotter, J. P. *Organizational Dynamics: Diagnosis and Intervention.* Reading, MA: Addison-Wesley, 1978.

Light, R. J. *The Harvard Assessment Seminars, Second Report.* Cambridge, MA: Harvard University, 1992.

Lookatch, R. P. "How to Talk to a Talking Head" in *Training & Development Journal,* September 1990, pp. 63-65.

Managers as Leaders. Harvard Business Review Special Collection #90084, 1988.

McCarthy, M. J. *Mastering the Information Age.* Los Angeles, CA: Jeremy P. Tarcher, 1991.

Mintzberg, H. "The Manager's Job: Folklore and Fact" in *Harvard Business Review,* March-April 1990.

Morgan, T. "Fears and Dependency Jostle in Shelters," *The New York Times,* November 4, 1991, pp. 1 and B2.

Napier, R. W. & Gershenfeld, M. K. *Groups: Theory and Experience.* Boston: Houghton Mifflin Co., 1973.

Nasar, S. "Employment in Service Industry for Boom of '80's Falters," *The New York Times,* January 2, 1992, p. 1.

National Society for Performance and Instruction (NSPI), *Introduction to Performance Technology,* vol. 1. Washington, D.C.: NSPI, 1986.

Nilson, C. *Training Program Workbook & Kit.* Englewood Cliffs, NJ: Prentice Hall, 1989.

Nilson, C. *Training for Non-Trainers.* NY: AMACOM, 1990.

Nilson, C. *How to Manage Training.* NY: AMACOM, 1991.

Nilson, C. *How to Start a Training Program in Your Growing Business.* NY: AMACOM, 1992.

Perkins, D. N. *Knowledge as Design.* Hillsdale, NJ: Lawrence Erlbaum Associates, 1986.

Personal Strengths Assessment Service, P.O. Drawer 397, Pacific Palisades, CA 92072.

Peters, T. *Thriving on Chaos.* NY: Alfred A. Knopf, 1987.

Quick, T. L. *The Manager's Motivation Desk Book.* NY: John Wiley & Sons, 1985.

Rakow, J. "Performance Aids: How to Make the Most of Them" in *Training/HRD,* September 1981, pp. 40-44.

Raybould, B. A. "A Case Study in Performance Support" in *CBT Directions,* October 1990, pp. 22-31.

Rosenberg, M. J. "Performance Technology, Working the System" in *Training,* February 1990, pp. 43-48.

Rowan, R. *The Intuitive Manager.* NY: Berkeley Books, 1986.

Schmidt, W. E. "Risk to Fetus Ruled as Barring Women from Jobs," *The New York Times,* October 3, 1989.

Senge, P. M. *The Fifth Discipline: The Art and Practice of the Learning Organization.* NY: Doubleday/Currency, 1990.

Shabecoff, P. "AT&T Barring Chemicals Depleting the Earth's Ozone," *The New York Times,* August 2, 1989, p. A12.

Smith, M. A. and Johnson, S. J. (eds.). *Valuing Differences in the Workplace: Theory to Practice Monograph Series.* University of Minnesota and American Society for Training and Development (ASTD), 1991.

Spitzer, D. R. *Improving Individual Performance.* Englewood Cliffs, NJ: Educational Technology Publications, 1986.

Springer, S. P. and Deutsch, G. *Left Brain, Right Brain.* San Francisco: W.H. Freeman and Co., 1981.

Suessmuth, P. *Ideas for Training Managers and Supervisors.* La Jolla, CA: University Associates, 1978.

Thomas, R. R., Jr. *Beyond Race and Gender.* NY: AMACOM, 1991.

Thorndike, R. L. & Hagen, E. P. *Measurement in Evaluation and Psychology.* NY: John Wiley & Sons, 1977.

Training America: Learning to Work for the 21st Century. Alexandria, VA: American Society for Training and Development (ASTD), 1989.

U.S. Congress, Office of Technology Assessment (OTA), *Worker Training,* Washington, D.C.: U.S. Government Printing Office, 1990.

U.S. Department of Congress, National Institute of Standards and Technology, Gaithersburg, MD, *1991 Application Guidelines Malcolm Baldrige National Quality Award.*

U.S. General Accounting Office, *Management Practices: U.S. Companies Improve Performance Through Quality Efforts,* Washington, D.C., May 1991.

Watson, T. J., Jr. *A Business and Its Beliefs,* McKinsey Foundation Lecture Series. NY: McGraw-Hill, 1963.

Wellins, R. S., Byhan, W. C., and Wilson, M. M. *Empowered Teams.* San Francisco, CA: Jossey-Bass, 1991.

Workforce 2000. Indianapolis, IN: Hudson Institute, 1987.

Zuboff, S. *In the Age of the Smart Machine: The Future of Work and Power.* NY: Basic Books, Inc., 1988.

Indices

Index of Training Techniques

Index

Q

R

S